£12.99

# Process and structure in higher education

During the 1980s the whole higher education scene in Britain shifted dramatically. This new edition of the well-known text by Tony Becher and Maurice Kogan presents a synoptic model of how the system as a whole now functions, and how its various components are interconnected.

Drawing on detailed interview data from leading figures in British higher education, on their inside knowledge and research, and on an extensive review of the relevant research literature, the authors explore the characteristic values and practices of the four main levels in the system – the central authorities, the institution, the basic unit and individual – and analyse the pattern of relationships between them. They note the changes that have taken place in the last decade, and look ahead to how the system seems likely to develop in the future. Although the analysis is based on the UK, much of it is relevant to higher education in other countries.

In its unravelling of complex issues such as academic freedom, the tensions between research and teaching, the influence of market forces on institutions of higher education, and the apparent resistance of leading universities to change, *Process and Structure in Higher Education* does much to demystify the nature of higher education. It will be of lively interest both to those engaged in academic activity and those concerned in its management.

D0226957

# Process and structure in higher education

Tony Becher and Maurice Kogan

## Second edition

London and New York

First published in 1992
by Routledge
11 New Fetter Lane, London EC4P 4EE

Simultaneously published in the USA and Canada
by Routledge
a division of Routledge, Chapman and Hall Inc.
29 West 35th Street, New York, NY 10001

© 1992 Tony Becher and Maurice Kogan

Typeset by LaserScript, Mitcham, Surrey
Printed and bound in Great Britain by Biddles Ltd,
Guildford and King's Lynn

*British Library Cataloguing in Publication Data*
Becher, Tony
    Process and structure in higher education. – 2nd. ed.
    1. Great Britain. Higher education
    I. Title II. Kogan, Maurice
    378.41

*Library of Congress Cataloging in Publication Data*
Becher, Tony.
    Process and structure in higher education/Tony Becher and
Maurice Kogan. – 2nd ed.
    p.  cm.
    Includes bibliographical references (p. ) and index.
    1. Education, Higher – Great Britain. 2. Higher education and
state – Great Britain. 3. Educational change – Great Britain.
I. Kogan, Maurice. II. Title.
LA636.8.B36 1991
378.41 – dc20                                                    90-29005
                                                                     CIP

ISBN 0–415–06461–9
      0–415–01804–8 (pbk)

# Contents

# Illustrations

# Preface to the second edition

The first edition of *Process and Structure* was published in 1980; the text itself had been largely completed a year before. In the decade that has passed since then British higher education – along with the higher education systems of other countries, and perhaps most noticeably Australia, the Netherlands and West Germany – has altered in a whole diversity of ways. The extent of the difference between the system at the beginning of the 1990s and that at the beginning of the 1980s would be graphically illustrated by comparing the present revised text with the original version.

When we came to prepare this new edition we were struck by the large corpus of references which were so quickly outdated, and the substantial number of statements which time and circumstance had made no longer valid. Entities once significant – the Local Education Authorities, the University Grants Committee, the Regional Advisory Councils and a variety of others – have disappeared or virtually disappeared from the higher education scene. One such agency, the National Advisory Body for Public Sector Higher Education, came and went between our two editions. The major structural innovations which have occurred over the period – including the establishment of the Polytechnics and Colleges Funding Council and the Universities Funding Council, the according of legally incorporated status to the polytechnics and other institutions – are charted in more detail in Chapter 3 below.

But besides a myriad of detailed changes, one major shift has been significant enough to cause us to modify our original representation of the higher education system. Ten years ago it was still possible to view the whole structure, in Britain at least, as reasonably autonomous: although we noted the importance of the surrounding context, it did not feature as an integral part of our model. Such a distancing of the enterprise from its environment is no longer tenable. The subsequent extent of external intervention in both the structures and the processes of British higher education makes it impossible to sustain the earlier claims for an independent, self-

Process and structure in higher education

determining network of institutions in which the basic unit reigns supreme.

We have had to take account of this particular source of difference in several places, but perhaps particularly in Chapters 1 to 3, and in our wholly rewritten Chapter 10. The latter replaces the earlier discussion of the extent to which the model we first presented might be applicable to other areas of social policy. We now conclude instead with a look towards the direction in which continuing changes seem most likely to point: in which attempts at strong central control will vie with attempts to create a system dominated by the values of the market.

For the rest, the corrections to the text are individually modest but collectively numerous: there is scarcely a page of what we originally wrote that has not called for some emendation and updating. But in addition to the changes occasioned by the march of recent history, there are other and sometimes significant differences of interpretation, brought about by our own enhanced familiarity with the subject-matter. In the period that has passed since our earlier collaboration, we have severally and jointly been engaged in a number of research studies which, though not directly relevant to the theme of this book, have had a bearing on our understanding of how the system functions. These include a major collaborative study, led by Maurice Kogan, of the relationships between higher education and the labour market (Boys *et al.*, 1988); a long-term investigation by Tony Becher of the cultures of academic disciplines (Becher, 1989); and a more recent enquiry, involving both of us alongside other colleagues, in the UK and in four other countries, into postgraduate education and research training (the results of which are as yet unpublished, but which we expect to appear within the next year or so).

We have been helped in our rethinking of the model and its implications by a grant from the Economic and Social Research Council, which enabled us to employ a modest amount of research assistance in updating our reference sources, to undertake a number of detailed consultations with key individuals in the British system, and to test our emergent ideas in a residential seminar with fellow-researchers from Europe and the USA. Our indebtedness to those who thus helped us is recorded below.

*Maurice Kogan*
*Tony Becher*
1991

# Acknowledgements

Those we had particularly to thank in connection with the first edition of this book included Margaret Archer, Eskil Björklund, Ann Bone, the late Lord Boyle, Geoffrey Caston, Clive Church, the then Sir Frederick Dainton, Hendrik Gideonse, Sally Harris, John Honey, Jan-Erik Lane, Jack Meadows, Barbara Nelson, Malcolm Parlett, Robert Pinker, Rune Premfors, Peter Scott, Geoffrey Squires, Martin Trow and Robert Woodbury. We were indebted to the Leverhulme Trust for a grant which supported our initial work.

For the second edition, we have further (and overlapping) obligations to record. We are grateful to John Ashworth, Christopher Ball, Clive Booth, Ron Dearing, Kenneth Edwards, Malcolm Frazer, Norman Hardyman, Martin Harris, Edward Parkes, John Kingman, Peter Knight, William Stubbs, Peter Swinnerton-Dyer, William Taylor and Leslie Wagner – all distinguished and busy people holding leading positions in higher education – who allowed themselves to be interviewed. The interviews were based on an open schedule of topics; full records of them were made and analysed by both authors. It was not appropriate to refer to them individually in a text which attempts to provide analytic modelling rather than an account of knowledgeable views held from different perspectives of current developments. But the interviews sharpened and helped us to challenge our own perceptions on key issues, and also confirmed our own judgements about the major shifts that had occurred over the last decade.

When the book was at an advanced draft stage we invited a group of experts to join us in making a critique of certain key chapters. We are indebted to the following for joining us for an extended seminar at the London Business School in September 1989: (from the Netherlands) Frans van Vught; (from West Germany) Claudius Gellert; (from Sweden) Eskil Björklund, Torsten Nybohm, Rune Premfors; (from the UK) Ronald Barnett, Richard Bird, John Brennan, Oliver Fulton, Mary Henkel, Robin

Middlehurst, Guy Neave, Geoffrey Squires, Bruce Williams; (from the USA) Burton R. Clark, Roger Geiger and Martin Trow.

We also invited four expert readers to look at the final text. We are grateful to Graeme Moodie, Michael Shattock, Leslie Wagner and Gareth Williams for their stringent and constructive suggestions.

In all of our work on higher education studies we have been conscious of the growth over the last fifteen years of a supportive and able international network of scholars. The Society for Research into Higher Education has increasingly contributed to this development, as did the associated series of conferences organised by Professor Gareth Williams under the aegis of the Leverhulme Trust Fund. We note for particular mention the lead given to higher education studies by Eskil Björklund of the Swedish National Board of Colleges and Universities, Martin Trow of the University of California at Berkeley and Burton R. Clark of the University of California at Los Angeles.

Finally, we are greatly indebted to Penny Youll who provided us with an impressive bibliographic and critical back-up; to Mary Henkel for further critical comments; to Keeley Jones and Carole Bullen, Brunel undergraduates on work placement for our project; and to Sally Harris who, as with our 1980 study, displayed prodigious administrative and secretarial skills in getting the project into the field and out into publication.

# Abbreviations

| | |
|---|---|
| ABRC | Advisory Board for Research Councils |
| ACOST | Advisory Council on Science and Technology |
| APR | Age Participation Rate |
| CCETSW | Central Council for Education and Training in Social Work |
| CIHE | Council for Industry and Higher Education |
| CNAA | Council for National Academic Awards |
| CVCP | Committee of Vice-Chancellors and Principals |
| DES | Department of Education and Science |
| HEIs | Higher Education Institutions |
| HMI | Her Majesty's Inspectorate |
| LEAs | Local Education Authorities |
| MSC | Manpower Services Commission |
| NAB | National Advisory Body for Public Sector Higher Education |
| NFER | National Foundation for Educational Research |
| OECD | Organisation for Economic Co-operation and Development |
| PCFC | Polytechnic and Colleges Funding Council |
| PIs | Performance Indicators |
| SCOEG | Standing Conference of Employers of Graduates |
| SERC | Science and Engineering Research Council |
| SRHE | Society for Research into Higher Education |
| UFC | Universities Funding Council |
| UGC | University Grants Committee |

# 1 Introduction

## THE BOUNDARIES OF OUR TERRITORY

In many countries higher education accommodates a substantial and steadily increasing number of students, and takes up a large proportion of the national budget. It offers most of its recipients enhanced vocational opportunities and is held to enrich their personal and social lives. It also helps in the production of national wealth through the training it provides in specialised skills and through the contribution it makes to research and the advancement of technology.

These are all good reasons for taking higher education seriously. Much has been written in relation to the external justifications for higher education, viewed as an enterprise within its wider society. However, this book has a different set of considerations in view: namely, an attempt to understand the internal nature of higher education, and its diverse and distinct components, conceived as a system with its own internal logic. The focus is on how the workings of that system can best be understood and explained, in terms of that internal logic as much as of any extrinsic rationale.

To say this is not to deny that higher education needs to be firmly set within its social and economic context. As it has grown, so the demands it makes on society for resources, and the corresponding expectations which society has of the benefits it can offer in return, have become more significant. The system cannot be treated as if it were closed and self-contained; nor is it possible to ignore or to play down its interaction with its external environment. But given our prime concern to make sense of its inherent structure and of the processes which that structure embodies, the perspective we have chosen to adopt is an internalist one: what happens outside the system is viewed predominantly in terms of how it relates to what happens inside.

The book is explicitly limited in time and place. That is to say, it concerns the academic scene in Britain at the outset of the 1990s, rather than higher education in other parts of the world, or in the past or future. This relatively restricted framework reflects our own direct familiarity with the subject-matter. We have nevertheless been concerned to avoid taking a narrowly parochial view. Our discussions are set against a historical background in Chapter 3. There are references at a number of relevant places throughout the text to other national systems. And in our final chapter, we attempt to extrapolate from current trends to possible future developments.

Since our main emphasis is on the clarification of basic structures and the illumination of underlying processes, rather than on a description of the existing state of affairs, our analysis can claim to have a wider currency than the specific here and now from which it happens to have been developed. The essential elements which go to make up a system of higher education – the individual teachers, the departments and other basic units, the component institutions, the central agencies for management and control – do not differ dramatically from one point to another in the history of Britain in the past generation, or even from one point to another in the geography of the advanced countries at the present time. Nor do the relationships, tensions and divergencies between those various elements change or fluctuate in a way which would preclude any meaningful generalisation. A number of our observations, though based on one country, have relevance to higher education as a whole.

We have drawn our illustrative examples mainly from the universities rather than the polytechnics because in their longer history they have displayed a wider range of relationships with the central authorities. Now, with increasing convergence in the UK between the two sets of institutions and their funding bodies, their values and governing mechanisms do not differ significantly. Our purpose in any case is to present common components for analysis rather than provide a taxonomic account of different institutions within the current UK system.

## THE NOTION OF A SYSTEM OF HIGHER EDUCATION

A system of higher education, rigorously defined, would generate common goals or objectives related to all levels of its functioning, and would incorporate strong enough authority to ensure that they were met. But the metaphor, when applied to higher education, should not be taken too literally. It implies a degree of organisational tidiness which is very rarely achieved in practice. In common with most other social institutions, the shape of higher education is as much a consequence of historical accretion and continuing transactions across institutional boundaries as it is of long-term rational planning (Archer, 1979). As already acknowledged, it has to be seen as an open, rather than a closed system. The metaphor has to be further qualified, in that the internal structures of most national forms of academic provision are no less untidy than their external boundaries. The component elements seldom mesh neatly one with another. There are discernible contradictions, duplications and gaps in coverage; pluralistic (and sometimes mutually competing) goals; and an absence of structures for administrative control. On this score, higher education must be further typified as a loosely coupled system (Baldridge *et al.*, 1978; Cohen and March, 1974; Weick, 1976).

This much – that higher education is both open and loosely coupled – can be said with confidence about the contemporary scene in general. However, there are also important distinctions to be noted between existing systems in one country and another. The main differentiating characteristics can conveniently be placed on two dimensions, with particular reference points identified along them.

The first dimension relates to access. The traditional – and thus familiar – end of the scale is denoted by Trow (1974) as an elite system; this is echoed by Teichler's (1988) reference to an elitist model. The contrasting end point is labelled by Trow as universal higher education. Teichler adopts a variety of terms, of which perhaps 'open' and 'soft' come nearest to catching the same general sense.

The intermediate situation is typified by Trow as mass higher education. Teichler offers a more complex picture, differentiating between diversified systems (which accommodate 'a multitude of somewhat permeable institutions somewhat overlapping in their function, while being distinctive in their major goals as well as in their academic standards') and integrated systems (involving 'the admission of students with different prerequisites and abilities to the same institutions ... students would share some common experience and finally acquire degrees, which would differ in academic standards to a lesser extent than in the case of a diversified structure'). He suggests that integrated systems have in the event proved 'much less popular' and have only been partially implemented.

The second dimension is that of governance and control. Clark (1983) identifies an autonomous model, based on control by an 'academic oligarchy'; Neave (1986) similarly singles out institutional autonomy as a defining characteristic. Further along the spectrum Clark also writes of a contrasting market model, and Neave of self-regulation through a 'systems-learning model' (that is, autonomy within external constraints). Clark identifies a reliance on statism or state authority as intermediate between autonomy and the market. We shall return to these distinctions as our argument proceeds.

## PURPOSES AND PERSPECTIVES

In our focus on components of the higher education system and on the nature of the relationships between those components, we have found it useful to present the essential features of our analysis in diagrammatic form. The resulting model is designed to reflect the underlying features rather than the complex topographical details of the landscape.

The contrast may be illustrated by noting some distinctions between a detailed street map of London and a London Transport map of the underground system. The latter is a drastic simplification of reality, with all detail pruned away except that portraying the intercommunication between different stations. Even distances and directions are ignored in the interests of topological simplicity and clarity. To anyone needing to find his or her way round the underground railways, it is a superbly efficient device (as anyone who has struggled to follow the topographically realistic map of the Paris metro will readily acknowledge). But for someone wanting to trace a route on foot or by surface transport, the underground map is useless – only a map which accurately represents distances and directions, with accompanying details of street names and landmarks, will do. That in its turn, however, while it may portray all the relevant stations (and even perhaps the routes), is for the underground traveller a poor substitute for the map of the tube.

This book sets out to be more like a London underground map than a street plan. It could be characterised in terms of an emphasis on conceptual clarification rather than description, an endeavour to link the macro-structure of higher education with its micro-structure, a concern with the furtherance of sound policy-making and an interest in trying to understand not only the differing value perspectives within academia as a whole, but also the ways in which acceptable resolutions can be reached between them.

In some of the following chapters we consider aspects of the historical background to British higher education, examine the nature and incidence of innovations within the system, and review the impact of evaluation, accountability and resource allocation procedures. We discuss these not as issues in their own right so much as elements necessary to a coherent understanding of the academic enterprise. Our approach to each such theme is of necessity limited, in being instrumental to a different end.

Although we do not set out to look in any comprehensive way at the evolution of the system, or the occurrence of changes within it, or the mechanisms by which judgements are made and resources distributed, we do aspire to a reasonably thorough and self-contained examination of each of the four levels we have identified – namely, central authorities, institutions, basic units and individuals. Accordingly, a reader of any of the subject-specific chapters concerned (4 to 7) should – unlike the reader of any of the thematic chapters (3, 8 and 9) – come away with a fair idea of the norms and operations which characterise the particular level in question.

This contrast is made only to underline the differing functions, in the overall structure of the book, of subject-specific chapters and thematic chapters. The four levels serve as main elements in the explanation of how the system is articulated, and are therefore explored as subjects in themselves. The thematic chapters serve to underline and clarify the relationships between the various levels, and to show the system in a temporal perspective: it is through these chapters that we seek to convert a series of static camera-shots into a dynamic motion picture.

The nature and characteristics of the system as a whole, the way it works, some explanation of *why* it works in the way it does, and some insights into its component elements – all these form the subject-matter of Chapters 3 to 9. The remaining three chapters – 1, 2 and 10 – could be described as providing a surrounding frame. Chapter 2 presents the conceptual structure within which the subsequent analysis is carried out, and Chapter 10, as already remarked in the Preface, offers a speculative account of how the British higher education system might develop in the future. Taken in conjunction with our retrospective survey in Chapter 3, it acknowledges that our portrayal of the system as it now exists has to be seen as a transient phase in a constantly, if not rapidly, changing scenario.

What, then, could readers expect to gain by staying with us through the course of our exploration? They should, first, acquire a clarifying conceptual lens through which to view that which is already familiar, and through which to make better sense of anything unfamiliar which comes into their field of vision. Second, they should be able to pick up, apply and develop further some of the subsidiary distinctions which we draw in our more detailed accounts of the different levels within the system.

The achievement of both objectives depends on the successful delineation of the model or framework itself. It is to this task that we shall turn in our next chapter.

# 2 A model for higher education

## THE PURPOSES OF THE MODEL

This chapter presents a portrayal of higher education which attempts to meet the requirement of simplifying and making it more readily comprehensible while at the same time remaining true to reality. In so doing we adopt the terminology of constructing or setting out a model. The term 'model' has come to have a variety of different meanings. It is employed here in a non-technical sense, as a straightforward, but necessarily and deliberately simplified, set of categories for thinking about British higher education and looking at the relationships between its components. These categories, components and relationships can be compactly summarised in tabular form and it is the resulting figure to which we will refer as our model. No special powers or properties are ascribed to the model itself, other than those of conveniently presenting abstract ideas in concrete visual terms. It must, to be of any use, stand up to the test of being recognisable; it must succeed in reflecting without distortion important discontinuities in value; and above all it must provide a coherent overview of the complex phenomena of higher education. We are not attempting the more ambitious modelling familiar to economists or natural scientists which characteristically depicts inputs and outputs and the relationships between them in quantified terms.

Although the model has been developed in relation to the British scene in particular, it is offered as a conceptualisation at a sufficiently general level to serve with only limited modification for other analogous systems of higher education. It can, for example, clarify elements of the US public system of higher education in which each member state figures as a central authority; it encompasses less successfully the American private universities whose relationships with the federal or state authorities are far different from those of universities in the UK. It can, however, help describe the relationship between a US private university and its basic units and individual constituents.

The model is not intended to apply to organisational elements devoted solely to research, nor to those charged with carrying out a service function, as against basic units and individuals undertaking both research and teaching. It should remain possible, in the case of such elements, to distinguish their operational from their normative modes: but their structural characteristics and working processes will necessarily differ from those we discuss below.

## THE MODEL'S NATURE AND STATUS

Any attempt to subsume our arguments under a general, all-embracing theoretical perspective would be misplaced. We are not concerned to make law-like propositions about higher education which go beyond the available phenomena, and are thus verifiable or falsifiable in Popper's (1979) sense. The attempt is, rather, to rearrange the existing conceptual maps of higher education in such a way as to make more clearly evident those interconnections, interrelationships and inherent properties which are in one sense already known but in another not adequately recognised.

Two straightforward examples of this kind of conceptual mapping can be found in the general domain of social policy. The notion of the single-parent family has come widely into currency in the last few years, linking together the previously separate (but individually familiar) phenomena of young widowed mothers – or fathers – with dependent children, divorced parents and what were previously called unmarried mothers. The new terminology has underlined a previously neglected comparability – of the organisational and psychological stress created by coping with children in the absence of a spouse – but has ceased to separate the different subgroups in terms of social acceptability and moral praise and blame. Similarly, the concept of child abuse has brought together, within a single frame of reference, a set of phenomena which were hitherto treated as separate and diverse, linking physical, sexual and psychological maltreatment by adults of those deemed too young to be capable of adequate self-protective measures.

It would not, in these examples, be relevant to ask questions about truth or falsity, but only about the appropriateness of each concept to its situation, the extent to which it is useful and its degree of general acceptance. Analogously, in the case of the conceptual framework developed in this book, we would readily accept its evaluation in terms of whether it seems to fit the domain under review, whether it helps to make it more readily intelligible and whether it can usefully be taken up and developed by others in the same or related contexts. Its status has to be judged, we would argue, as a good or bad conceptual interpretation, rather than as a correct or incorrect predictive or *post hoc* theory, of how the education system works.

## MAIN DIMENSIONS AND COMPONENTS

The proposed model is two-dimensional, embracing modes as one dimension and levels of organisation as another. The modes are designed to reflect a familiar contrast, though one that is not easy to catch. We have chosen to mark it in terms of a distinction between norms and operations: between collective and individual values, aspirations and loyalties on the one hand and what might be called job requirements on the other. But the dichotomy is also close to that between belief and practice or what Argyris and Schön (1974) have termed espoused theories and theories in action; between value and fact, or ideal requirements as defined by morality and everyday requirements as defined by law.

The levels are in their turn designed to indicate the discrete clusters of norms and operations which differentiate one stratum of the organisation from another. The number of levels which can be discerned within the system is to some extent a matter of choice. Van de Graaff *et al.* (1978), for instance, distinguish six: the institute or department; the faculty or college or school; the university; the multicampus institution or federal system; the state government; and the national government. The regional level has assumed greater importance in some national systems, such as Germany and Spain. It could be argued, however, that the regions may be struggling to take over aspects of the national or central authority role. Our own categorisation adds the individual as a distinct organisational level, and elides Van de Graaff's six other categories into three: the basic unit, the institution and the central authority. The decision to restrict ourselves to these four levels was not an arbitrary one: besides our general inclination to be as parsimonious as reasonably possible in constructing the model, we would argue that all forms of governance above the institutional level have a reasonably coherent set of values and functions, and that the faculty level functions either as a molecular basic unit or as subsidiary to the institutional level according to context. To us, the condition for a particular organisational category of groups to form a level is that it has a distinctive value set and sufficient authority to promote it.

It will become evident in Chapters 6 and 7 that we regard the level of the basic unit, and to a lesser extent the individual level, as playing a crucial role in the system, since they embody most closely what may be termed the characteristic socio-technology of higher education. The institutional and central authority elements are important in their own right, as will be demonstrated in Chapters 4 and 5. They have their own value systems but do not as clearly reflect the inherent values of teaching and research as does the basic unit.

## THE LEVELS IN THE SYSTEM

We now turn to the business of assembling the model itself. In the discussions which follow we distinguish between the four elements already identified in the structure of any higher education system. The first is the central level, involving the various authorities who are between them charged with overall planning, resource allocation and the monitoring of standards. The second level is that of the individual institution, as defined in law (through its charters or instruments of governance) and by convention (through its various decision-making bodies).

We have called the third level the 'basic unit', because its precise nature varies between different institutions. In many traditional settings, it corresponds with subject-based departments, but in some institutions the basic unit is a more broadly constituted 'school of study'. In other contexts again, it may be defined by a course team – namely, an interdisciplinary group of teachers who collectively provide a major component of the undergraduate curriculum. The main characteristics of such basic units are that they have academic responsibility for an identifiable course or group of courses, that they have their own operating budgets (and some discretion in disposing of them) and that they exercise some element of choice in the recruitment of professional colleagues (and often also of students). They may in certain cases engage in collective research activities, but this is far from being a defining feature.

Finally, the system is composed of individuals: teaching and research staff, administrators, ancillary workers and students. We shall focus in our discussion on the teaching staff, since it is they who normally play the main role in shaping academic and curricular policy. In the first stage in the construction of the model, then, we have merely identified four elements representing the different structural levels within the system.

*Table 2.1* The structural components of the model

| Individual | Basic unit | Institution | Central authority |
| --- | --- | --- | --- |

Two considerations need to be emphasised in the interpretation of this part of the model. The first is that the elements are meant to represent functions rather than entities (to illustrate this, the same people may operate at some times as individual academics and at others as representing basic units; and particular institutions can, in certain aspects of what they do, depart from their institutional role to act as central authorities, or even as basic units). The second consideration is that the fourfold categorisation deliberately simplifies reality. It is evident that the more complex components – and especially the central authority and the institution – function in a variety of different styles and embody a diverse collection of entities, a point to which we shall return later.

## THE MODES AND THEIR ASPECTS

The second stage in the process depends on a less familiar set of distinctions. It separates two components in the everyday life of the academic world which are not in practice sharply distinguished. The first of these, which we have designated as the normative mode, relates to the monitoring and maintenance of values – to what people in the system count as important. The second, the operational mode, refers to the business of carrying out practical tasks at different levels within the system – to what people actually do, or are institutionally required to do.

Although these two modes obviously interact, their characteristics can be readily marked off one from another. Their inseparability in practice and clear differentiation in theory recall the familiar contrast between mind and body. Looked at in this light, the normative/operational distinction can be considered as denoting two facets of the same state of affairs. However, the best way to draw out the differences between them is perhaps within the context of discussing the model itself in more detail.

Each mode is further to be seen as having an internal and an external aspect. The internal aspect embodies the features which stem directly from the nature and purpose of the enterprise of higher education as a whole; the external denotes those which derive from outside sources. Thus we shall refer to external norms and external operations as being those which in some way impinge on the system from the outside, and to internal norms and internal operations as those which are integral to the system of higher education itself.

## THE CELLS OF THE MATRIX

We now have the basis of a sixteen-cell matrix which charts the two modes, each with their two aspects, against the four structural levels. Within this matrix we may distinguish an inner core of eight elements (internal) from an outer framework of the other eight (external).

The next step must be to fill out the cells of the matrix in sufficient detail to make it possible to discuss the interconnections between them. This task

*Figure 2.1* The elements of the model

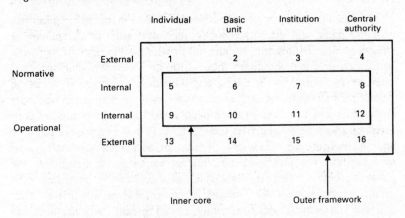

can be best tackled by taking the numbered elements in linked pairs and commenting on the nature and implications of each.

## Normative Mode

### (1) and (5): Individual level

The main internal characteristics at the individual level in the normative mode comprise meeting the expectations of the role in two ways. The teacher or researcher seeks to fulfil personal wants and realise personal expectations, linked with a general concern to maximise job satisfaction. In so doing, however, he or she will meet such role expectations as conducting original and non-trivial research, engaging in a disinterested pursuit of the truth, or teaching with an altruistic regard for students' development. However, there are also two distinguishable sets of external characteristics. In the first place, most individuals derive some sense of support from the main professional reference group to which they belong, and reciprocate by subscribing to the group's norms. This reference group is represented in our model as being external to the system itself, because it is cosmopolitan in its composition. In applied fields, it may embrace professional practitioners as well as academics; in pure fields it will commonly have an international constituency. In the second place, academics are susceptible to the prevailing social, economic and cultural values of their wider environment, and may internalise – or at least feel that they have to conform with – a number of these. As we shall argue later, the process is necessarily one of selection and accommodation, since personal, professional and societal norms may not always be compatible.

## *(2) and (6): Basic unit*

The basic unit, viewed in its normative mode, has the internal requirement of maintaining, and indeed promoting, its own distinctive disciplinary or subject values. To this end, it must fall in with the demands of its parent institution and accommodate these with its own particular sectional interests, as defined by the peer group immediately concerned. As in the case of the individual, its external norms are twofold, deriving in part from those of its wider professional community and in part from those of contemporary society at large. The societal norms are important in sustaining and underwriting the values of the basic unit, as against questioning their acceptability. The professional norms are important in comprising the collective credit system through which members of the immediate peer group, in concert with the network of comparable groups in the wider national and international community, obtain rewards, advancement and recognition. (Thus, for example, a history department in a given institution is concerned to endorse the canons of historical scholarship and codes of good professional practice in the subject. In doing so, its own standing will be preserved and enhanced; its individual members may also gain reputation, and perhaps promotion in other history departments in other institutions at home or abroad. Non-disciplinary subject areas may seek to reflect the diffuse norms of more than one discipline or those of the professional or practitioner group to which they belong.)

## *(3) and (7): Institutional level*

Academic institutions are engaged, in their internal normative aspect, in meeting the requirements of the central authority, in setting and monitoring rules of procedure and in the maintenance of 'due process'. They seek to ensure that proper behaviour is observed by their constituent basic units in relation to academic appointments, the use of funds, the selection of students, the protocols of assessment and the like, and that the activities of such units conform to the shared interests of the collective to which they belong. However, as we shall go on to argue in Chapter 5, partly as a result of pressure from the central authorities, institutions are increasingly likely to develop their own portfolios of values, related to such policies as the enterprise culture or management efficiency, and to lay down their own criteria of excellence. As far as external norms are concerned, institutions are expected – as are individuals and basic units – to take cognisance of the current social, economic and cultural values.

*(4) and (8): Central authority*

Much as academic institutions monitor – and to some extent guide – their basic units, the central authorities have the internal normative task of overseeing the standards of the institutions and, in periods when academic values are not stable and assured, of attempting to change the system itself to match external normative expectations. The external pressures to which the central authorities are subject tend to be predominantly economic, insofar as higher education makes substantial demands on public funds: but there are also political pressures and general social expectations of quality and relevance which they are called upon to meet.

At this point, we might conveniently summarise the elements in the normative mode, as in Table 2.2.

*Table 2.2* The elements in the normative mode

| *Individual* | *Basic unit* | *Institution* | *Central authority* |
|---|---|---|---|
| (1) | (2) | (3) | (4) |
| External: reflecting (a) professional norms; (b) social/ economic/cultural values | External: reflecting (a) professional norms; (b) social/ economic/cultural values | External: matching social/economic/ cultural values | External: meeting economic, political and social expectations |
| Internal: realising role expectations and personal goals | Internal: maintaining peer group norms and values | Internal: maintaining academic regulations | Internal: overseeing and maintaining standards of quality, relevance and effectiveness |
| (5) | (6) | (7) | (8) |

## Operational Mode

*(9) and (13): Individual level*

At the individual level, the main internal operational demands lie in the performance of the traditional academic tasks of teaching and research and scholarship: but individuals may also have calls on their services in both institutional and extra-institutional contexts, as when they act as members of internal committees or are concerned in placing their knowledge and expertise at the disposal of the outside community. The external operational pressures which affect the activities of individual academics derive from the social, economic and cultural requirements imposed on the overall pattern of work. We shall explore these considerations in more detail in Chapter 7.

### (10) and (14): Basic unit

In operational terms, the key internal function of the basic unit is to define the nature and content of the unit's everyday practice, and especially that relating to teaching and caring for students. It is thus concerned primarily with issues of the curriculum, teaching and learning, but also with the collective research profile of its members of staff. It has to specify the working programme in sufficient detail to make it capable of implementation, and to translate the results in terms of individual tasks. The basic unit is in its turn subject to external operational pressures in terms of the requirements of its potential clients outside the higher education system: pressures which may take a variety of forms – economic, social and cultural – according to the context in question.

### (11) and (15): Institution

The institution has an internal operational concern for the maintenance and development of its constituent elements and its range of established activities, mainly through the differential allocation of money and personnel between basic units. It has a key role to play in forward planning, insofar as a changing environment will allow any meaningful planning to take place. The institution is further called upon to implement policy decisions at the central level in return for the resources required for development. Extrinsic operational pressures at the institutional level may be local or national in form: they might include proposals for industrial research contracts, demands that the institutions concerned should play a more active role in solving current social problems, or expectations that they will promote or contribute to aspects of cultural development.

### (12) and (16): Central authority

The central authorities have operational responsibilities internal to the system in accounting for the public funds made available for higher education and optimising the use of existing resources by allocating them between their constituent institutions. They are also in certain instances charged with authorising proposals for new developments or laying down specifications for new courses. The external operational demands placed on them tend broadly to reflect the economic and social expectations to which reference has already been made.

A summary of the elements in the operational mode is shown in Table 2.3.

*Table 2.3* The elements in the operational mode

| Individual | Basic unit | Institution | Central authority |
|---|---|---|---|
| (9) | (10) | (11) | (12) |
| Internal: performance of teaching/research/ service roles | Internal: student provision/ programming of curriculum and research | Internal: maintenance of institution/forward planning/ implementation of policy | Internal: optimisation of resource use/ sponsorship of developments |
| External: responding to social/economic/ cultural requirements | External: responding to social/economic/ cultural requirements | External: responding to social/economic cultural requirements | External: meeting social and economic demands |
| (13) | (14) | (15) | (16) |

## RELATIONSHIPS BETWEEN ELEMENTS

Before this initial exploration of the model is completed, it remains to say something more about the relationships between adjacent elements in the matrix we have just discussed. We may distinguish two sets of such relationships: those which are vertical and those which are horizontal. In the latter case, we confine our attention to those which link the elements in what we earlier (see Figure 2.1) termed the inner core, as distinct from those in the outer framework.

Looking first at the horizontal links, it has been implicit in our discussion of the normative mode that the relevant relationships involve appraisal or judgement. Thus basic units relate normatively to individuals in terms of matching an individual's standards against the values of the group (elements 5 and 6). Institutions and basic units are linked in terms of procedural judgements in which the units must be seen to conform to institutional codes of practice and to be striving towards institutionally agreed outcomes (elements 6 and 7). Central authorities carry out their monitoring function in relation to institutions by evaluating the general effectiveness of their basic units and by appraising their overall competence (elements 7 and 8).

In comparable ways, the main relationships in the operational mode can be characterised in terms of the allocation of resources, responsibilities and tasks. The individual's activities are set out in terms of the operational demands of the basic unit to which he or she belongs (elements 9 and 10). The basic unit is related operationally to the institution in terms of the specification of its budget and the institutional requirements on its curricular and/or research programmes (elements 10 and 11). Each institution is to a greater or lesser extent dependent on the allocation of public funds from the pool available for the system as a whole and on the specification by the central authorities of desired modes of course provision (elements 11 and 12). This is so even where the central authority relies on academic peer assessments to guide its choices: the final decision nevertheless rests formally with the authority itself.

The vertical relationships are more complex, and less easy to define. The outer framework – comprising both external norms and external operational requirements – impinges on the inner core of the system in a variety of ways. The configuration of norms at any given level is, as we have argued, partly a consequence of value formation (or re-formation) through a broad range of societal pressures; partly, where appropriate, through more specific pressures from the relevant professional community; and partly from the internal dynamic and value formation of the system and its components. Similarly, the pattern of operations may be internally determined but also reflect external requirements: commonly through the commissioning by external agencies of teaching and research activities at the level of the individual and the basic unit, and in terms of more generally programmatic developments at the level of the institution and the central authorities.

Within the inner core itself, it may be contended that as long as the internal normative and operational modes are in phase with one another, the system as a whole remains in dynamic equilibrium: if not in harmony, then at least in a state of balanced tension – a point we deal with fully in Chapter 8. However, when the two modes become significantly out of phase, some form of adjustment is necessary to restore the possibility of normal functioning. Herein lies one of the major sources of innovation within the system, although, obviously, more drastic and radical forms of change, perhaps derived from external pressures, also occur. We shall explore this topic further in Chapter 8. In principle, one would expect the normative level to exercise dominance over the operational, in that value preferences tend to be represented through actions, rather than actions defining value preferences. However, given that external factors also affect the normative–operational relationships, there are many instances in which internal operations arguably condition internal norms.

The vertical relationships within the inner core, then, may in part be characterised in terms of developmental changes designed to re-create the equilibrium between norms and operations. At the individual level (elements 5 and 9), the emphasis is on how developments in practice interrelate with modifications in role expectations (an example would be the changes in a researcher's emphasis and approach brought about by some new apprehension of the research field). The interaction between the normative and operational modes at the level of the basic unit (elements 6 and 10) may quite commonly be characterised by changes in curricula as group values develop in such a way as to question current activities (an example would be the effect on undergraduate courses of the increasing predilection for a quantitative emphasis in pure economics). At the institutional level (elements 7 and 11), the characteristic product of a tension between norms and operations is some change in academic or administrative organisation, designed to bring what is done more closely into line with what is held desirable. The comparable task at the level of the central authorities (elements 8 and 12) – namely, matching operational provision (itself partly a product of external demands) with normative requirements (which are to some extent affected by external expectations) – has on occasion to be tackled by a major structural reform (as in Sweden in the 1970s and in Britain in the 1980s).

## THE COMPLETION OF THE MODEL

The various considerations brought forward so far can be summarised by presenting them as Figure 2.2. The model which we have now set out contains no features which have not already been discussed. However, the act of bringing them together in a relatively compact form will, we hope, make it easier to keep the system as a whole in view – and hence to grasp more clearly the nature of its components and the interrelationships between them. We shall be putting this possibility to the test in the chapters which follow.

## SOME JUSTIFICATIONS AND QUALIFICATIONS

The point has already been made that the proposed model is not the only conceivable, or the only allowable, representation of the higher education system in Britain. There could well be different models, not necessarily in competition with one another, but concerned to emphasise different features and to develop distinct but not necessarily incompatible interpretations of shared phenomena.

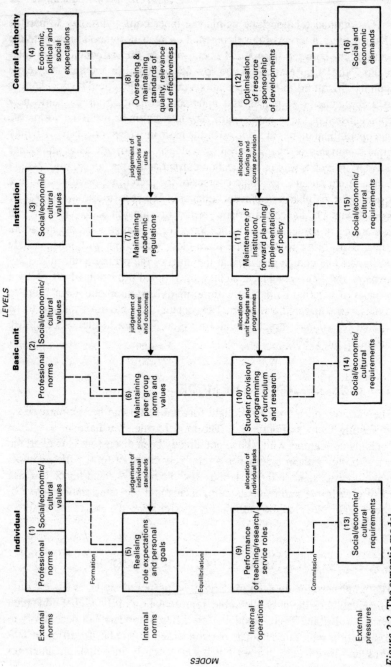

*Figure 2.2* The synoptic model

Central Authority

(4) Economic, political and social expectations

(8) Overseeing & maintaining standards of quality, relevance and effectiveness

(12) Optimisation of resource sponsorship of developments

(16) Social and economic demands

Institution

(3) Social/economic/cultural values

(7) Maintaining academic regulations

(11) Maintenance of institution/forward planning/implementation of policy

(15) Social/economic/cultural requirements

LEVELS

Basic unit

(2) Social/economic/cultural values / Professional norms

(6) Maintaining peer group norms and values

(10) Student provision/programming of curriculum and research

(14) Social/economic/cultural requirements

Individual

(1) Professional norms / Social/economic/cultural values

(5) Realising role expectations and personal goals

(9) Performance of teaching/research/service roles

(13) Social/economic/cultural requirements

External norms

Internal norms

Internal operations

External pressures

Formation

Equilibriation

Commission

judgement of institutions and units

allocation of funding and course provision

judgement of procedures and outcomes

allocation of unit budgets and programmes

judgement of individual standards

allocation of individual tasks

MODES

One might now ask whether the four levels defined in the model are generally useful. In the first place, a number of systems outside the UK (for example, those of former Federal Germany and Canada) have nothing exactly corresponding to the level of 'central authority'. Similarly, in some small monotechnic colleges in the UK, the level of 'basic unit' seems hardly to exist; in some very large institutions the position is complicated by the apparent existence of sub-institutions.

Earlier in this chapter we remarked that the levels should be seen as denoting different functions within the system, and not as categorising particular entities: the same individual or corporate group might be identified at one time as performing a role at one level, and at another time, a different role at another level. However, it seems necessary – in addition to this particular means of giving flexibility to our descriptive vocabulary – to introduce a further ruling to take into account the type of objection just outlined. We shall therefore have recourse to the mathematician's notion of a 'degenerate case' – although we shall use the term 'special case' to avoid possible connotations of debauchery or disintegration.

Insofar as we might wish to extend our model to other systems roughly comparable with that of Britain, we could say that, just as a straight line is a special (degenerate) case of a circle – that is, a circle with infinite radius – so too a system without any single central authority constitutes a special case of the model. It will usually have a series of governing authorities (trustees for private institutions, state administrations for public) rather than a single and unifying one. Nevertheless these authorities severally will discharge the kinds of functions attributed in our model to the unitary central agency. The absence of basic units in small institutions can be seen as another special case in which the second and third levels are combined.

If the apparent absence of a particular level is usefully regarded as a special case of the model, the suggested addition of further levels raises different problems about the ways in which values, entering through the normative mode, are expressed in operational form. We should not elaborate levels beyond those necessary for explanation: thus in the UK system, we would not regard the relevant Secretaries of State, or the Cabinet of which they are members, or the Parliament to which they are answerable, as constituting separate levels from the Department of Education and Science or the Funding Councils and Research Councils through which public funds are channelled. Equally, the existence of federal institutions (such as the universities of London and Wales) does not call for an elaboration of the model, since the functions ascribed by the model to the institution are in these instances distributed within the conglomerate structure. There is no distinctive set of values which differentiates the federal from the component entities.

In this context, a distinction may be drawn between the constitutional framework of higher education – which can be depicted as a particular constellation of managerial elements arranged in formally designated organisational tiers – and the underlying structure of the system, which our model seeks to portray. While the number of tiers is a matter of administrative definition, the number of levels (as we have defined the concept) can be marked off in terms of significant differences in value sets.

The distinctions may be summarised as follows. The central authority is responsible for collating the demands of society on the higher education system, in terms of its consumers (the employers of graduates and the potential students) and of its sponsors (the taxpaying public and its elected representatives). It must also ensure that the system meets such demands to an acceptable degree. The institution (as we shall later argue in Chapter 5) has and increasingly promulgates its own distinctive values. Among its tasks is to maintain and develop a collective mission, style and reputation, incorporating but reaching beyond those of its constituent basic units; and as part of this to respond to internal and external demands by the initiation of new units and new programmes. It also has an important secondary task, of acting in its fiduciary role of collating values and monitoring the procedures of constituent units. The basic unit has the very different responsibility of responding to and maintaining academic norms within its particular field of relevance. And the values of the individual are again separable from, though comprising part of, those of the basic unit.

The dichotomy embodied in the model between the two modes, normative and operational, can also be called into question. For example, the allocation of resources within an institution can properly be seen as a value-laden activity – in other words, one which reflects the judgement of merit as well as answering functional needs. But even allowing for the close interrelationships between the normative and the operational modes, there is a familiar and recognisable difference between the rationale of a group or organisation and what it does in practice: between its values and its tasks. The distinction is useful precisely because it separates for the purposes of analysis two different perspectives from which the workings of the higher education system and its constituents can be viewed. The duality is in no sense meant to imply that we are dealing with two separate systems, or two systems which are interconnected in some mysterious way: it is, as we suggested earlier, the same system, analysed from two different perspectives.

The remaining constituent of the model – namely, the set of relationships between the different levels and different modes – is similarly open to qualification. Our model implies that the only connecting links are those between adjacent elements. But there can also be links between components other than those directly shown – for example, between institution and individual, leapfrogging the basic unit, in the internal normative mode; or diagonally between central authority in the internal normative mode and institution in the internal operational mode. Our model is drawn to illustrate the key essentials but is not intended to deny these possibilities.

A point which may deserve re-emphasising is the importance of the outer framework in relation to the inner core. As has already been suggested, external professional norms play a central part in maintaining the value coherence and promoting the status of basic units, and in giving individuals a clear sense of identity and purpose. But in many systems even greater significance attaches to the wider social context in which higher education finds itself.[1] This exercises its most direct influence on the central authority, but it also has a bearing on the institution, the basic unit and the individual within the system.

A society which holds higher education in considerable esteem will give rise to a very different morale within academia from that generated by a society which denies its academic institutions any significance in the scheme of things. More specifically, institutions whose graduates do well on the job market will tend to have more confidence than those whose record in this respect is poor; the fortunes of particular basic units will wax and wane with the extent to which their particular areas of coverage match or fail to match the prevailing social mood; and the individual academics' self-esteem will to some extent be affected by the comparability of their salary scales with those of other professionals, including fellow-academics in other countries.

Such considerations, though external to the values of higher education *per se*, undeniably influence those values and the ways in which they are operationalised. Our model therefore takes the social, economic and cultural background as essential to the understanding of how the academic enterprise has developed, and how it currently functions.

## NOTES

1 What we described in Chapter 1 as institutionally autonomous forms of higher education offer an apparent exception to this general claim: but it must be remarked that, even in their case, autonomy is contingent on the general readiness of society to license it, and to meet the costs of doing so without conditions attached. In strongly market-driven systems, the impact of external social norms is more evident and more pervasive.

# 3  The development of higher education in the UK: changing purposes since 1945

## THE HISTORICAL CONTEXT

Implicit in our model is the assumption that, although higher education changes in response to the social expectations placed on it, authoritatively by government and persuasively by others, it also demonstrates a contra-functionalism, a different view of society and its needs, embodied in the obstinacies of the academic way of life. The higher education system allows for the pursuit of values at the different levels and these do not constitute a hierarchy from one level to another. The beliefs dominant in the central authorities at any one time may not therefore be those which drive the institutions and the basic units. Higher education nurtures beliefs that the growth and transmission of knowledge are legitimate in themselves, not depending for their right to flourish on stated public demands; and that it is a proper function of academic institutions to act as centres of alternative opinions within the political system. This constitutes what some call higher education's essentialism.

The antinomy here is evidence of society's need (or higher education's ability to convince society of its need) to nourish criticism from the same sources that it sustains for its supply of skilled manpower and leadership. Higher education is not alone in embodying such a contradiction. The judiciary, for example, are both 'lions under the throne' – in Francis Bacon's phrase – and testers and critics of the way in which public authorities implement the law.

It is perhaps the multiple layers in this assumption which history can help us to unpack. For not only does higher education assume that it might put up a critical view of society's needs; it has also assumed that it is licensed to interpret society's needs through its power to use public resources to create and administer the curriculum and devise its own research agendas according to academic criteria. Paradoxically, it was during the period of growing funding by the public authorities in the 1950s and 1960s that university freedom increased most vigorously. Academic criteria were thought to be happily convergent with the needs of society and the economy; a degree in English literature or anthropology, for example, was acceptable to both the world of scholarship and of employment. Academic values were assumed by many leading practitioners to be invariant and unassailable; social values might change whilst academic procedures would guarantee intellectual stability and integrity during processes of change that were organic and incremental.

In recent years, however, those assumptions have been weakened in two ways. First, the allocation of resources for research has become more directly influenced by the central authorities' and industry's views of what ought to be investigated – even in the most prestigious subject areas in the most prestigious institutions (Brennan and Henkel, 1988). Second, the curriculum is now under direct pressure for its employment relevance from the Manpower Services Commission (1987). Government has thus sought to revise the traditional view of academic development.

In elaborating our model we may identify a number of stages in the history of British higher education from 1945 (Stewart, 1989). The first is that of gradual expansion and the pressures that resulted from it until the Robbins Report (1963) converted gradual expansion into stated policy.

## ACADEMIC NORMS UNDER PRESSURE FROM EXPANSION

The 1939–45 War was the starting point for changes which eventually became codified and promulgated in the 1960s. Some of the University Grants Committee's statements in the early post-war years reflect the changes that took place:

> there was an artificial extension of university activities ... directly related to the various and developing needs of the war machine ... there has emerged from the war a new and sustained public interest in the universities and a strong realization of the unique contribution they had to offer to the national well-being, whether in peace or war. Any conception that may have existed of the universities as places of cultural luxury catering for a small and privileged class had faded away and will not return. A heightened sense of social justice generated by the war has opened the door more widely than ever before.
>
> (University Grants Committee, 1948)

At this time, it might be noted, the competent authorities were promoting the 'opportunity', or the 'soft', concept of equality which sought to ensure that the able, from whatever social class, would find their way to university and thence to the heights of the social system.

The UGC's last report before the war (1936) had looked forward to a period in which 'quantitative growth would be less rapid than hitherto and it will be possible for the universities to concentrate their attention on questions of quality'. In 1948 too, whilst, as noted, sponsoring some expansion, 'the dominating task which confronts the universities is that of maintaining, and ultimately of improving, the quality of university education notwithstanding a pressure in student numbers hitherto unknown' (UGC, 1948). The UGC and the universities were thus driven by three potentially conflicting motives. First, society needed educated manpower; compared with other countries, Britain's output of graduates was disconcertingly low. A second aim should be to achieve a much greater measure of social and educational equality than existed before the war. Third, academic balance and quality must be retained.

On the first of these points, the Barlow Committee (1946) proposed a doubling of output of scientists and technologists. It argued for an increase of the university system from 50,000 to 90,000 places as soon as possible; it is, indeed, a mistake to assume that all was stagnant before the 1960s. Two years after the Barlow recommendation, in 1948/49, there were already 83,000 students. The increases were mainly to be found in the provincial universities although, for example, Oxford had increased its overall numbers by 50 per cent over the pre-war total.

In specifying the changes in scale necessary to meet the new social and economic objectives, the central authorities did not avoid setting academic norms, though the UGC would always claim it indicated rather than prescribed. In the early post-war years, the aim was to ensure a good spread of disciplines within institutions so that there was contact between students in different fields (UGC, 1948). The UGC therefore resisted the notion of technological universities for a long time. It was concerned about quality and shared the views of the Barlow Committee that 'in few other fields are numbers of so little value compared to quality properly developed.... Moreover, before a student enters the university, intelligence must be trained and the associated personal qualities matured to a standard that we would not wish to see lowered' (UGC, 1948).

Joining the debate, the Committee of Vice-Chancellors and Principals (CVCP), in a note on university planning and finance for the decade 1947–56, warned that 'academic standards once lowered are not retrievable, and Gresham's law applies to them'. The Barlow Committee had, however, thought that 'on the evidence of certain intelligence tests there is ample reserve of intelligence to allow university numbers to be doubled and standards to be raised concurrently'. The UGC's own view was that 'no reliable conclusions concerning the future supply of students of a provable quality can be drawn from the present situation'.

In any event, the Education Act of 1944 would increase the numbers of pupils in full-time education until 18 and thus increase the supply of potential undergraduates. Not only would ability be tested, but also 'character, temperament and wider qualities of mind'. The UGC duly endorsed the egalitarian impulses to which the war gave rise:

> It is clearly desirable to exclude one type of student whom the possession of means once entitled to secure admittance: that is the riotously living pass-man, sometimes of athletic promise, on whom the university as an agency of culture made small dint.

These statements indicate how far the central authorities – here the UGC – accommodated to social and economic demands. The institutions in their turn responded, and at a cost. The standards of life in the universities deteriorated with the increased numbers. The UGC was anxious lest the quality of staff, the teacher–pupil ratios, the buildings and the provision of office accommodation should worsen and the improvement in quality to which it had looked forward in its last pre-war report would be further postponed. Before the war, for example, the staffing ratio at Oxbridge had changed from 1:11 in 1934/35 to 1:10 in 1938/39. Similar developments took place elsewhere in the early post-war period; there were, in some universities, however, no rooms for discussion groups or individual tuition and there were long queues in the refectories. The life of a professor was not one of gilded charm. In one place, as many as four professors occupied one not very large office. Junior staff might be four to six – or even, in one university, nine – to a room. Ratios again became more favourable in the 1950s.

The UGC report for 1935–47 anticipated the time, twenty years hence, when the current increases in the numbers of staff in the universities would produce major problems. In fact promotion blockages never occurred in the 1960s because of further expansion of the universities; they were to come in the 1980s when there were absolute reductions in staffing establishments. The UGC also deplored the heavy demands of administration placed on professors and heads of departments. As a result, research was in danger of being undertaken only by junior staff. There were too many calls to serve on committees outside the universities. The increase in load on non-professorial staff was perhaps one of the reasons why universities were asked to keep such staff informed of current academic and financial issues and to foster in them, by whatever means possible, a sense of administrative responsibility. At this stage, however, there was no hint that junior academics had any part to play in the government of their universities.

The central authorities were concerned with more than the increase in numbers. For example, the UGC deplored postgraduate studies that

reflected only the 'specific endowment of research', or 'narrowly special-
ized fields of enquiry not all of which have particular educational value', or
'over-emphasis on original work, however trivial'. Interestingly, it took the
view that 'the risk of absorption in sterile forms of so-called research is
greater in the arts than in science and technology'.

The UGC was in effect operating on two conflicting premises. It had
views about matters of academic substance, but was always concerned that
the institutions and basic units should make the running: it was for them to
propose while the UGC disposed. This doctrine persisted, if with decreas-
ing power, until the late 1970s. The UGC's reading of social needs and of
desirable academic developments, including the maintenance of particular
academic norms and styles, led it to make operational decisions. It did so
reluctantly, maintaining the assumption that its allocations were deficiency
grants. Nevertheless, it must decide which institutions or basic units to
support; all institutions were excellent but some were more excellent than
others. Moreover, from 1945 onwards the UGC was required to identify
developments that should be promoted: for example, its backing, in terms
of specially earmarked funds, was crucial for the development of social
sciences after the war.

In using its power, the UGC developed pragmatic principles from which
to work. The criterion of need meant that small and financially weak
institutions received a higher proportion of grant than their student numbers
would otherwise justify. This principle, however, was qualified. Writing in
1948, the UGC stated that its intention had been to help those who were
able to find money for themselves, to support quality and thus direct money
where it seemed most likely to produce the best results. 'We did not regard
it as a proper object of policy to use our financial influence in such a way
as to obliterate existing variations of academic prestige' (UGC, 1948).
Thus, the norms to be endorsed were not only those of national need but
also that of intellectual quality as perceived by the institutions themselves,
their peers who judged them and their benefactors who might be attracted
to excellence. The UGC articulated the values of academe and acted on
them.

## GROWTH AND NORM-SETTING

The academic principle of excellence and elitism was, however, in tension
with the social need for rapid growth. In the first post-war period of
expansion, the smaller universities and colleges took a large part of the
increase in student population. Thus numbers influenced a pattern hitherto
based on prestige. Inevitably this reduced the rewards that a sympathetic
state gave to those who pursued excellence, although the UGC moved only

reluctantly from the earlier criterion. It did not much want to equalise professorial salaries, and in this as in other things 'it seemed to some of us questionable whether government funds should be used for the purpose of depriving certain universities of advantages which they had built up over a long period' (UGC, 1948). But other considerations pointed towards an opposite conclusion. Unless the weaker universities and colleges were enabled to offer salaries more nearly comparable with those prevailing elsewhere, they would obviously find difficulty in attracting to their chairs more than a very small proportion of men and women of first-class attainment.

In the years following the immediate post-war period (1947–52) the rate of growth slowed down. The UGC thought that the student population might have reached a peak. It also hoped that when the upward movement was resumed the increase might be gradual (UGC, 1953). Thus there would be a period in which to consolidate, develop and experiment. The essential functions of universities would continue to be those of doing original work, of creating knowledge and of producing the next generation of scholars and leaders. Such developments as were contemplated were educational rather than social: students should have a broader education. The UGC sustained the liberal and humanistic view of an elite system. It did not take up or advocate, for example, closer relationships between universities and their immediate communities, or emphasise the vocational aspects of education.

During the early 1950s, with numbers much increased (science and technology doubled and arts subjects grew by 68 per cent between 1938 and 1952) the UGC began to wrestle with the difficulties of estimating employment demands. There was now 1 in 31 of the relevant age group, compared with 1 in 60 before the war, entering university in Great Britain; should the proportion grow further? The UGC noted that the Committee on Scientific Manpower (Barlow Report, 1946) had not thought it wise to aim at raising the university student population in the country to the American scale 'at the cost of so great a decline in entrance standards'. The UGC would welcome an increase, but subject to three conditions. First, it would want to ensure that there would be satisfactory employment for graduates. Second, accommodation and equipment should be adequate. Third, there should be no decline in standards. At the beginning of 1953 the UGC argued that the proportions of both the really good and of the really poor students were lower. There were many more second-class candidates. There could not be great increases in numbers without reducing quality (UGC, 1953).

The Committee's associated concern with academic independence was reflected in indirect ways. In particular, money reaching universities from government rather than from private benefactors or the UGC was thought of as tainted. There might be no immediate danger from taking on a larger number of government contracts, but only because most government research took place outside the universities. It should not, however, be overdone. Again, the UGC was reluctant to earmark funds for particular developments. The universities should determine their own excellences and not be over-responsive to central influence.

In the 1950s the universities and the emergent institutions within the public sector increasingly came under public view, partly because of the political ascendancy of those (such as David Eccles, a Minister of Education in the 1950s) who believed in an opportunity state, directly related to economic growth. Industry began to recruit many more graduate trainees, and the university began to figure in the minds of students more as a means of employment than as a civilising community.

At the same time, the universities experienced the problems created by increased dependency on the state, which caused the UGC itself to become more involved in systematic policy-making. University salaries were made uniform. Because in the 1960s many new institutions received charters, the UGC was compelled to take, and to express, a view of what universities should be like. For example, in deciding to encourage the creation of a university college at Sussex, it took account of where it should be located and of the optimum size and range of courses it should offer. Some demands for universities to be established elsewhere were turned down. The process of vetting such bids inevitably caused the UGC to build up criteria.

The assertion of stronger central policy was a direct consequence of growth. More A-level passes in the schools meant greater pressure for places. Yet the standards of what the universities provided were rising, as measured by such indicators as the increasing number of students able to be accommodated away from home and the improvement in staffing ratios from 1:10.2 in 1939 to 1:8.6 in 1952, and then to 1:7.2 in 1957. The resulting increases in cost led inevitably to more control over resources (UGC, 1958).

With all of this, the norm of university autonomy remained strong. The UGC deprecated any attempt to regard research as an activity separate from teaching, 'partly because it might give the impression that useful guidance could be given from the centre on the balance of effort between teaching and research' (UGC, 1958). It hoped that the universities would continue to ensure that the acceptance of outside support was consistent with the balanced development of their work. (Only some twenty years later, government demands for relevant research were made manifest not only through the UGC but even through the research councils, hitherto the main sources of independent academic finance in Britain.)

The UGC still remained resistant to new forms of higher education. As we have noted, it did not at first embrace willingly the notion of the technological university. 'We should regard the isolation of the institutions confined to a narrow range of subjects as unfavourable to high attainment' (UGC, 1958). So it pressed forward instead with the expansion of Imperial College, London (itself not far from being a technological university).

Throughout this period the UGC was able to promote expansion whilst maintaining the classic relationship between state and universities, in which the UGC was regarded by the universities as the guardian of their liberties – the buffer between government and universities, as one UGC chairman put it – and by government as responsible for seeing that increasing sums from the public purse were spent to the best advantage in the national interest. The mode of influence from the centre was that of negotiation rather than of managerial diktat.

The UGC report for 1962–67 (UGC, 1968) remarked on three distinct phases of development which could be identified since 1946. Until 1953 the UGC refurbished the universities for those whose education had been interrupted. If it was not to be business as usual, higher education was certainly not to spring too far out of the classic mould, even though newly available to a larger proportion of the population. Between 1952 and 1962 there was 'the trend' of voluntary staying-on at school, which brought pressure from qualified entrants for expansion. And now the UGC noted how the trend was being overtaken by the 'bulge' caused by the increase in birth rate immediately after the war. Already a university population of 200,000 was being contemplated. The UGC cautiously wondered whether the economy would be able to take the strain of these increases and whether particular subject needs might not be too strongly asserted against balanced development. It began, too, 'to pay close attention to developments elsewhere in the national structure of higher education'.

## EXPANSION AND THE BINARY PRINCIPLE

It is perhaps ironic that a proposal for a wide ranging inquiry into the universities in 1958 was headed off by Treasury opposition on the grounds that it would injure their autonomy and call into question the role of the UGC (David Walker, quoting Minutes of a Cabinet Committee, 1958, *Times Higher Educational Supplement*, 6 January 1989). The Robbins Report of 1963, as the UGC remarked, did not institute expansion in the universities or in the public sector institutions. At the end of 1967, well before the Report's recommendations had worked their way through the system, there were already 184,000 students and nearly 24,000 academic staff in the universities. The report instead established, publicly and authoritatively, the principles of development for higher education in this country. The Robbins Committee was itself an example of how central

authorities classically develop policy by co-opting both those who are
assumed to speak for societal needs and those who respond to professional
norms. The chairman was a leading academic but government assessors
were deeply involved. So, too, were other members who were academics
and representatives of local government and the schools. Among other
things, the report created the case for the preparation for degrees, and their
subsequent conferment, by bodies other than universities. Although for the
most part it advocated university-led expansion, the universities were none
the less compelled to consider their plans in relationship to those of other
institutions.

Anthony Crosland's Woolwich speech, made on 17 April 1965, set the
seal on this policy:

> On the one hand we have what has come to be called the autonomous
> sector, represented by the universities, in whose ranks, of course, I now
> include the colleges of advanced technology. On the other hand we have
> the public sector, represented by the leading technical colleges and the
> colleges of education. The Government accepts this dual system as
> being fundamentally the right one, with each sector making its own
> distinctive contribution to the whole. We infinitely prefer it to the
> alternative concept of a unitary system, hierarchically arranged on the
> 'ladder' principle, with the universities at the top and the other institu-
> tions down below.

The UGC voiced no opposition to the notion of a binary system and in
so doing accepted what some would regard as artificial differentiations.
The universities were to be more national than local in their recruitment,
more free to determine their own field of academic activity and standards,
and had their freedoms safeguarded by an independent University Grants
Committee. The non-university sector would teach undergraduate courses
in conjunction with non-degree work and would thus be 'vertically comprehensive'. It would be regionally or locally oriented, largely controlled
and directly financed by public authorities. It would meet national needs
but also the requirements of local industry and other forms of local demand.

These proposals were finally endorsed in the White Paper of May 1965,
*A Plan for Polytechnics and Other Colleges*. At this point, the UGC became
apprehensive as it saw how large would be the increase in the number of
full-time degree courses to be provided within the public sector. The
pressures on the universities from the competing sector developed at the
very time when the money available to nourish higher education became
more difficult to guarantee.

The creation of the binary system can be viewed as a dramatic intervention in both the norms and operations of higher education, and as an

affirmation that public purposes should be determined and acted on outside higher education. It can also be seen as a governmental assertion of the antinomy, discussed at the beginning of this chapter, between academic independence and conformity to social demands.

The universities themselves had diverse origins. Some were set up on the initiatives of groups of scholars, and others on the initiative of civic or private or ecclesiastical authorities. In contrast, 'the technical colleges were more the children of towns, or rather of town councils, administrative bodies which wanted to administer the new institutions, to press them and keep them in the mould which they saw as most appropriate to the demands of the city' (Giles, 1977). Hence their service tradition and Crosland's attempt to establish a separate sector for a different purpose, but one of equal merit. The polytechnics derived in part from an attempt to achieve equal educational opportunity for all, including those candidates of merit who did not find it easy to come in through the traditional route to the universities. The non-university institutions were intended, too, to provide for innovation in the field of higher education in ways of which the universities were felt to be incapable. They represented a form of pressure by the government. At this stage, the government would not and could not instruct the universities to change their ways. Instead, it set up an alternative system to bring about by other means what was thought to be necessary in the public interest. The polytechnics would have to fit their advanced courses into regional plans, and submit to a measure of local authority control and DES building programmes, and so be more firmly planned than the universities could be. They would incidentally have the advantage of being less expensive, and provide a means of rapidly meeting demand.

The case of the polytechnics demonstrates, however, that the basic characteristics of higher education cannot easily be overridden. The polytechnics opened the way to many developments to which the universities were not, at least at first, hospitable: more open access; part-time degrees; modular curricula; courses which were more formally planned, validated and monitored; a wider range of subjects and a much larger proportion of part-time students. After twenty-five years of development the two sectors still maintained important differences: the universities produced 90 per cent of those with postgraduate degrees and the polytechnics still had a much larger proportion of part-time students. Yet the polytechnics steadily moved towards the modes and aspirations of the universities in what Burgess and Pratt (1974) have called 'academic drift'. The universities in their turn moved towards meeting identifiable market needs. In effect, the distinctions between the two types of institution had within a decade become blurred, and the system, in the perception of staff, students and employers, came to resemble increasingly the 'ladder' which Crosland had deplored. By the latter 1980s both convergence between and a new stratification within the two sectors had become evident.

The Council for National Academic Awards (CNAA), founded in 1964 to regulate standards for, and to award, degrees outside universities, adopted norms not far different from those that any Senate would apply to the behaviour of basic units, while remaining open to innovations in curricular content. Indeed, its Charter proclaimed the intention to sustain similar standards; and in its first decade the great majority of its subject members were from universities. Accordingly, it sought to achieve comparability across all advanced higher education institutions, through its visitations and its panels which approved courses, as well as through its insistence on the use of external examiners. It urged resource standards as well as academic freedom for the polytechnics and their departments. In effect, it followed university traditions, practices and criteria, as the Robbins Committee had intended it should. Although it acted throughout its first decade as 'a relatively passive institution, more content to be the recipient of external pressure than the active initiator of policy' (Davis, 1979), its role became more assertive towards the end of the 1960s. Later it argued that comparability with university standards required sustained support and encouragement for research in the polytechnics. And in the 1980s, as the pressure of external evaluation made itself felt in the universities, the CNAA, responding in part to external pressure and criticism, increasingly liberalised its procedures in favour of institutional self-evaluation of courses (partly, at least, in response to institutional irritation with detailed control). But that movement was itself overtaken by the managerial drives of the Polytechnics and Colleges Funding Council (PCFC) established under the 1988 Education Reform Act.

## THE CHANGING NORMS

As the polytechnics developed and the Robbins planning figures were first achieved and then overtaken, the social context began to shift. The Robbins principle of open access to all those who were qualified greatly altered the scope and ethos of higher education. The assertion of the public ethic, of meeting the needs of society through more economically and socially relevant studies, came to be regarded as a particular function of the polytechnics, although all of the post-war UGC reports give some evidence of its previous recognition in the universities.

At the same time, the changes in client groups and the reciprocal weakening of authority in traditional institutions affected the whole academic milieu. Thus, if higher education traditionally was private, elite and eclectic in its purposes (and such was the part truth, part caricature of its pre-expansion nature), it had certainly become far more open and socially responsive at the end of the period of expansion. Even before the economic blizzards of the early 1970s academia seemed ready to acknowledge the need to respond to society's demands – always on the understanding that it would do so in its own ways, rather than those perceived by the central authorities, whose monopoly of understanding on these matters universities persistently questioned.

## CHANGES IN CENTRAL AUTHORITIES

The power of government grew with expansion. But government inter-vention had always been possible, if more often concerned with the con-stitutional arrangements than with the purposes of higher education. There were interventions by governments through the succession of Royal Com-missions in the nineteenth and twentieth centuries: these strongly affected the development of the Scottish universities (1826); the universities of Oxford and Cambridge (1850); the University of London (1909) and the University of Wales (1916). There was a Privy Council 'trial' in 1902 to determine whether the Victoria University should be divided into separate autonomous universities in Lancashire and Yorkshire (Ashby and Ander-son, 1974). Controversies over the relationship between St Andrews Uni-versity and Dundee University College led to a special UGC visitation in 1951 and a subsequent Royal Commission to settle the matter (UGC, 1953).

More than this, the Establishment has never shied from redefining the purposes of higher education. Even in the early years of the present century Haldane and others argued for a connected system of education in univer-sities, schools and colleges, to be organised in regions, each with a uni-versity as a 'brain and intelligence' of the whole, with teacher training as part of the university function. It was proposed that the organisation should be decentralised and that the pattern of curricula should both provide culture and apply scientific and other forms of knowledge to practical life. Haldane was more interventionist than most, but this duality had been preached by Matthew Arnold thirty years before and was later to be advocated by Lyon Playfair, T. H. Huxley and Henry Roscoe. (In contrast, Lord Davey, chairman of the commission charged with making statutes for the University of London in 1898, doubted 'whether the two objects – culture and professional training – can be carried on concurrently in a university' (Ashby and Anderson, 1974)). Thus even when university autonomy persisted most strongly, there was never a concept of academic freedom that eschewed connections with practical problems or professional training.

From the beginning of the post-war period, the UGC had no illusions about the implications of increased government support. Before the Second World War the sums given to the universities had been small, even if they were on the increase. Grants were intended, as the UGC itself noted (UGC, 1948), not to stimulate active policies of expansion and development but to encourage and facilitate improvements which the universities could make within a relatively stable financial framework. Government grants did not dictate the pace of progress. Between the two wars state interference and control were at a minimum. In 1938 grants were about one-third of the universities' total revenue. But by 1946 the Committee of Vice-Chancellors (in a note to universities on policy and finance) was able to assert that

> Universities entirely accept the view that the government has not only the right but the duty to satisfy itself that every field of study which in the national interest ought to be cultivated in Great Britain is in fact being cultivated in the university system and that the resources which are placed at the disposal of universities are being used with full regard both to efficiency and economy.

In the event, the UGC chose to perform these functions on behalf of government, not by direction but by stimulation, co-ordination and advice.

The most important evidence of the negotiative style was the maintenance of the quinquennial grant system. Universities received a block grant for recurrent expenses (capital grants were negotiated separately) to last for a five-year period. Supplementation for unavoidable increases in such costs as university salaries could, however, be allowed. The quinquennial system released both institutions and central authorities from detailed annual control and enabled the universities to pursue their own ends, once agreed in broad outline with the UGC, over a reasonably long planning period.

The UGC's decisions nevertheless answered to changes in the style and purpose of the central authorities as a whole. The second half of the 1960s was the period of manpower planning, of the ill-fated National Plan (1965), of optimism about the capability of planners to predict needs and specify institutions which would meet them. The Committee did not itself feel able to translate general expressions of need into particular numbers and types of output. For guidance on national and manpower requirements, it looked to the government through the Department of Education and Science – although it thought, realistically enough, that because demand could not be predicted, flexibility in the training of university graduates was necessary.

The UGC believed, as did the Robbins Committee, that entry to university courses was something over which universities had no direct control and that the size and balance of the flow of candidates to admission could not be closely related to national needs for graduate manpower. In this connection, one of the Robbins principles – the misleadingly named principle of 'social demand', which became government policy – was all-important: 'Courses of higher education should be available for all those who are qualified by ability and attainment to pursue them and who wish to do so.'

In its post-war reports, the UGC frequently referred to its role *vis-à-vis* the universities and government. The Committee thought it essential that it should be able to make a regular review in depth of university needs and university efficiency, both collectively and between one university and another (UGC, 1968). It stood firm on the quinquennial freedoms for over two decades, as well as on the principle of its being a buffer or shock-absorber between government and the universities. Anthony Crosland did not controvert this principle when he decided in 1967 that the universities should be open to audit. The Committee had in any case always been more than a buffer between government and institutions. It ensured some degree of connection through what some would call loose-coupling, between central authority policies and academic development. The functions of the UGC inevitably changed with the changes in the university system's scope and size. The increase of university institutions from twenty-four in 1944 to forty-three in 1967 made it all the more necessary that the Committee should exercise a positive role. It also had to consider what was being offered in non-university institutions. The universities began to see themselves as only a part, 'if a distinguished part' (UGC, 1968) of the nation's provision for higher education. The creation of the technological universities had already widened both the popular and the professional notions of what universities were for. On top of all this, the UGC saw the need to take cognisance of what the five research councils which also reported to the DES might do.

These developments caused inevitable changes in the structural position of the UGC and its relation to government. At first, there seemed to be no significant implication in the transfer of central government responsibility for universities from the Treasury to the DES which followed a minority report from the Robbins Committee. It was supposed to allow university education to be related to developments elsewhere, and to enable DES ministers to argue with the Treasury, which lost the embarrassment of being a spending department negotiating with itself about allocations. It was only later that a more directive style began to be adopted. This is commonly thought to have occurred with the allocations announced in 1967, when UGC preferences on the balance between different subjects and between the numbers of undergraduates and postgraduates were first stated in detail in a General Memorandum of Guidance (Shattock and Berdahl, 1984). It is anybody's guess whether the quinquennial arrangements would have survived, even in the absence of inflation and the associated financial retrenchment which precipitated a new system of short-term budgeting for universities in the early 1970s.

In 1976 the UGC had to report a conclusive downturn in the process of growth and a series of *ad hoc* decisions related to changing national pressures: 'As a result there is a deep and damaging sense of uncertainty which can only be removed by the restoration of the long term planning horizons': a viewpoint repeated in the Croham Report twelve years later. It was accepted that the taxpayers should receive full value for money. By the early 1970s, the UGC was already exerting influence on universities to specialise and concentrate their offerings. This led to adjustments in the number of places in particular subjects such as agriculture and forestry, area studies, mining, metallurgy and agricultural economics, although such measures were not unknown before. The UGC began to take account of developments on the other side of the binary line which were brought into its deliberations through discussion with the DES (UGC, 1977). But it continued strongly to defend the principle of university autonomy, which was not only a recognition of academic freedom but also, it maintained, exemplified good management practice.

## THE STATE ASSERTS ITSELF

The Robbins Report did not so much radically change these assumptions as legitimise them and promote them into explicit policy. Its associated research by Bowen (Robbins, 1963) clarified the assumption that there was a link between investment in higher education and the economy. The enquiries under the Committee's aegis, and those carried out independently by Douglas (1964), broke the belief that there was a limited reservoir of talent and created the conviction that instead there was a 'widow's cruse' providing a regular flow of the talent to meet the number of places that might be provided. In principle, there need be no limit to the stock of educability upon which higher education could depend, and it must follow in a democratic society concerned with equality of opportunity that all who wanted to enter higher education and were appropriately qualified should be allowed to do so. The Robbins Report has subsequently been criticised for not facing the financial consequences of unlimited qualified entry (Carswell, 1985).

But by the end of the 1960s, confidence in the objectives and operational capacities of higher education began to decline. With increased uncertainty in the economy at large, the demand for graduates stopped growing (Williams, 1984) and with it the pressure for places. Radical student behaviour undoubtedly contributed further to public questioning of the value of higher education. Although the resulting period of disruption was short-lived, and involved only a small minority of students, its aftermath is held still to affect the ability of some of the better UK universities to recruit able students. The oil crisis of the early 1970s was one of the factors which helped precipitate the collapse of the quinquennial system of grants which had symbolised society's willingness to trust the universities to meet social needs at the same time as they satisfied academic wants.

None the less, a number of positive changes took place during this period. The public sector of higher education grew in quantitative strength and in acceptability. On one important index, the equality function began to be successfully served: the number of undergraduate places taken by women rose from 25 per cent to over 40 per cent between 1960 and 1988 (Fulton, 1988), although the social class composition of recruitment hardly changed. 'Sectoral' or publicly commissioned research grew in quantity. By the end of the 1970s, the independent research capacity of higher education was to be drastically reduced through government action, and even the limiting assumptions about commissioned and policy-related research, embodied in the Rothschild Report (1971), were replaced by sharply instrumental programmes. But until the change of administration in 1979, government seemed prepared to contemplate the increased growth of higher education and of spontaneous student recruitment as if it were a self-sufficient good (Oakes, 1978). It produced different models of how to cope with a brief expansion followed by a slump in number, through, for example, 'tunnelling through the hump'.

Throughout the 1970s, therefore, the activities of higher education sustained a sometimes uneasy but broadly consensual balance between the social and economic needs which might be imputed to the central authorities and the internal drives of academic endeavour. Poor economic performance was beginning to upset the earlier optimism about a whole range of public sector programmes. Sometimes willingly, sometimes cautiously and under pressure, higher education edged towards becoming a mass as opposed to an elite system and one increasingly responsive to social needs.

## THE COLDER CLIMATE

Up to this point (the early 1980s), the history of higher education in the UK conformed to the outlines of our model in Chapter 2. But the subsequent working of British higher education represents a sharp turning away from the whole of its previous history – a history which was admittedly idiosyncratic to the UK. As Neave (1986) recounts, in the Continental European countries the revolutions of the late eighteenth and nineteenth centuries ensured that the university was incorporated in the national bureaucracy. By contrast, in the UK,

> the status of academia as a property owning corporation of scholars, the purest expression of which was in the two Ancient British universities, was preserved.... Until the first World War, British political life had no concept of 'The State' as a distributive or regulative entity ... and ... particularly in the field of education ... there existed a broadly held view which regarded education ... as ill-served by state intervention.

Instead there developed the idea of the facilitatory state which would provide resources to universities whose freedom would be enjoyed within an area of negotiation largely controlled by the universities themselves. The resulting autonomy was both institutional and individual, and embodied in charters and collegial self-government.

In their normative mode the central authorities set and maintained standards of quality, relevance and effectiveness for the system and its constituent institutions until the late 1970s. They did so discreetly and even diffidently through the judgements made on the distribution of resources by academics working through informal peer review. The broad determination of policy depended on the centre's interpretation of social and economic interests and demands which were signalled, if imperfectly and unsystematically, through the political system and the policy communities of which the government forms part.

Government, however, reached many of its judgements on the assumption that what academics thought to be good research and teaching was likely to be good for the economy and society. The judgements of government amalgamated with those of academics co-opted through membership of the central bodies. It can, moreover, be questioned whether in the period from 1945 to 1980 higher education constituted a system in more than a notional sense: the linkages of value and authority were relatively loose.

A new pattern began to emerge from the early 1980s onwards. Government reduced the resources available to higher education whilst insisting that it met increased demands. At every point of control, the centre asserted itself: on the numbers of students to be recruited; on higher education's duty to evaluate its activities; on a selective reapportionment of resources for research although research councils had long moved towards selectivity (Shattock, 1989); on the development of entrepreneurial activities and attitudes; and by the insistence on efficiency and managerialism in place of the mixture of collegial and hierarchical governance. The central authorities grew certain that their own values, which were assumed to equate with societal values, should be the starting point for higher education's objectives, which would be imposed on both teaching and research through a set of explicit, directionally funded policies. Even the modes of internal management and quality control were no longer to be left to academics to decide for themselves: institutions and their basic units became more accountable to the centre.

In the university sector, the rule of the academics was to be broken in the provisions of the Education Reform Act 1988, with the replacement of the University Grants Committee by the Universities Funding Council – much as, in the polytechnics and colleges sector, the rule of the local authorities was broken by the replacement of the National Advisory Body for Public Sector Higher Education (NAB) by the Polytechnics and Colleges Funding Council (PCFC). To a discerning eye there could be previous intimations of the UGC's mortality, dating from the early 1960s (Moodie, 1983, 1987). Of the eighteen UGC members, thirteen were academics, three were industrialists and two represented local authorities. It was led by a distinguished academic of vice-chancellorial level. The Universities Funding Council (UFC) was intended instead to be under the chairmanship of an industrialist. In fact a hybrid personality, the Vice-Chancellor of Cranfield Institute of Technology but with industrial connections, was appointed, and the former Chairman, an academic, became Chief Executive. The new body had fifteen members comprising nine academics, five industrialists and one polytechnic director. The local authority interest disappeared. An infrastructure of committees was not assumed.

The PCFC, established at the same time, replaced the NAB. Like the UFC it was committed to some form of contract funding, and it appeared, at initiation, to be more specific about certain policies such as rewarding institutions which increased access to different groups of students. A new funding regime and a new planning process were initiated. Strategic plans had to be submitted to the PCFC and polytechnics and colleges could no longer simply react to targets for individual academic programme areas. Both the Councils' non-academic membership would be biased towards industry and business.

New university staff were not to be offered the tenure which their predecessors had enjoyed. At the same time, government maintained that it was not interested in creating a 'command' model of higher education, but rather one in which institutions could compete and earn their own rewards in the academic market place.

## CONTEXTUAL FACTORS

The most obvious contextual issue of higher education policy in the 1980s was demography. Higher education policy has always been extremely sensitive to the numbers of potential students presenting themselves.

Educational demography always has two components – that created by the numbers in the main age cohort from which students are recruited and that created by a combination of student demand and governmental, institutional and employment incentives. The first of these factors was not as important as the second, except inasmuch as anticipation of a drastic reduction in student numbers from the later 1980s onwards affected the policy discussion (Oakes Report, DES, 1978).

From 1982/83 to 1988/89 the number of 18-year-olds had declined by 10 per cent and was due to drop by a further 24 per cent by the mid-1990s: but, to the surprise of some, the numbers coming forward for higher education continued to increase in the 1980s. This enabled government radically to change the policies which had seemed likely to be endorsed in the early part of the decade. It first took credit for the enhanced recruitment and then decided that the system should accommodate a much higher proportion of the available population. The Age Participation Rate (APR) would thus increase from about 14 per cent of school leavers to whatever could be reached – figures between 23 per cent and 30 per cent by the end of the 1990s were quoted by ministers. This would call for no great expansion because the APR would grow against a reduced age cohort, and, in any case, higher education had shown that it would take in more students without more generous funding, though protesting all the while that a reduced unit of resource would result in lower standards.

By the end of the 1980s the prospect of so drastic a change in recruitment pattern had had a significant effect. Proposals were made that the funding bodies should reward institutions which recruited applicants with lower A-level scores and those with non-traditional qualifications (Fulton and Ellwood, 1989). The academic gold standard implied by Robbins' principle of social demand would thus be abandoned. British higher education would move from the borderline between an elite and a mass system to being well on the way towards a universal system.[1] With it, the case for an explicit stratification of institutions, differentiating those concentrating on teaching from those concentrating on research, would become plausible.

If demography was one salient contextual factor, ideology provided another. Throughout the 1970s the traditional assumptions about the Welfare State – of which higher education formed one element – remained firm, if somewhat battered by economic hazards and growing lack of confidence in the capacity of public systems to deliver services with sufficient responsiveness and economy. The 1979 Conservative government arrived with a mandate to roll back the frontiers of the state. Moreover, whilst every previous government had gone through at least the form of working with the policy communities affected by changes of policy, this government was impatient of negotiation and of protests on the effects of drastic changes (Young, 1989).

The universities were no longer liked or trusted as they had been in the heyday of expansion. By contrast, the polytechnics were given more freedom through their incorporation, and seemed more in favour with the government. This feeling was not exclusive to Conservative ministers: the universities found no constituency prepared to come to their aid, even when they were subjected to the consequences of the most drastic government ideology. By the early 1990s many of those working in universities were feeling undervalued and out of political and social favour, a phenomenon common to other European countries as well (Taylor, 1987). In higher education at large staff considered themselves underpaid even in comparison with those in other publicly funded occupations.

## THE EFFECT OF CUTS IN FUNDING

The first moves of government to reduce the financial commitment to higher education appear to have been less a result of specific higher education policy than of a general Treasury-led movement to limit public expenditure. University grants had already suffered from a 10 per cent reduction through failures to compensate fully for inflation in the 1970s. The period 1972–77 was the last in which even the illusion of quinquennial funding of the universities had been sustained. The fact that it had been allowed at all was evidence of the trust with which government had treated the universities throughout the period of their great expansion. In 1973–74 there were particularly fierce cutbacks. In 1974, the award of a committee on public sector teaching salaries (Houghton, 1974) created, for the first time – if temporarily – higher salaries in the public than in the university sector and the government's reluctance in removing this 'anomaly' was rightly seen as evidence of changing attitudes towards the universities. The year 1974–75 became the final one in which substantial capital funds were available through the UGC (Moore, 1987).

In 1979 the process of charging overseas students a higher fee than that required of home-based students, begun in 1967 by Anthony Crosland, was carried to its extreme and also used as a further means of cutting government subsidy. Institutions lost funds on the assumption that they could be recouped by recruiting the same number of overseas students in 1980 as before, even though fees would be much higher. This decision was taken with no apparent regard for the way in which it discriminated against institutions recruiting many such students or for the more general effects on Britain's role as a major world provider of higher education. Taking together the reduction in recurrent grant for overseas student fees and the cuts imposed in 1981, the universities lost between 13 and 15 per cent of their income over the three years, depending on how many overseas students were recruited. It took some years to restore their numbers, which finished up being redistributed differently between institutions.

The year 1981 was one of drastic policy change. A positive reduction in university places for the first time became inevitable. The members of the UGC were required by the government to make a painful decision. It was left to them whether to reduce student numbers or to reduce the unit of resource (the notional amount allocated per student which included provision for research). In a much-criticised decision (for example, Kogan and Kogan, 1983) they decided to reduce student numbers by about 20,000 (in the event, nothing approaching that reduction occurred). It has been argued (Moore, 1987) that had this not been done the government would have thought the UGC to be failing in its main function. The cuts in funds and the consequent reduction in student places took place at a time of peak demand from school leavers, and the polytechnics rapidly took advantage of the lack of control over their own admissions to recruit many of the students who were thus unexpectedly refused university places.

The cuts were visited differentially on the universities. Most technological universities did badly. Others, such as Keele, fell foul of the new policy criteria which particularly penalised those institutions with a bias towards the arts and social sciences (Stewart, 1989). The UGC allocations were significant in that they purported to incorporate quality judgements, thus beginning the process of stratifying universities and departments which became more explicit in the 1986 research grading exercise. In the latter, the UGC graded cost centres (clusters of subject disciplines) in four bands, and published the results, a procedure repeated with variations in 1989. Within a five-year period, some 14 per cent of UGC funds to universities were to be distributed according to the hierarchy of esteem established by such gradings. The notion that all British universities formed part of an elite group was thus called in question.

## PLANNING AND GOVERNANCE

The pressures produced by demographic uncertainties and the less predictable elements of ideology, associated with reduced funding and variable policies on access, were reflected in changing patterns of governance and planning. In summary, these were the creation of more explicit planning mechanisms at the centre; the insinuation of particular educational and research objectives by government; and the requirement that institutions become more efficient through the strengthening of managerial structures and techniques.

In different degrees there has been, at least since 1945, national planning of higher education. Certain sectors such as teacher and medical education have been funded on the basis of the estimated numbers of new recruits needed. Inasmuch as government funded, or allowed others such as local authorities to fund, places in higher education, some kind of predictive frame for student numbers and the accompanying resources had to be erected. In the main, however, the system lacked the ingredients necessary for a comprehensive planning structure until the late 1970s.

Different elements of a more systematic schema began to come into place in the 1980s. Public sector higher education had been planned directly by the DES, which approved courses of advanced studies in the poly-technics and colleges on the advice rendered (*ad hoc*, rather than as part of a national plan) by regional staff inspectors and Regional Advisory Coun-cils. They assessed student demand, the possible incidence of duplicated provision and the likely quality of what would be provided. There was, however, no effective control over money spent: LEAs could charge a central pool, to which they all contributed, for the costs of providing higher education through their colleges. In 1978 the Oakes working group (Oakes, 1978) recommended that a national planning body should be set up for local authority colleges. Oakes brought DES policies into the open, added sup-port for the creation of a body analogous to the UGC, and reduced the direct planning role of the DES (McVicar, 1989).

The Oakes proposals were abandoned with the fall of the Labour government in 1979. None the less, in 1980 the new government decided to limit the size of the pool. A representative group convened by the DES then found it necessary to determine how to distribute the now restricted resource to institutions. 'In the absence of any ministerial planning strategy this group was obliged to devise a formula which allocated resources against historic student numbers ... and which incorporated an element of discrimination against colleges with high unit costs' (Booth, 1987).

The consequent creation of the NAB and its eventual demise in 1989 illustrate the way in which higher education in the UK was progressively placed within central control. Previously, the public sector had been demand- rather than policy-led. An earlier minister for Higher Education had rejected the case for any central agency, on the grounds that weaker institutions could be left to wither on the vine. But parliamentary pressure and the manifest need for some planning machinery caused a reversal of this *laissez-faire* policy. DES officials put out for consultation (DES, 1981) two plans, one of which would allow the control and funding of public sector higher education to remain with LEAs whilst, under the other plan, public sector institutions would receive funds directly from the DES on the advice of a body analogous to the UGC. In a compromise scheme the LEAs were secured a strong role in policy-making for the sector through their membership of the NAB. The NAB's terms of reference were to advise the Secretary of State on the academic provision to be made in institutions, the apportionment of the Advanced Further Education pool, and the approval of advanced courses. A two-tier structure consisting of a committee, an essentially political body, chaired by the minister and with six LEA political representatives, was placed over a board whose chairman was on the committee and whose members came from the DES, the LEAs and a range of other interests (Booth, 1987).

The LEAs owned the institutions, and membership of the NAB required them to participate in a national planning frame. By all accounts they did this vigorously. They legitimated national resource allocations. If there was one particular objective which they promoted above others, it was wider access: it was this, as much as local pride, that made the LEA representatives support dispersion rather than concentration of resources. Such conflicts as occurred were between central and local authority perspectives rather than on party lines.

The decision to transform the NAB into the PCFC was wholly political. By 1986, tension had built up over the choice between sustaining an acceptable unit of resource and expanding numbers. In the spring of that year the NAB published proposals for the 1987 planning exercise, showing that, on the resources allowed by the government, 10,000 student places would have to disappear. At a moment uncomfortably close to the 1987 general election, government felt bound to yield by providing an increased allocation: but the episode helped to number the days of LEA control (McVicar, 1989), which was in any case being reduced throughout a range of other functions. The Committee of Directors of Polytechnics had for some time been pressing for freedom from their LEAs. In the 1988 Act, the government decided to allow the polytechnics and certain other institutions to become incorporated bodies, divested of LEA ownership and control. At the same time, it replaced the NAB by the PCFC, which had no LEA representatives; its members were chosen instead on a personal basis. Thus was expunged a key assumption underlying Crosland's creation of the binary system, that a public sector under the local authorities could serve public purposes in a way not to be entrusted to the universities.

The changes in the UGC were as significant as those in the allocation system of the public sector. From 1967 onwards, observers have noted an increasing propensity to offer guidance to and create a plan for the universities (for example, Shattock and Berdahl, 1984). However, the universities still retained considerable freedom throughout the 1970s, albeit with much reduced financial subventions from the centre. Guidance could still be ignored, and universities that used their block recurrent grants in their own ways might find themselves restored to grace if their development proved successful. No reduction of provision was assumed, even if the students were less easy to recruit and the unit of resource somewhat weaker than in the 1960s. Attempts by government to suggest modifications of objectives and ways of working (as in Shirley Williams' thirteen points, which included, for example, proposals for two-year degree courses) were easily brushed aside. A sector not so much opposed to as disdainful of government intervention left itself open to subsequent counter-attack. Meanwhile, bit by bit the national policy lines and priorities between the main subject fields were beginning to be asserted.

It was, however, the 1981 reductions that led to a wholesale change of mode. 'Whilst the UGC had been dirigiste upwards before, for example, over the capital grants in expansionist days, it now had to become dirigiste downwards, giving guidance on student numbers in much narrower subject groupings than before' (Moore, 1987). By 1985, the UGC had become a full-blooded planning organisation which required universities to respond in the same mode. It called for statements of overall objectives for the planning period, a detailing of research achievements and plans, forecasts of student numbers in various subject groups and financial forecasts up to July 1990. This type of request became normal and frequent. The universities were pressed without remission not only for data but also for declarations of their intentions. The May 1985 letter spelled out the UGC's intended method of allocating grants. One of the components was to be a research resource based partly on the ability to earn research grants and partly on the UGC's judgement of research quality. This factor was to have an increasing effect on the support given to individual universities from 1986 onwards. The letter also outlined the first selectivity exercise which introduced explicit institutional and departmental rankings. At the same time, in 1986, as we have noted, the UGC published ratings of the research standing of all university 'cost centres'; the use of that designation of higher education units is significant in itself. That act of public evaluation seemed intended to put resources into those centres deemed excellent, to punish and deflect trade from those deemed to be below par and to assure a punitive DES that academics would respond to ministers' notions of accountability and not simply bask in the informal rules of the Republic of Science. It represented a decisive move towards formula funding. It also heralded the stronger stratification of universities and basic units which would in any case be accentuated by the very publication of the gradings. There was considerable academic hostility against the methods used, the secrecy surrounding the ranking procedure and the denial of provision for appeals (Smith, 1987).

The premium on research selectivity was to become greater as higher education passed through the 1980s. The UGC undertook (UGC, 1987) to report annually to the Secretary of State on universities' arrangements for drawing up and carrying out plans for the selective distribution of the resources they devoted to research. It was taken for granted that research can be planned and that its successful inauguration depends on the predictions of those who cause plans to be drawn up for the consideration of committees. In its letter to the Secretary of State, the UGC stated that

> it intends to monitor two aspects of the selective distribution by universities of their resources for research: (i) the machinery for planning and implementing research priorities within the university; and (ii) the distribution of resources among departments, and the extent to which it is correlated with the UGC's research assessments.

It then went on to give a detailed account of the effects of its 'Strategy Advice'. About a dozen institutions, it reported to its ministerial sponsors, had been unsatisfactory for one or more of three reasons: inadequate detail; lack of clarity; indications of lack of progress in implementing research selectivity.

This is centralist dirigisme in which a predominantly academic committee acted as if it were appropriate to report to a minister on the managerial competence of its fellow academics. It leaves no doubt of the growing reach, and authoritarian stance, of the central authorities over what had come to be regarded as the terrains of disciplinary groups acting through peer review.

The Advisory Board for Research Councils (ABRC) attempted to create a strategy for the research base (ABRC, 1987) which laid emphasis on programme grants, sought to differentiate between research, teaching and 'mixed' Higher Education Institutions (HEIs), and to create Interdisciplinary Research Centres. Not only did the UGC and the ABRC show a growing tendency to set the objectives for research but themselves came under the hand of more determined policy directions from the inner circle of government, led by the Prime Minister's Office, the Cabinet Office and the Advisory Council on Science and Technology (ACOST), a body designed to promote research strategically tilted towards the needs of the economy, chaired by an industrialist. With the encouragement of the DES the five research councils set Corporate Plans and applied performance measures to their work. The ABRC encouraged them to sponsor research which met council- – and government- – devised objectives rather than proposals put up by the researchers themselves. The concern for co-ordination even led to a proposal that all five councils should be merged into a single overarching council.

During the UGC's latter years its functions went beyond the strenuous and detailed determination of resource planning. At the behest of the DES it put pressure on the universities to move to models of strong management in both their structures and behaviour. A joint committee of the UGC and the Committee of Vice-Chancellors and Principals produced a report (Jarratt, 1985) which took the managerial doctrine to an extreme. Vice-Chancellors were to adopt the role of chief executives to whom deans and heads of departments would report as line managers. The universities would create and work under a corporate plan that would be formulated by a small group drawn from the lay council and the senior academic management. The report was explicitly hostile to the power of departments. It urged the use of performance indicators, but failed to mention the functions of teachers, researchers or students – an omission not repeated in the less well publicised equivalent NAB report (NAB, 1987). Its implementation was a requirement the UGC placed on universities, a few of which adopted it with avidity. The requirements for universities to respond to endless UGC enquiries, to meet the demands for selectivity, and to satisfy the Jarratt definition of efficiency, undoubtedly increased the power of the university administration at the expense of the senior academics and the academically led committee systems.

Alongside these developments came an insistence on more rigorous control of academic standards in universities. The public sector was moving, or perhaps being moved, towards more flexible and sophisticated forms of institutional and course validation (Lindop, 1985); at about the same time, the CVCP set up codes of practice on the maintenance and monitoring of standards, including external examining and the arrangements for postgraduate training and research (Reynolds, 1986). In this respect, as in others, the two sectors began to converge.

## NORMS AND OPERATIONS

Over the period of our review, from 1945 to 1989, British higher education displayed dramatic changes in its policies and ways of working. The measure of the changes can be seen in the 1987 White Paper (DES, 1987a). There were to be more students. The need for quality and efficiency was held to justify more selectively funded research 'targeted with attention to prospects for commercial exploitation'. Government was to make money available through the funding councils on contracts and to monitor performance on those contracts. Institutions which made themselves useful to business would be rewarded. This policy was reinforced by the creation of an Enterprise Initiative which provided grants to a total of £100 million for higher education institutions prepared to 'inbed [*sic*] initiative into the curriculum' (Manpower Services Commission, 1987).

The system had changed from being a small group of universities and of public institutions, loosely held together, catering for a minuscule proportion of the population, to a largely centralised system with a sizeable recruitment. Academic norms and modes of self-governance had given way to powerful objective-setting by the central authorities. At the same time, institutions were being invited to respond to the needs and demands of the markets constituted by students and research sponsors, described by the Secretary of State in 1989 as 'a movement towards mass higher education accompanied by greater institutional differentiation and diversification in a market-led and multi-funded setting' (Baker, 1989). The extent to which traditional academic values and ways of working would actually change under these prescriptions remained to be seen.

How does this account of changes in the central authorities' relations with higher education institutions relate to our model? From 1945 the central authorities acted in terms of their own norms concerning equality and student access, and the role of higher education in the economy. Accordingly they commanded the operational decisions on the large-scale expansion of numbers, the endorsement of new institutions and new types of courses and groupings of subjects. They controlled the important if somewhat artificial divisions between private concerns and public purposes as entailed in the binary system. Policies laid down by the central authorities were translated from the normative into the operational mode through the conferment of status upon different institutions, through laying down their governing systems, through allocating funds for the buildings and staff essential to running the system.

The normative and operational functioning of the central authorities had never, therefore, been in doubt. There are two main changes which our historical account displays. First, whereas the normative assumptions underlying operational decisions were once implicit, they later became explicit (if not always unambiguous). In the view of many we have consulted, the norm of peer control of academic content remained strong (see also Boys *et al.*, 1988) but was now directly pressed by the central authorities' social and educational agenda. Second, whereas the central authorities were earlier prepared to concede to the basic units and individuals, at least in universities, powerful degrees of self-determination within an order negotiated largely on the basic units' behalf by the institutions with the central authorities, they now sought to determine the norms pursued by the academics. And towards the end of the 1980s, it was they who began to insist that academic decision-making be guided by market and enterprise considerations as well as by those of academic excellence: a point to which we shall return in Chapter 10.

## NOTES

1  Trow's definitions of these stages (Trow, 1970) depends on age-enrolment rates. But comparisons between the stage reached in different countries need to be made cautiously because UK enrolment rates produce proportionately higher graduation rates; so-called full-time students in many countries are *de facto* part-timers because substantially engaged in paid employment; and the definition of what constitutes a higher education institution, and thus higher education, is highly variable between countries.

# 4    The working of the whole system

## THE CENTRAL AUTHORITIES AND THE MODEL

In this chapter we outline the central functions of British higher education and consider the ways in which central authorities work with other levels. We also consider whether and how higher education institutions are part of a structure that behaves systematically, in the sense that it strives to achieve compatibility between each of the levels in terms of objectives, processes and products.

If the higher education system was once an informally linked range of institutions, what elements now exist which form a higher education system? As both Clark (1983) and Becher (1985) have implied, it would be wrong to look for too tidy and rigid a definition. But we assume that a system rigorously defined has common values, or at least agreement on the range of values to be tolerated, that it makes values operational through the creation of goals or objectives which can guide the evaluation of performance of parts of the system and the allocation of resources to them. It incorporates sufficient authority to ensure that common goals are met.

In Figure 4.1 we illustrate the components and relationships of the central authorities as established in the model set out in Chapter 2. The central authorities are portrayed as maintaining certain norms concerned with standards of quality, relevance and effectiveness which are conditioned by the external norms of economic, political and social expectations. These condition specific judgements about the quality of individual institutions, courses and units which the central authorities make operational through allocation of funding and course provision. Decisions about which institutions to expand and which courses to maintain and develop, although allocative in their modes and consequences, are themselves a reflection of normative judgements. In the operational mode, the central authorities also respond directly to economic and social demands through access policies, man- power planning and the like.

*Figure 4.1* The functions of the central authorities

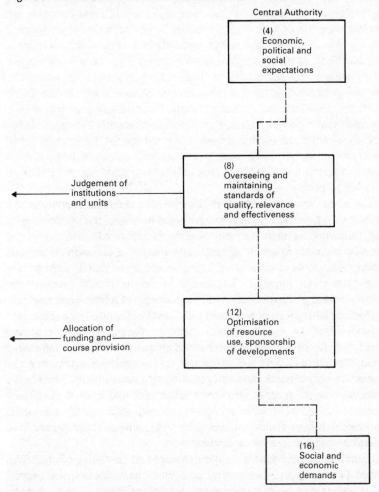

# CENTRAL AUTHORITIES AND THE SETTING OF NATIONAL OBJECTIVES

The normative content of decision-making by the central authorities has become progressively more overt. Throughout the period of expansion the objectives stated in the Robbins Report (1963) were implicitly accepted by the central authorities. The four main objectives then accepted were: instruction in skills suitable to play a part in the general division of labour; the promotion of powers of the mind; the advancement of learning; and the transmission of a common culture and common standards of citizenship.

Since then, additional objectives have come into discussion, although they are not always accepted to the same degree by different governments. Thus the objective of wide access responds both to economic objectives and to those of increased social equality, particularly if its increase will enhance the educational chances of hitherto under-recruited groups such as women, older people and ethnic minorities. The connection between higher education and economic development came into serious doubt in the 1970s (Williams, 1984) and the central authorities accordingly were less willing to assume that higher education must continue inexorably to expand. However, the sharp demographic decline projected for the 1990s (which had already begun in the 1980s) made access to a wider range of the population more acceptable, and indeed essential unless the system were to be allowed to shrink by perhaps a quarter.

The advancement of learning for its own sake is no longer considered a social good so overriding that resources are to be given for it unhesitatingly. Nor, following the increased stratification of higher education, can it be said that exposure to it will automatically transmit a common culture and common standards of citizenship. Some would argue that it ought to promote even wider ranges of knowledge criteria than now predominate; others would urge the restoration of elite concepts of learning and research.

Do these national objectives hold at the level of the institution, basic unit and individual? Do the central authorities use their authority to reinforce them? In different degrees, all institutions are at least implicitly committed to the Robbins objectives and, albeit to a somewhat lesser extent, to wider access; the Polytechnics and Colleges Funding Council (PCFC) makes it a prime indicator of success. Objectives at the basic unit level, it can be said (Boys *et al.*, 1988), remain modelled predominantly on the traditional academic values of disinterested enquiry and teaching related primarily to individual rather than to skills development

In the 1980s, government's coyness abated and the setting of objectives ceased to be implicit. But central authorities have always made social policy judgements in deter- mining the numbers of places to be funded and the levels of student support to be allowed. There was always, too, an implicit concern for manpower outcomes in the prescription of numbers to be taught within the broad subject areas (first made known to the universities in 1967) and the pro- portions of undergraduate and graduate places. The central authorities were making a normative judgement each time they divided allocations of resource and places between the polytechnic and the university sectors. The determination to assert objectives which directly affect the research and curriculum agenda has already been noted. Authority is exercised through power to allocate.

Despite the sharp and decisive fluctuations of policy that can be, and have been, induced by changes in political control and the more general social and economic climate, the central authorities seek to defend the basic academic norms. In common with the institutions, they have the fiduciary role of maintaining the system. In theory at least, the claims of all interest groups and the merits of all proposals for change are weighed in the balance before any decisive move is made and in principle, too, government is reckoned to be predictable, accountable and equitable at the same time as it responds to social change. To some extent, therefore, the radical changes induced by government in the 1980s were a deviation from the classic position of the central authorities.

## THE DIVISION OF TASKS BETWEEN GOVERNMENT AND THE INTERMEDIARY BODIES

In their normative mode the functions of the central authorities are evaluative and judgemental; those in the operational mode are concerned with allocating resources and sanctioning new developments or imposing reductions. In some systems of higher education, one agency of government both evaluates and allocates, although there can hardly be a system which does not co-opt academics into the making of judgements about academic quality and academic requirements. In the UK a clear distinction is made between what the organs of central government decide through their own machinery, and what decisions are delegated to the intermediate central authorities which occupy a position between government and the individual institution.

The central government decides the level of resources which will meet what it considers to be social and economic needs; it also formulates such framework policies as how many places shall be financed in the different sectors of higher education, what resources to provide for each and therefore the quality of provision. Increasingly, too, it expresses views on the deeper purposes and modes of functioning of the system in a way not known before the 1980s.

Having made the framework decisions, however, it hands over the specific negotiations with and allocations to institutions to its two principal funding bodies and to five research councils which themselves work under an increasingly co-ordinative system (Kogan and Henkel, forthcoming). Other funding agencies, such as the Training Agency, have also been part of the intermediary system of central authorities which set norms and make allocations within government.

No allocation is made without some value judgement at its base and the make-up of intermediate bodies is therefore likely to reflect the values which central government wishes to assert for higher education policy. In Chapter 3, we have described the reconstitution of the two main funding councils, the Universities Funding Council and the Polytechnics and Colleges Funding Council. The strong insertion of non-academic economic and social interests in the membership of the UFC and the removal from the PCFC of its predecessor body's Local Education Authority representation are explicit expressions of the social and economic desiderata within which central government wishes to act.

If the funding councils, among which should be included the research councils under the Advisory Board for Research Councils, are concerned with converting governmental norms into operational decisions on the allocation of resources and other provision, there is a second species of intermediary body almost wholly concerned with normative judgements undertaken on the basis of explicit evaluations. Some evaluative mechanisms are lodged within institutions themselves; universities, for example, have power by their Charters to award degrees. Public sector institutions do not, and must either have their qualifications validated by universities or by the Council for National Academic Awards (CNAA). The CNAA operates on peer judgements. In recent years it has granted many institutions the power to validate their own courses and assessment procedures within criteria set down by the Council, which still awards the degrees.

## CENTRAL AUTHORITIES AND PEER REVIEW

Central authorities depend for their evaluations on two peer systems. Academic peer groups occupy an ambiguous position within higher education. We have seen that some of their leading members are co-opted by the central authorities to assess the academic promise of the relevant basic units; at the same time, they are expected to contribute to authoritative decisions, delegated by government to the central authorities, on the allocation of institutional resources. Here we may note the caveat expressed by Burton R. Clark (1978) that 'it is better to assume that order is variously determined, rather than produced by administration alone'. In many higher education systems, he writes, there are national and centralised bureaucracies: but 'always underneath that superstructure which lodged power in ministerial hands, there was the understructure of guild-like faculty units which lodged local power in professorial hands'. But as Clark later observed (1983), academics are subject to a matrix of their own guild-like structures which provide professional networks outside the institution and which now tap into the larger governing system. In the UK we can see some tension between the guild, the co-optative and the managerial systems, aspects of which will be explored further in Chapter 10.

Peer review operates strongly and widely through external examining, through the vetting of academic publications for learned journals and the like, and through the system by which academics are appointed and promoted. This is the 'invisible college' at work. A second and more formalised peer system is that of the CNAA and professional bodies in certain areas such as medicine, social work and the law and teaching, which validate courses or approve institutions which validate their own courses. Control over substantive content is allocated to intermediary bodies such as the General Medical Council, or the Central Council for Education and Training in Social Work (CCETSW), which administer different degrees of peer and practitioner control. Some agencies are backed by legislation enabling them to license practitioners or by Royal Charters giving them legal autonomy. Their judgements may be used to validate content or to underpin decisions by funding bodies on whether or not to allocate resources.

## HIGHER EDUCATION AND THE REST OF CENTRAL GOVERNMENT

The central authorities are themselves part of a larger government machine. Ministerial responsibility for higher education rests with the Secretary of State for Education and Science and his or her Department, the DES. The Secretary of State appoints the two main funding councils and also the Advisory Board for Research Councils (ABRC). The ABRC co-ordinates the overall policies for the five research councils. But this DES infrastructure itself responds to ministerial consideration of science and technology priorities under the Prime Minister's leadership. It does so with the assistance of an expanded independent advisory body – the Advisory Council on Science and Technology (ACOST) – whose remit is to advise across 'the whole of scientific and technological endeavour, international as well as British'. ACOST is expected to establish working relationships with departmental advisory bodies, including the ABRC. Its secretariat is located in the Cabinet Office and reports to the Chief Scientific Adviser to the government. It also has close links with the Treasury, which (in concert with the Cabinet Office) requires the DES and the ABRC to set research objectives and to assess performance as well as to control budgets. A Science and Technology Assessment Office helps departments, the research councils and the UFC to assess their R and D expenditures and evaluate the results. The ambition is to establish clear objectives for expenditure and develop systematic criteria for assessing and managing research.

The research functions of higher education are thus considered to be part of policy concerns extending well beyond the province of higher education itself. Similarly, higher education's teaching functions, once regarded as primarily the responsibility of institutions and basic units, are the subject of not only the PCFC and, less directly, the UFC (through its persuasion of the CVCP to produce codes of practice on external examining and a unit for the assessment of teaching performance) but also of government departments outside the DES. The Department of Employment, through its strongly funded and empowered Training Agency, asserted particular views of the education curriculum. These entered the system partly through the award of contracts to institutions prepared to develop curricula in terms of the enterprise culture, and partly through the DES's encouragement of institutions that will consult the needs of business in determining their programmes.

There are differing views of the status of the DES in relationship to the rest of Whitehall as it pursues its tasks of governing the higher education system. Its relative isolation and weakness in the wider government structure are thought to have a reciprocal effect – by some deemed a strength and by others a weakness – of bringing it closer to its higher education constituents. The DES's place in Whitehall is also affected by the fact that it responds to policies of which higher education is only a part (Kogan, 1987). Thus the government claimed that the reductions in university expenditure in 1981 were only one element of a Treasury-led drive for economy (Kogan and Kogan, 1983). Other government departments contribute to decisions in respect of certain key occupations where manpower calculations are deemed to be plausible, such as social work and the health professions.

## INPUTS TO THE CENTRAL AUTHORITIES

The central authorities can be viewed in terms of a yet wider set of institutions. In the past a series of Royal Commissions, as we noted in Chapter 3, concerned themselves with the development of individual universities. The Percy Committee (1945), the Barlow Committee (1946) and the Robbins Committee (1963) illustrate how government reached outside itself into the established academic and social elite for advice and legitimation. It did so in order to develop, to confirm but also to make concessions to, changing norms within the larger society which needed a wider social imprimatur before they could be adopted as policies through the normative and operational modes.

In Figure 4.1 (page 51), the central authorities are portrayed as maintaining certain norms which are conditioned by contemporary social and economic desiderata, and which take the form of general judgements about requisite institutional standards. These in their turn condition the specific judgements about the quality of individual institutions, courses and units which the central authorities render operational through allocations and approvals. Decisions about which institutions to expand and which courses to maintain and develop, although allocative in their consequences, are themselves a reflection of normative judgements. Chapter 3 has already provided us with a historical review of how these processes are set into action.

In theory, the centre responds to different inputs which change over time and which constitute the environment within which the normative mode is formed and modulated. Chapter 3 described many of the changes which bore the impress of movements in society, the economy and the political system over the post-war generation. But whilst we can detect the outcomes of political operations at the centre, it is vexingly difficult to relate them to inputs to the central authorities. The changes have been momentous: transition from an elite towards a mass system; the growth of a wide range of institutions; the increased power of the state and its insistence on the pursuit of certain, particularly economic, objectives; the onset of managerialism as largely dictated by the centre; and selectivity policies. We should naturally look on government as picking up and 'reducing', in Easton's (1965) term, external influences into policies, and we should look for markets and unorganised constituencies as well as organised interest groups which operate indirectly as 'interests' and 'forces' to be interpreted by government. Such factors might include the media's influence on higher education's future. The chances of mutual understanding have been described as small, partly because the respective cultures are different. 'Higher education's culture is elitist, private, reasonable.... The media's is populist, public, emotional' (Scott, 1987). So far, however, no historian has traced the impact of such interests and forces in the UK or in any other western European country where dramatic change in the higher education system has occurred.

Nor can the question of how issues emerge and how higher education interlocks with the larger political system be easily answered. There are clearly inputs to higher education from its sponsoring environments. The larger system does not look to higher education to maintain support for it, except inasmuch as it provides the economy with the necessary skilled manpower. Premfors (1980) found, at the central level, that many commentators exaggerated the extent to which higher education became an issue in national politics; there is little evidence in any country that party political differences made any difference to the history of higher education during its period of expansion. In the 1980s, however, many countries which had long allowed 'organic' development in higher education experienced radical policy changes: Australia, the UK and many of the other west European systems threw over the Welfare State assumptions that

had hitherto underpinned higher education policies and introduced combinations of managerial and quasi-market forms of governance. These can
be viewed as spasmodic and episodic examples: in general, there seems to
have been no internal logic to convert higher education into a subset of the
larger political system (Kogan, 1984). Major 'corporatist' interests of
labour and capital have been more significantly involved in the politics of
higher education in Sweden than in France or the UK or the USA. The
central politicians and bureaucrats have had more influence, to the detriment of academics in national policy-making.

In higher education, according to Premfors (1980), 'the freedom of
action for elites, and even individuals, seems relatively greater than in areas
of greater political salience'. Each of the policy surges which we have
described seems to have come out of a quite small group of decision-
makers. In the UK, earlier expansion resulted from pressure from the
schools and such official bodies as the Secondary School Examinations
Council, and some pressure, too, from those concerned with the planning of
science policy. In the 1960s, for example, the Science Policy Advisory
Council persuaded successive governments to increase dramatically the
provision of places in higher education for the study of science and technology (Gummett, 1980); liberal and expansionist ministers picked up the
theme. The trade unions gave only generalised support to the expansion of
higher education and made no particularly large issue of it, or, indeed, of
recent cuts and other radical changes. The massive expansion in the 1960s
was endorsed with virtually no political debate after a process of legitimation which included the appointment, by the Prime Minister, of the
Robbins Committee and the instant acceptance of its expansionist recommendations. It is not easy to identify presentation of wants by client groups,
stake-holders or the development of constituencies in any of the periods of
change in Britain. Instead, ministers seemed to sniff the wind and then
determine the direction of policy. Even now, when the economic function
of higher education is so important, ministers have largely ignored the
cautions expressed by employer-related organisations (Standing Conference of Employers of Graduates, 1985, and Council for Industry and
Higher Education, 1987).

Nor does central policy appear to take much account of pressure groups,
varying as they do in legitimacy and power. The heads of institutions are
represented through the Committee of Vice-Chancellors and Principals and
the Committee of Directors of Polytechnics. They have faced uncommonly
difficult tasks in recent years. They must press the central authorities on
matters of concern which they share with employees, such as levels of
funding, of salaries and of conditions of service. At the same time they act
as management, a position to which they have been strongly compelled in

recent years. They respond to the main substantive issues which emerge through the policy system, although it is never easy to create a single opinion from the multiple views of their constituents. For the most part, they have thought it wise to tack to the wind, as government has inflicted on them research selectivity cuts and an emphasis on particular subjects. In recent years, wider university interests have been presented by the formation of a body representing the Chairs of University Councils, a group noted as lacking a voice at the time of the 1981 cuts (Butler, 1982).

Neither have students or teachers generated sufficient power to affect central policy. The Association of University Teachers and the National Association of Teachers in Further and Higher Education protested vigorously as the value of salaries declined whilst the pressures placed on teachers increased. For the first time in history 'industrial action' was called by higher education teachers in 1989. But their claims, weakened by the vagaries of economic and demographic performance since the expansion of the 1960s, became marginal to the concerns of the central authorities, which sought instead to interpret the opinions and needs of those who run the economy.

## CO-OPTED ACADEMICS

A particular input to higher education policy and the making of allocations has been that of co-opted academics. Advisory committees have always co-opted influential academics. They have also been recruited to the main funding bodies, classically the University Grants Committee. The UGC negotiated on major allocative decisions with government, but then its largely academic membership made judgements about how the consequent detailed allocations should be made. But increasingly the role of the UGC was diminished by the creation of such bodies as the Advisory Board for Research Councils and the Advisory Council for Applied Research and Development (Shattock, 1987). Similar academic judgements were provided for the NAB. Although academic memberships were reduced in the new funding bodies, academics are still required to offer judgements to both of the funding bodies. The CNAA, which has validated public sector institutions and courses, depends strongly upon co-opted academics.

These arrangements have provided a well-functioning link between academic judgements and allocations, between the normative and operational modes of working. But reductions and selectivity have made co-optation a less comfortable notion. As soon as academics are required to discriminate publicly between cost centres and institutions, they become suspect in the eyes of their peers. A few members of the academic elite are now wholly associated with the policy-making and actions of central government which must affect their standing with their colleagues. To some extent, HM Inspectorate, in its assessment of polytechnics and colleges, acts from a knowledge base similar to that of co-opted academics involved in peer review. They differ, however, in the authority which they possess inasmuch as whilst they are closer to the central authorities, their judgements feed into, rather than directly determine, allocations and approvals. There are also differences in professional credibility.

## CHANGING RELATIONSHIPS BETWEEN THE CENTRE AND THE INSTITUTIONS

Our model allows for the exercise of authority by one level over another through the conversion of evaluative judgements, in the normative mode, to decisions on allocations of funding and course provision in the operational mode. It also allows, through the exercise of professional, social and economic and cultural norms at all levels, and through the co-option of academics to the evaluative activities of the central and institutional authorities, for interchange and a degree of negotiation about the prescriptions that are adopted. Until the fundamental changes in arrangements in the 1980s culminating in the 1988 Education Reform Act there were no written regulations governing the relationships between the central authorities and the universities and a minimum of legal prescriptions governing similar relationships with public sector institutions. There was subsequently more deference to legally based prescription and what can only be described as a wariness in the relationship between central authorities and their higher education clients, resulting from reduced resources, selective policies and the insistence on evaluation and accountability.

## SELECTIVITY

A key strategy in strengthening the grip of the centre over the system has been the policy of selectivity. The UGC's 1986 exercise in research selectivity heralded the strong stratification of universities and basic units. It exemplified the centre's growing determination to plan, through stratification, and to demand accountability. In 1987 universities were called upon by the UGC to develop research planning in spite of many doubts that research could be planned or that its successful development depended upon planning by committees. The Committee promised the Secretary of State that it would monitor the selective distribution of resources by universities by assessing their machinery for planning and implementing priorities and by appraising the extent to which the resulting allocations correlated with the UGC's own research assessments and, as noted in Chapter 3, dutifully reported to its ministerial sponsors that a dozen institutions had failed to meet the standard.

These developments could be represented as a response from the central authorities to social expectations about the nature of higher education in the form of a reinterpretation of the standards of quality, relevance and effectiveness against which institutions and units might expect to be judged. Such standards, insofar as they exist, legitimate the central authorities in making judgements on quality to which they can attach decisions about differential allocations of resources. The changes also marked a shift towards monitoring the managerial competence of institutions.

From the time of the Robbins Report and before, all universities were thought to be roughly comparable in quality. This comparability would be assured by the peer review which governed access to senior academic positions, to research and other awards, and by the system of examining designed to safeguard degree standards. If there was always a steep hierarchy of institutions, by every official manifestation parity of outcomes within broad boundaries was assumed. For example, a CNAA degree was deemed officially comparable with a degree awarded by Oxford, in terms of acceptance for employment in the public sector or in recruitment to academic posts. Although some universities were regarded as superior to others in their research records, all received (in principle if not in practice) the same levels of funding on the assumption that all university teachers, unlike those in public sector institutions, were engaged in research. Insofar as the centre steered the system on its underlying economic and social purposes, it trusted academic intermediaries to make the evaluations upon which funds were allocated for those purposes. This was possible because it assumed that what academics deemed to be interesting or useful was also likely to contribute to social ends.

In more recent years the centre has demanded evidence of academic competence as well as management efficiency through measures of differing degrees of prescriptiveness (Becher and Kogan, 1987). Thus far it has not followed the French, Swedish or Dutch in controlling the framework of the taught curriculum, a set of controls now being anyway removed in many countries (van Vught, 1988). It has instead left it to the universities to develop their own control mechanisms for the assessment and supervision of students, including the procedures for external examining (Reynolds, 1986), and to create a unit which will assess universities' mechanisms for assuring quality in teaching (Committee of Vice-Chancellors and Principals, 1990). At the same time, the central authorities have imposed an appraisal system for staff, in addition to the informal peer review traditionally undertaken. Such policies for research and teaching selectivity are important not only in their own right but also for the kind of mechanisms then created and the relationships which they entail.

## COURSES AND CURRICULUM

The capacity of the system to control the life of the universities and polytechnics has been developed and strengthened in two other ways. One concerns the balance between different kinds of courses. The DES White Paper of 1987 was explicit: 'Meeting the needs of the economy is not the sole purpose of higher education, nor can higher education alone achieve what is needed. But this aim ... must be vigorously pursued.' The White Paper urged much closer communication between academic staff and people in business at all levels: 'These connections can lead to more suitable teaching, to research and technology transfer.... They also help to foster positive attitudes to enterprise. The Government and its central funding agencies will do all they can to encourage and reward approaches by higher education institutions which bring them closer to the world of business.'

This surge of interest in the curriculum has been reinforced by the activities of the Training Agency, a quango (now disbanded) which reported to the Department of Employment rather than the DES. In 1987 it launched the Enterprise in Higher Education Initiative; at the cost of £100 million this was 'to enable higher education institutions to ... embed activities that promote enterprise into the work of the institutions'. An important effect might be to make academics think more seriously about the curriculum and the skills that could be transferred to the world of employment. Institutions receiving or seeking funds found themselves subject to audit of the most intimate aspects of curriculum objectives and content. The content of the curriculum remained, however, largely in the hands of the teachers whose reactions to the pressures from outside were generally to accommodate and assimilate them on their own terms and without hostility or negativism (Boys *et al.*, 1988).

## THE SPONSORSHIP OF RESEARCH

The central authorities may use different lines of regulation and negotiation in respect of teaching and research. Until 1980, research was implied rather than specified as an element of funding in the general resource allocations made to university institutions. Staffing levels, building, equipment allowances, discretion to give sabbatical leave, constitutional inbuilt provision for research: they were directly associated with, and a residue of, provision for teaching.

Research is financed in a variety of ways. First, the five research councils, established under royal charter and operating by peer review, receive funds from which they distribute research grants and studentships within broad policies agreed with government. Second – as noted above – the funding councils include some indirect provision for research. Third, central government provides additional research funding through contracts negotiated with institutions and basic units for specific pieces of work: this mode is adopted, too, by industrial sponsors. Lastly, further marginal sums can be obtained from private foundations, who tend to use their funds as 'risk money' on projects considered to be more innovative or unorthodox than those which attract support from the research councils, or on proposals which are unrelated to – and even critical of – government policies. Basic units receiving private foundation money have been supported by UFC contributions to overheads.

The value assumptions of individual academic enquiry, or of investigation of 'pure' research topics, rarely come into conflict with the other norms of institutions and basic units. Contract research, whether sponsored by government or industry, is, however, a different case. Its rapid growth has had discernible effects on the relationships between individuals, basic units, institutions and the central authorities. The central authorities may note with favour that a particular institution encourages its basic units to engage in research activities compatible with social needs. The peer groups to which such units belong may take the contrasting view, that too close a relationship with the field of action is deleterious to academic standards. But in this area central government and its intermediaries have attempted to create a decisive shift in academic behaviour, and the distaste for contract research expressed by the UGC in the immediate post-1945 period has long since abated.

In the past the research networks, both those developed by central government interests and those relating to the research councils, depended in large measure on academic judgements of the viability and validity of research projects. After the mid-1980s, however, new policy priorities began to affect the mode of research support. There was an emphasis on strategic research – that is, research which was 'curiosity driven and although it may have wealth creating results ... unpredictable both in time and field. Strategic research is not targeted as specific wealth creation but lies in areas in which the emergence of application may be expected though not predicted' (Science and Engineering Research Council, 1989). Priority was given to research relating to economic concerns, and a strong set of co-ordinating instruments, within the Cabinet Office, and elsewhere, were created to attempt to secure this objective. A further element of policy was the concentration of research activity in centres where both economy and excellence could be pursued.

The institutional consequences of these objectives were significant. The research councils deferred to the Advisory Board for Research Councils which, for example, insisted that they adopt performance indicators by which they could measure their own effectiveness. The individual research councils created corporate plans on which they were interrogated by the ABRC, itself closely tied into central government policy. The responsive mode, by which research councils and other bodies depend upon academics to make the running in offering subjects for research funding, gave way to a strongly objectives-led system. In consequence of this normative and institutional shift the management of research within universities, through research committees and the like, changed accordingly, at least in form.

## GOVERNANCE AND MANAGEMENT

A further change in the system's approach to its constituent institutions can be seen in the area of governance and management. The history of the demise of the UGC and the NAB and their replacement by the UFC and the PCFC has already been related. The change of titles signified the advent of funding for specific purposes laid down by the centre and in return for evaluated performance.

Changes in the principal bodies are less significant than changes in the style and content of the relationship with institutions and the behaviour which the centre has sought to impose on them. The universities, putatively private institutions under royal charter, always less managerial than the polytechnics, have found their modes of managerial behaviour subject to instruction from the centre. They were to submit Academic Plans for scrutiny; so were the polytechnics and colleges, but they at first resisted this demand from the PCFC more strongly than did the universities from the UGC/UFC. The Vice-Chancellors were to be Chief Executives rather than the *primi inter pares* of a scholarly community. Senior academics were to take their places in a hierarchy of senior and middle managers. Performance was to be measured by quantitative indicators as well as by peer judgement. The system of deficiency grants was to be replaced by a system of contracting which would lead to, among other things, 'greater precision in the specification of what is expected of institutions in return for public funding' (DES, 1987b).

## MODELS OF CENTRAL GOVERNMENT INFLUENCE: THE IMPLEMENTATION GAP

As the British government moved from its role as facilitator to one of leading the system, the resulting pattern of relationships was not that simply of a quasi-managerial hierarchy in which policies were laid down at the centre for pursuit by those at the periphery. Institutions must submit academic plans and work within the frameworks of increasingly tight substantive and resource policies. They were required to follow instruction on questions of institutional behaviour and structure. To all intents and purposes this seemed to be a 'command model', but two major qualifications must be placed against that inference.

First, the style, content and quality of teaching, scholarship and research continued to originate from the motivation and ability of the individual teacher and researcher. Teachers were not hostile to some of the more recently advocated central ideologies, such as deference to the needs of employment (Boys *et al.*, 1988). On the whole, however, they continued to assimilate the changes in social and economic values on their own terms and in their own ways. Their modes of behaviour would be affected by the system of rewards and punishments now conditioning academic behaviour, including technical devices such as performance indicators which were known to favour particular modes of the presentation of performance. But, ultimately, it seemed that the objectives were more prone to outside influences than the modes of performance.

Second, government itself was ambivalent. It imposed important elements of a command model but soon afterwards introduced a system of market forces which, in theory, enabled institutions to go their own way to success or failure. These included changes in student finance so that a higher proportion of resources would reach institutions through the exercise of applicants' preferences for places as well as through the preferences of those who might sponsor research.

## THE RELATIONSHIPS BETWEEN CENTRAL AUTHORITIES AND OTHER LEVELS

In principle, there are three ways in which a central authority may relate to the institutions for which it is responsible. The first is by adopting a managerial approach in which the central authority gives instructions, allocates resources to specific ends, and rewards and punishes according to the degree of conformity to its instructions. The armed forces and social security would be examples in many democracies. This has not until recently been a pattern accepted in most higher education systems. The second approach relies on a sizeable measure of consensus on functions, objectives and processes, so that prescription is unnecessary, and unconditional grants can be given for new developments. This free grant pattern was prevalent in a number of countries before higher education became an acknowledged component of social planning and a major charge to the public purse, but no longer obtains in most of them. The third strategy rests on the acceptance of divergencies of values and hence of the necessity for negotiations between the various components of a pluralistic system. As we have noted, however strong the bureaucracy may appear, the professional guild or some other peer grouping remains potent. However, its power is now severely challenged in many systems by such devices as performance measurement, the provision of higher education resources in return for contractual obligations and the like.

In terms of our model, the recent history of many countries, among which the UK is the strongest example, shows that it is well within the capacity of central government to use different modes of authority in asserting central policies. The classic model is that of negotiation between the norms set up as a result of interchange between all levels in the system, reflecting the professional norms expressed by the academics, and the social, economic and political expectations of those outside. The normative elements of negotiation remain even when direct managerial prescription is adopted or when quasi-market systems are established. The more dirigiste planning mode has proved of dubious effectiveness: planning, it is held, has been tested to destruction – its credibility began to be lost when it was realised that the 1984/85 selectivity exercise involved the submission of over a million pieces of paper. But this softening of the command model has taken place after a period of draconian control and remodelling of the system under the leadership of central government in a way hitherto never experienced.

# 5   The institution

## IS THE INSTITUTION A VIABLE LEVEL?

The academic institution is the principal legal entity through which most of the functions of higher education are performed. In terms of our model it is that body by which a group of basic units are authoritatively held together.

The model deployed in Chapter 2 and, indeed, much of the literature (see, for example, Moodie and Eustace, 1974; Clark, 1983) has concentrated on three levels of authority and of value setting in higher education. In the classical models of higher education the norms are assumed to be determined either by single teachers or researchers, or by academics collectively within their basic units, or nationally, in response to social and economic desiderata, by central authorities. Except in the case of private institutions – so important in the USA – where the institution determines its own relationship with the economic, social and cultural environments, this has seemed to leave the institution somewhat short of functions as a value-setter. Determining curriculum – a function of the basic unit – or determining whether an institution shall be enabled to grow or stay still – a decision for the central authorities – are substantive decisions. Mediating between the two seems to be secondary, non-substantive, almost intransitive, in the sense that the object of the exercise is at least one remove away.

In the 1980s power at the institutional level inevitably grew. Indeed, the trend was observed in the 1970s (see, for example, Baldridge *et al.*, 1978), but it was accelerated by demands for academic accountability from a growingly powerful national system, and the need for decisions to be made about the implementation of cuts and reorientations of effort. For the most part, it was those institutions with strong leadership that seemed best able to survive the period of cuts (Sizer, 1987). Yet it still has to be considered whether that growth of institutional power was a temporary phenomenon, responding to the need for crisis management. The issue remains how far the institution has a substantive existence and a distinct purpose or how far it is, in effect, a holding company, a legal and organisational formula designed to authorise and control the activities of its units.

The existence and identity of a level is established by the extent to which it has discernible norms of its own; whether it performs discernible operations or tasks which are compatible, if not in perfect fit, with those values; and whether it has authority to act in the normative mode by making evaluations of, and in the operational mode by making allocations to, its affiliated basic units and individuals. The recent history of higher education shows that the institutional level has strengthened its hold over each of these defining characteristics.

## THE TWO FACES OF LEADERSHIP

The complex and ambiguous relationship of basic units and individuals to institutions emerges in such phrases as 'organised anarchy' (Cohen and March, 1974), collegium, bureaucracy and 'federated professionalism'. All of these ascriptions have some truth in them, as have the two principal versions of how institutions work.

The first, mainly held in previous times by those outside higher education – particularly as they viewed the almost total dependence on public funds of most higher education activities – assumed that institutions would respond as unities to the leadership and management of a vice-chancellor or director. For all that they might acknowledge the complexities, the central authorities themselves acted on the assumption that their requests, or guidance, or prescriptions, would be followed, provided that they addressed themselves to a visibly nodal point of authority in an institution; and in fact the chief administrator was nearly always able to secure a decision from his institution which matched the expectations of the funding body. Pressures from the external environment have made for a definite shift of authority towards the institutional leadership. These have included the demands for stronger management, the early retirement schemes, the weakening of tenure, and the writing of detailed institutional plans, all of which have reduced the power of the basic units and their individual members in favour of the institution. During the period of cuts in the 1980s the quality of leadership was discerned as a critical determinant of survival (Sizer, 1987b). It is seen as an often missing but essential element in institutional well-being (Trow, 1984, 1985).

The doctrine of the managerial authority of institutional leadership was succinctly stated in the Jarratt Report (1985), which specified that the vice-chancellors should be chief executives, that there should be a corporate plan in which lay members of council together with the vice-chancellor and his senior management team should lay down the objectives of the university, and that the power of departments should give way to more corporate planning. Its recommendations sought to eliminate the functional duality of academic life in which there are both collective and highly individual concerns. It postulated a role in which leadership is not disputed, a view which many regard as callow managerialism, based upon an insufficient organisational analysis.

A second version rested on a denial of such internal authority as existed. It represented the institution as being wholly collegial – if not now, in any particular institution, then in some favoured institutions in a golden age before managerialism began to assert itself in the 1970s. This view assumed an academic staff whose mode of working was, on the face of it, antithetical to management, hierarchy or bureaucracy.

Both versions contain elements of reality and are reflected in the Janus-like role of a vice-chancellor, principal or director; the dual systems of hierarchy and collegium running through the system; and the ways in which both individuals and committees operate within hierarchy and collegium.

In Britain, unlike some of the Continental systems, a vice-chancellor or director is appointed on meritocratic rather than democratic principles and by a small selection committee representing the council or governing body and senate or the academic board, rather than the whole collegium of academics. Institutional leaders are usually given tenure until retirement age although some are now appointed on a shorter-term contract. In terms of salary, conditions of service, functional as well as symbolic status, the institutional leader is in a position to lead.

Institutional leaders have dual expectations placed on them. In the traditional mode of working they are responsible for making sure that the institution sustains and, where possible, develops itself. Accordingly, they have to account for the way in which it runs, both to its dominantly lay council or governing body and (if not logically or formally then oper-ationally) to the central authorities from whom they must seek funds (Seldin, 1988). At the same time, they must mediate among strongly idiosyncratic academics whose pre-eminence in their own professional spheres is likely to be among the institution's most important assets. The university vice- chancellor or polytechnic director has thus always been, at one and the same time, required to be a leader but the first among equals within the institution; an entrepreneur with external funders and, sometimes, within the university or polytechnic itself; an administrative service-giver to those who maintain the primary tasks and operations of the institution; and a norm-setter, particularly for those requirements not professed within the existing basic units.

The authority and power of institutional leaders are various, as are their functions. They may use the appeal of one academic to another or may act autocratically in exercising discipline on a wayward group of colleagues, for whose actions they are to some extent accountable. They possess certain tactical advantages which lift them clear of the collegium. Institutional leaders are the key figures at all important committees, and the chairmen of many. This gives them informal authority to veto proposals. They have the advantage of being entitled to attend any meetings they choose and of being best informed about the total range of activities. They also have the moral authority of being able to assert a case for co-ordination to counteract the effects of idiosyncratic particularism. Not only are they regarded from the outside as the most important figure in the institution; internally, they occupy a pivotal position between management, the collegium and the lay governors or councillors, particularly when there is competition amongst otherwise strong and ungovernable heads of the basic units. Their managerial authority is not far less and is to some extent more than that possessed by leaders in other public institutions. They can decisively shape the nature of a basic unit when there is a change in its headship. They usually chair all appointments and promotions boards. They decide, usually on delegation from the governors or council, the award of salary increments to senior members of staff.

One of their functions is certainly to represent the institution across the boundaries to the wider outside world, including that of government and the central funding bodies. The kind of decisions that now fall to leaders are not those made most easily within a collegial forum, for they may require hard decisions about activities that should cease or be taken up at a different pace, and sponsoring changes in parts of the institution's range which would not occur through the traditional process of organic development. The institutional leader must be able to be strong in the face of personnel and staff issues and industrial relations. The modes of corporate planning, represented through the writing of academic plans and the like, and the administration of performance measurement, again require strong leadership and managerial capacity, to be backed up by appropriately qualified staff.

This consideration of leadership roles does not dispose, however, of the issue of who 'owns' the institution. Whilst all institutions must now be more explicitly accountable to bodies outside themselves, the task of leadership in higher education in its essential functions remains one which can only be appropriately carried out through consensual forms. Decisions may have to be made which go against the consensus. But the decisions that are thought to hold most firmly in institutions where individual creativity and commitment to scholarly pursuits remain the norms are not best established through modes of hierarchy. Good management is not seen, in fact, as endorsing the particular instrumental art forms which have been pronounced by the central authorities as appropriate.

Expectations on leadership vary between institutions. At one time, a sharp distinction between universities and polytechnics could be discerned. Polytechnics have always had stronger central directorates and the academic boards were correspondingly weaker than their university counterparts. Under the Education Reform Act 1988, the need to account, if in somewhat attenuated ways, to local education authorities has gone. None the less, the managerial mode remains dominant. Faculties or schools are often larger and more heterogeneous in function than their university equivalents. Deans are often full-time administrators, working in hierarchical relationship to the director, and less likely to occupy the role of a convenor of colleagues than some heads or chairmen of university departments, schools or faculties.

The roles of vice-chancellors have varied between universities. A vice-chancellor in a federal university certainly has a role different from that of a vice-chancellor in a unitary university. For example, university appointments, which are key points of control and development within any institution, are made by the colleges, basic units and the university faculties acting jointly. In other fields, too, there are interlocking powers and functions. For example, an Oxbridge or London college has purchase on its own development, on buildings and student numbers, but the university mediates UFC and other external fundings to the different disciplinary systems and to the colleges, apart from such private endowments as they might find themselves. The vice-chancellor and university administration thus have to act as brokers between heads of houses, the university faculty and the basic units within the colleges. The leadership (let alone the managerial function) is less clear-cut than in a unitary institution.

## COLLEGIUM AND HIERARCHY, COMMITTEE AND EXECUTIVE

In all three cases – unitary or federal university or polytechnic – the components of collegium and hierarchy are present. The balance between each may, however, vary, and the resulting styles may be entirely different. Hierarchy is a stronger element in traditionally administered polytechnics, but so it was in some of the pre-war and post-war civic and Scottish universities. The ancient universities of Oxford and Cambridge have always been strongly collegial in form. Even there, however, seniority of academic status may create an actual hierarchy of power. Collegial structures are paralleled by departmental and faculty systems, which have become stronger in recent years, particularly in laboratory subjects, where managerial authority emerges in forms not far different from those to be found in science or technology departments in more hierarchically organised institutions.

Hierarchy assumes that the individuals in designated roles possess authority to affect the behaviour of others. Collegium designates a structure in which members have equal authority to participate in decisions which are binding on each of them. It usually implies that individuals have discretion to perform their main operations in their own way, subject only to minimal collegial controls (on, for example, the use of resources and the observance of proper procedures in the admission, teaching and assessing of students).

As a consequence of the duality of hierarchy and collegium, academic institutions contain systems of executive roles and systems of committees. They seldom resolve the overlaps and conflicts between them in any logical way. The executive structure links the head of the institution, the heads of basic units and individual members of teaching staff. This structure of mainly part-time academic managers is closely interlocked with the full-time administrative system staffed by career administrators and headed by such senior permanent officials as the registrar and bursar.

The equivocal status of the vice-chancellor has been reflected in roles lower down the executive hierarchy. In the past, deans were not thought of as possessing managerial authority over heads of departments. Instead they would have to persuade basic units to make collective decisions to be put into action. Unit heads were equal in status, with an equal voice in senate, and decanal authority had to be exercised informally. Characteristically, the deans would work within small oligarchic mechanisms (such as deans' or heads of schools' meetings) and then assert their views collectively, with the support of the vice-chancellor, when matters arose in the senate or its committees. They might have to depend for the success of policies which they regarded as in the collective interest, but which the basic units left to themselves would not agree, on being present at key meetings, on developing political expertise and on exercising it in the various committees to which they had access. At any one time, however, the decisions reached by deans could be changed or challenged within equivalent meetings of heads of basic units, or in the course boards at which members of basic units were in the majority, or in resource committees where the deans themselves might not be a dominant group. So even their informal leadership might be exercised with difficulty.

In many institutions the picture given above still holds. But the need to respond to external challenges and to implement priorities has meant that the infrastructure beneath the head of an institution has become correspondingly stronger. The authority of the dean and of the faculty is in some

institutions reinforced as the mechanism through which institutional policies are implemented, but with a sufficient degree of knowledge about the
subject-matter to make the decision making plausible (Boys *et al.*, 1988).
There is also now a flow of normative literature (Jarratt Report, 1985;
Lockwood and Davies, 1985) which reinforces the notion of deans as being
'middle managers'.

In spite of these tightenings of managerial lines, authority within higher
education remains fragmentary. Heads of institutions have always
possessed powers, although exercised only with difficulty, to act against
staff who are in serious default of duty. They have unquestionably influenced futures of individual members of staff by the exercise of power in the
promotion and other reward systems. But the difficulty of using sanctions
and rewards has been that many academics, such as professors and other
heads of basic units, are at the peak of their profession, with tenure and no
need for further advancement. In recent years, however, there has been
explicit provision for institutions to bestow differential salaries. On the
assumption that, unlike the more distinguished American universities, the
power of reward will remain with the institutional leader rather than with
committees of professors, this might begin to give the former more purchase over senior academic staff.

The relationship between the head of a basic unit and an individual
teacher within that unit is also imprecisely defined and subject to negotiation. In the normal way, the contracts of academic teachers merely state
that they will work under the direction of unit heads without further
specifying the powers of those heads or the duties of those teachers. For the
most part, senior academics have the power to affect the rewards that the
institution may give to its members, but virtually no power to impose
sanctions of the kind usually attributed to a manager within any other kind
of hierarchy. But given that resources are constrained, and that distribution
of them will be made by the institutional hierarchy, the capacity to apply
pressure on individual members of staff has increased.

The executive and administrative systems interlock in complex ways
with the committee structure. The most senior committee – the council or
equivalent body – always has a lay majority. Its powers over academic
substance are minimal, although that has not always been so, and the close
attention to be paid by governing bodies and councils to the measurement
of performance and the making of a corporate plan may lead to greater
involvement. So far, there is little evidence that the lay members have been
able, or have wished, to exercise any such power (Boys *et al.*, 1988).
However, the governing body has significant authority to sanction or restrict resources such as academic establishment, buildings and finance,
although it will normally act here on the advice of the head of the

institution. Its control over resources and its fiduciary role (through which it defends and monitors the general organisational behaviour of the institution) puts it into an equivocal relationship with the senate. That body, which consists wholly of academics, mostly senior, is the prime collegium in the institution. It may not set the normative modes by which the basic units work, but it prescribes and sanctions the frameworks within which the basic units formulate both their norms and their operations. It operates subordinate committees which carry effective executive powers, subject to reiterative scrutiny by the senate itself, on academic issues derived largely from the basic units. Most universities have joint council and senate committees concerned with planning and resources, through which control over allocations is maintained.

The primary mode of the committee system is collegial. However, just as the executive structure described above is not a pure hierarchy, so the committee network is not that of a pure collegium operating at different levels. The more senior the committee, the more senior are individual members of it. Many of the more important decisions are beyond the capacity of large bodies such as the council or senate to formulate, and so have to be hammered out in subsidiary groupings.

The linking of executive with committee means that many individual roles are themselves dual. A head of a basic unit, or the head of a faculty or a school (who is best thought of as a convenor of heads of basic units), operates both hierarchically, inasmuch as he or she possesses the power to direct and to affect the prospects of individual teachers, and collegially, inasmuch as he or she has to reach agreement with colleagues on many of the major academic and allocative decisions.

The executive and the committee structures alike are thus shot through with both collegium and hierarchy. Moreover, as we have remarked, the relationships between the two can change as institutions go through different periods of history. When an institution is first set up, both its executive and its committee systems wield considerable power. Over time, institutions yield some of that power to the developing basic units, and some to the central administration.

## ADMINISTRATIVE STAFF

Institutions have always depended on the work of their non-academic administrators. The vice-chancellor or director is seen as the chief executive, accountable to the council or governing body, and also, but less certainly because he or she sits as its chairperson, to the senate or academic council. Immediately beneath him or her an academic hierarchy may be led by pro vice-chancellors or a vice-principal, and an administrative hierarchy will be led by a registrar.

The administrators' role has become more important as the power of academic units and individuals has been subordinated to institutional norm-setting, planning, modes and controls. Officially administrators may draw their authority from their positions as 'staff officers' to the vice-chancellors or directors or to the committees to which they act as secretaries. Registrars are protected in the statutes as the secretary of council and senate, which some construe as giving them degrees of independence from vice-chancellorial direction. In actuality, they formulate plans and see that they are carried out: this gives them an entrée into norm-setting even if the final say is not theirs. They monitor incomes and expenditures as finance officers. They are responsible for the upkeep of the physical fabric and its exploitation through non-academic letting.

The growing power of non-academic administrators raises the question whether they develop functions and values which are separable from those of the heads of institutions and other academic decision-makers whose work they service. Institutional heads are expected to concern themselves with both institutional and academic issues, whilst administrators, under the control of vice-chancellors and directors, specialise in operational issues concerning the maintenance and development of the institution as such and on the running of the non-academic services. Maintaining and developing the institution appeal to values entailed in the public service ethic; these include ensuring equitable treatment between competing groups and a fiduciary concern for the proper spending of resources and for the maintenance of due process (Kogan, 1975). Their ability to advance such value positions as against those of academics whose preoccupations are largely otherwise depends greatly on the institution's ethos and ways of working. They increasingly occupy, too, important areas of activity on the changing boundaries of the institution. Developing entrepreneurial activities, 'going into Europe', sharpening the institution's capacity to get research contracts and grants, all involve the co-operation and willingness of academics. They are often, however, causes advanced primarily by administrators.

## ACADEMIES AS POLITICAL ORGANISATIONS

There is, then, in traditional academic organisations, at most an uncertain allocation of tasks through a complex system of roles in which the powers of managers are exercised over subordinates. Wherever authority exists, it may be held subject to collegial structures such as those of the senate, or of other influential groups, some of whose members may be quite junior within the academic executive system. The formal as well as the informal organisation allows for the most important decisions to be the result of collegial procedures.

The interplay between executive and committee, hierarchy and collegium, cannot be easily rendered down into a straightforward and predictable structure. To understand the ways in which academic institutions function, we may need to consider other forms of analysis. One of these, developed by Baldridge *et al.* (1978), concentrates on political models of decision-making within higher education institutions. The research in question concludes that higher education is different from other enterprises in having more ambiguous and contested goals, in working with unclear technologies, in serving clients instead of working for profit, and in the fact that both the workforce and the decision-making process are dominated by professionals.

Baldridge and his colleagues thus partly assimilate the view of Cohen and March (1974) that academic institutions are not 'bureaucracies' but 'organised anarchies'. But within the organised anarchy decisions have to be reached, they contend, as the result of a political process in which various interest groups struggle for influence. To enumerate some of the important similarities between academic institutions and small-scale political entities, most individual constituents for most of the time, and some for all of the time, are not directly concerned in the shaping of policy. Allied to this, participation is fluid, in the sense that all but a politically committed few get involved only with particular issues over relatively short periods. As in the wider society, interests and loyalties tend to be fragmented, except in the case of internal schism or external threat. Value conflicts are a normal feature of the community; and, as we have seen, the degree to which direct authority can be exercised is very limited. The system is far from self-contained, being susceptible in a variety of ways to outside influences and pressures. Baldridge notes, too, how political processes give rise to regulations or regularities which themselves lead to structuration into institutional forms and established procedures.

The political analogy has the advantage of embodying the twin conceptions of collegium and hierarchy, or community and organisation, but going beyond them to account for the curiosities within academic institutions of policy-making and the exercise of power. The relationships are brought still more sharply into focus by F.G. Bailey's metaphor of the three arenas of academic discourse – front-stage, back-stage and under-stage (Bailey, 1977). He points out that most of the public, permanent, large and representational committees in any institution exist to sanction decisions taken elsewhere, and to provide scope for ritualistic and high-minded assertions of value and purpose. This, the front-stage arena, embodies the institution's main political functions. The hard, detailed bargaining, designed to yield a working compromise, typically takes place in smaller, *ad hoc* or temporary groupings whose members are appointed or co-opted rather than elected. This, the under-stage arena, manifests the main organisational features of the institution. But the important tasks of forming alliances, making or breaking reputations, and creating a groundswell of opinion takes place back-stage, where the members of the scholarly community congregate to exchange their gossip.

As we have pointed out, however, the intention of maintenance systems such as those advocated by the Jarratt Report is to simplify and stratify into hierarchical management such relatively loose and complex relationships. The political element has been thought to be implicit in academic life because of the functional necessities of the kind of work undertaken in higher education. The creation of chief executives, objectives setting, and the like, plainly constitutes a counter-theme.

## THE FUNCTIONS OF THE INSTITUTION

The uncertainty expressed at the beginning of this chapter about the institution as a distinct level within higher education seems to be reinforced by its ambiguities of structure and modes of working. Yet even in easier and more collegial times decisions have certainly been made – some of which may be of crucial importance to the welfare of the whole enterprise – which far transcend the concerns of any basic unit and clearly do not derive from the wishes of the central authorities.

## THE NORMATIVE MODE

In the normative mode, the institution relates its own assessments to central authorities' appraisals of the need for, and the quality expected of, particular courses and units. These central appraisals are informed by considerations of national economic and social needs and by views, usually based on peer-group judgement, on what constitute good academic standards. In Chapters 3 and 4 we noted how institutions may be expected to respond to, and give a lead to, basic units on sets of first-order values concerning the role of the institution and its units in the economy – for example, by participating in exercises intended to substantiate the enterprise culture, by widening access to various social groups, or by being more responsive to market forces impinging upon the institution's teaching, research and consultancy. In the past, the institution set the frame for academic development when first building itself up, or when senior academics moved out of headships: but it was primarily concerned to apply rules ensuring that the

*Figure 5.1* The functions of the institution

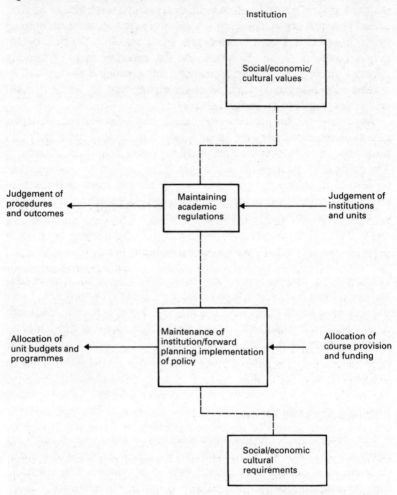

basic units worked effectively within academic values of the disinterested pursuit of truth and the just allocation of academic status through examin- ations and the like. Now, however, universities and polytechnics are called upon to be in the front line of economic and social policy and to demon- strate that they are so.

The traditional functions of the institution entail the pursuit of second- order values; that is, values concerned with ensuring its own maintenance and the reputable behaviour of its units. Thus it establishes academic regulations and generates the norms of academic behaviour expected of its component elements. It also makes judgements of its own concerning the ways in which it can best meet the needs it perceives. The institution has a further fiduciary role. Its physical assets and its money income are seen as being held in trust for the pursuit of academic goals. This causes it to attend to the intellectual and the ethical reputation, as well as the financial probity, of work undertaken under its aegis.

The institution must secure an adequate balance between its different subject areas and between research, development and teaching activity, as it always has done. At the same time, however, it must concern itself with ensuring financial survival, which may include winning contracts and recruiting students for short courses as well as for degree courses, whilst at the same time maintaining its academic reputation (Davies, 1987; Duncan, 1987).

In this connection, a view has to be reached on the proper relationship to be maintained with the outside community, and on how the enterprise as a whole should develop. Should it, for example, seek to resist or strive to accommodate to market pressures? Should it attempt to influence social and industrial practice by developing a strong technological emphasis, or should it seek to be a humanising force by sustaining the traditions of liberal education? Should it regard itself predominantly as a community of scholars or should it meet the demands of students and non-academic members of staff who seek a share in policy-making? These questions, though expressed in the language of the normative mode, may nevertheless carry far-reaching operational consequences. For example, decisions to accept or ignore the market demand for courses necessarily affect the pattern of resources to be put into teaching and research.

Finally, the institution viewed in the normative mode must concern itself with due academic process. It is this set of norms that gives it the functions that may be described as rule-setting. A basic unit responsible for teaching and research in, say, physics or political science will be expected to recruit good physics or political science teachers and students. No other group within the institution has the expertise to do so for it. The institution nevertheless lays down rules by which recruitment is effected in accordance with general academic norms. It is important to recognise, though, that policies on such issues as the advertising of staff vacancies, or the need for external assessment of degree awards, are not *simply* rules: they incorporate values of institutional maintenance and standard-setting. They do not embody the same norms as those used by the peer groups in determining competence in physics or political science, but refer instead to such civic virtues as equity and due process. They are similar to the concerns which underlie the institution's fiduciary and reputational roles.

The problem remains whether the institution itself contributes distinctively towards the values within the higher education system as a whole. Three points might be made in this connection, deriving from the functions we have already distinguished within the normative mode.

First, we have already noted that rule-setting involves institutional values such as those of maintaining equity and due process. Second, there is the developmental function of assessing current operations against changing needs and environments. The institution must, in fact, look out for, initiate and nurture developments which are in the collective interest but lie outside the purview of the discipline-bound practitioner. The institution might think it right in a particular context to work more closely with the community, to take a more active role in civic change and development. At such a time, a vice-chancellor may have to lure a professor away from his laboratory or his study to listen to the expressed needs of local councillors or of industry. The institution may have to push through 'unwanted' developments which would change the existing pattern of resource priorities, such as a department of management studies, which all theoretical social scientists of pure heart would feel bound to resist, or a special engineering course, whose advent would not be taken kindly by those whose engineering was thus seen not to be 'special'.

In pursuing this function, the institution certainly takes on obligations which are separable from those of any other level. It is the institution which acts as the point upon which external pressure is exercised. It also has to reconcile expectations of both the central authorities and the basic units. At the same time, however, the institution draws strength from its relationship with outside agencies and sources of power.

In performing its developmental role an institution must have the capacity to seize opportunity quickly – a new course, or chair or line of research – and, if necessary, to redistribute funds accordingly. The central authorities cannot move fast enough: moreover, they lack the knowledge of, and immediate control over, what is possible at the institutional level. The institution must also take a view on such matters beyond the concern of basic units as the scale of the enterprise as a whole: whether it should seek to be intimate and elite, or large and service-giving; whether it should, corporately, aim to cater for part-time and mature, perhaps not too well-qualified, students, or whether it should gear its courses to young full-time entrants with orthodox qualifications; and whether it should adopt particular modes of government, or forms of participation which seem likely to affect the pattern of relationships within the basic units themselves.

These issues become particularly salient in view of the challenges presented to institutions to take a lead in technological innovation, to convert fundamental knowledge into 'strategic knowledge' which relates not only to technological innovation but also to policy analysis and professional development. These priorities for the higher education institution (Lynton and Elman, 1987) require not only an examination of the corporate mission but also the creation of organisational forms which cut across internal disciplinary formations such as departments. What has been called by Lynton and Elman 'mobilising internally for effective outreach' would involve drawing on a number of disciplines and pulling them together in a way which enables them not only to share otherwise diffuse and disparate knowledge but also to form themselves into effective working groups that can court external sponsorship. In practice, there are powerful factors which discourage individuals and basic units from linking up with others. Overwhelmingly, the power and reputation of a subject department rest on the judgement of its disciplinary peers and not on those who present social and technological problems from the outside. Much of the 'outreach' work involved is likely to be development rather than the type of prestigious investigation funded by research councils. It must lie with the institution, therefore, to use the marginal resources which it always keeps in hand for development, or, perhaps, to make an even stronger decision to divert resources from existing disciplinary groups to such efforts. Promotional activities of this kind are a more significant part of the roles of institutions in a competitive and outward-looking phase of their existence.

The third point which justifies the presentation of the institution as a distinctive level in the model relates to the creation of a public persona. Every university, polytechnic and college has to market itself, not only to potential recruits and to possible benefactors, but also to the polity at large. Some have done this brilliantly and others badly. More generally it may be argued that higher education as a whole has been incompetent at building up a political constituency which can come to its aid when it is under duress (Butler, 1982). Creating a reputation and earning general esteem is not a substantive task in its own right, but it helps to support and make more potent the main activities of an institution. The task of image-building is partly achieved through ritual – the award of honorary degrees, the degree congregation, the public appearances of vice-chancellors and senior academics speaking not only on their specialist subjects but on the plight of humanity more generally. It seeks to reinforce the impression that while some departments might be excellent and others pretty poor, the whole is a force for culture, knowledge and social development. The projection of such a view is clearly a task for the institution rather than the basic unit.

## THE OPERATIONAL MODE

The institution, in the operational mode, is shown as negotiating with and receiving allocations from the central authorities and implementing their policies. It also develops the organisational forms, maintains the institution, allocates budgets and programmes to the basic units and undertakes forward planning.

The institution makes a case for resources and receives them from the central authorities and from other agencies. In so doing, it collates and adjudicates between the demands of the basic units. The central authorities build up judgements, not only about where individual subjects can best be advanced, but also about the total shape and size of individual institutions. An institution must therefore promote a view not only of its basic units but also of its overall development, in a form which will be convincing to the central authorities. (In the past, institutions sought to convince private benefactors or civic authorities in much the same way.)

Until the changes of the 1980s, the universities, if not the polytechnics and colleges, could distribute money, buildings and manpower to the basic units in any way they thought fit. The central authorities may have set criteria and given 'guidance' on the balances to be struck between the different groups of disciplines, between postgraduate and undergraduate numbers, and so on. Now, however, such allocations have to be construed carefully within the prescriptions laid down by the funding councils, especially insofar as specific performance contracts are adopted by the PCFC and UFC.

Institutions hold property and have all the responsibilities of a large employer of academic and non-academic staff. They also have contractual and other relationships with students and are legal entities responsible in law for the decisions they make and the resources they employ.

## THE OUTSIDE ENVIRONMENT

Institutions work within a diversity of environments, some of which are given formal expression but many of which are not. Chapter 4 has described the impact of the most immediately important elements in the external environment; namely, the funding bodies and research councils whose expressions of government policy reach institutions through the specific grants they award and whose authority is expressed through the degrees of control and the amount of monitoring which they apply to them. The relationships in both the normative and operational modes are explicit and have become more so. The CNAA and the professional validating bodies operate almost wholly in the normative mode, coming closer in to the institutions themselves. The formally created relationship between a university and its relevant laity is the council, sanctioned by royal charter and enjoying specific powers over the university's finance and resources. Since 1989 polytechnics and colleges, divested of local authority control, have entered into a relationship similar to that obtaining in the universities.

The functions and composition of councils and governing bodies again reflect various assumptions about the relationships between higher education and society. Collegiate institutions may be entirely self-governing in that they hold money in trust which they administer through their own college meetings of fellows. Non-collegiate universities are required to defer on all matters of finance, buildings and establishments to a council that may be partly nominated by the vice-chancellor and members of academic staff but whose majority comes from groups specified by charter and is deemed to represent different groups in society. Polytechnic governing bodies also comprise memberships laid down in their articles of government approved by the central authorities.

The intensity of control and the balance of authority between council and senate, governing body and academic board cannot be predicted from the formal statement of functions. Council and governing body have a fiduciary role over anything that smacks of resources. But resource allocations are a metaphor for the allocation of values. The extent to which it is academe, and the extent to which it is society (as represented by the lay majority body), which makes the running, is variable and volatile.

Other environmental forces include the challenges posed by strong market demands for courses, the pressure put by professional licensing bodies on course boards in certain applied subjects, and the emphasis given to certain themes as a result of financial sponsoring from industry, commerce or the government. Baldridge *et al.* (1978) have shown how different institutional systems in the USA are affected by a variety of environmental relationships relatively unfamiliar in Britain. The relationship between institutions and the political leadership of the community, the changing financial base as between private and public money, the changing pool of clients, the changing pattern of industrial relations and the unionisation of different staff groups, the extent to which social decision-making is subject to the intervention of the courts – a characteristic strongly established in the USA, but growing steadily in the UK – all these are factors which could have an effect on the ways in which institutions behave.

The notion of a market-led system must exercise a strong influence on the relationship between institutions and the external environment. Those who believe it worth their while greatly to expand student numbers are, against a declining age participation group, required to market their wares. The extent to which courses are modified to meet a wider range of applicants is signalled in the development by institutions of access courses and flexible admission requirements as against the former gold standard of good A levels in GCE.

The concept of the entrepreneurial and adaptive university has been elaborated in the USA (Davies, 1987). It is based on open systems theory and the assumed necessity of maintaining a state of creative equilibrium with the environment. It involves, especially in turbulent times, scanning political, social or economic stimuli and adjusting to keep pace with environmental changes. Such an organisation, it is claimed, is able to 'keep its external ... reference groups happy and committed'. It is proactive and opportunistic, and has a predictive capability and a strong service orientation encapsulated in a definitive university mission.

The entrepreneurial institution does not fit comfortably within the dominant UK tradition. The conversion of some of the more traditional institutions towards it would involve exceptionally strong institutional leadership. Linkages with the external world can be found, however, even in the more prestigious institutions. Science parks which now exist in significant numbers in the USA, the UK and other European countries are an attempt to ensure that there will be technology transfer, and the exploitation of institutional resources in the market place (Dalton, 1987). Other midway institutions include joint venture companies, research institutes which may have semi-autonomy from the institution, integrated degrees in which set periods of work take place outside the institution, externally sponsored master's programmes, tailor-made short courses and loans from industry to students (Pearson *et al.*, 1984).

The higher education institution has, then, become more rather than less complex. The underlying guild structure described by Clark (1978) persists, and is likely to do so because of the need for such an organisation if higher education's tasks are to be performed efficiently. At the same time, the demands for accountability, the demonstration of effectiveness, and the need for responsiveness to the outside world in some measure justify the stronger managerial role of the institutional leader. And cutting across both leadership and the collegial forms are the patterns of activity and resulting organisational structures that behaviour in a market demands.

## INSTITUTIONAL PLANNING

Planning by institutions, although unobtrusive, took place throughout the 1960s and 1970s as bids were put together for funding by the central authorities and distributions were made to the basic units. In the 1980s, however, institutional planning became far more explicit, for two reasons. First, the contraction of resources required priorities to be set. Second, the demands for institutional accountability to the central authorities made the creation of systematic machinery for academic planning virtually mandatory.

The fall in the number of overseas students caused by the government decision to increase their fee levels in 1979 sharpened the need for institutions to reappraise their own provision if they were to keep their market share. The subsequent fall in the 18-year-old cohort has also required institutions to reconsider where to secure their recruitment and on what terms. Financial stringency increases the pressure on subject areas where student demand is low, and favours a transfer of resources to areas where potential recruitment is strong. From 1990, institutions have been required to bid for the funding of student places and thus to formulate course-by-course judgements on what they can afford to provide.

In such circumstances, institutional leaders are called upon to make the best guesses that can be defended to their governing bodies or councils and their senates or academic boards. They have to work within several constraints. They must assess likely student demand, they must consider employers' interests and they must take account of national requirements as asserted and priced by government and the intermediary bodies. Thus universities have been encouraged to increase the number of their research students, and this is, indeed, necessary if the higher education staffing at the turn of the century is to be adequate. At the same time they must widen access for 18-year-olds. The creation of an academic plan has become an earnest of public accountability: a symbol on the basis of which an institution can be judged by the central authorities, by its client groups and by its own members. It has been suggested that a strategic plan of this kind can become a device of considerable value (Moore, 1989). It forces the institution's managers to concentrate upon the critical criteria for performance, to consider the fundamental changes taking place in higher education, to articulate their implications for the institution and to formulate appropriate responses. If the forward thinking is done well in advance, resource changes can be programmed smoothly over a number of years. The plan establishes criteria by which performance can be assessed.

Granted the need for more sophisticated and sensitive planning, the conflict of management and hierarchy versus academic professionalism and collegium reasserts itself. Even if the institutional leadership and the administrators who work for the leadership must inevitably occupy a more dominant role than hitherto, who then owns the product of their activities? It would be possible for a strong managerial and planning team to defer either to a hierarchy led by a council or governing body or to the collegium of practitioners within the institution, or to a combination of both. In practice, of course, those with full-time command over complex data and argument will succeed. But if they fail to consult others concerned, they might later face problems of implementation. Each line of an academic plan or of a budget or of a manpower projection involves activities by individual academics. The future of an institution remains an aggregate of academic activity rather than managerial planning. At least one research study has come to the conclusion that 'collegiality promotes consistent behaviour within the system' and that 'universities are paradoxically extremely stable at the broadest level and in a state of perpetual change at the narrowest' (Hardy *et al.*, 1984). A balance between logic and politics, as represented by planning at the centre and creative work at the production level, seems all the more necessary.

# 6 Basic units

## THE NATURE OF BASIC UNITS

Any full understanding of how the higher education system works must
depend on an understanding of the basic units which together make up its
constituent institutions. By basic units we mean the smallest component
elements which have a corporate life of their own. Their identifying characteristics would normally include an administrative existence (a designated
head or chairman, a separately accounted budget); a physical existence (an
identifiable set of premises); and an academic existence (a range of undergraduate training programmes, usually some provision for graduate work
and sometimes a collective research activity). A unit would not be regarded
as basic, in our sense, if it contained within it two more sub-units showing
such characteristics (for example, a department of anatomy might constitute a basic unit, but a medical school would be an amalgam of a number
of such units).

In traditional university structures, the basic unit would usually be taken
as the individual subject department, rather than the faculty bringing
together a number of cognate departments. However, this is not a hard-and-
fast rule, since some long-established universities use the term 'faculty'
where others would use 'department' (for example, as in 'faculty of economics' where there are no sub-units). Some more recent institutions have
developed alternative structures, in which the constituent elements are
more broadly based 'schools of study', 'course teams' and the like. Hence
the need to use a neutral term, such as 'basic unit', in discussing the nature
of the individual elements which make up the institution as a whole.

Basic units are especially important in the determination of professional
values, and in the maintenance and development of particular areas of
academic expertise (Trow, 1976). Although they are by no means all alike
in either their normative or their operational aspects, their main differences
from one another can be charted along a relatively limited number of

*Figure 6.1* The functions of the basic unit

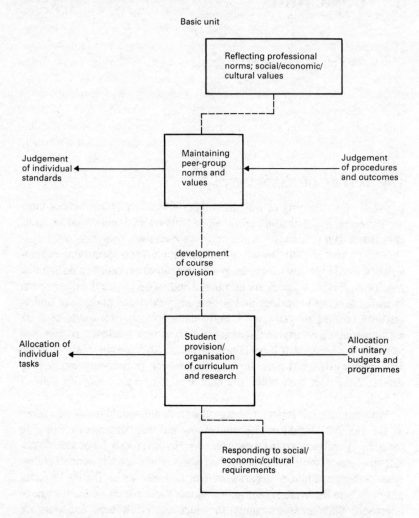

Basic unit

Reflecting professional norms; social/economic/cultural values

Judgement of individual standards ← Maintaining peer-group norms and values ← Judgement of procedures and outcomes

development of course provision

Allocation of individual tasks ← Student provision/organisation of curriculum and research ← Allocation of unitary budgets and programmes

Responding to social/economic/cultural requirements

dimensions. Our first purpose here will be to identify the dimensions and to describe the range of variation which each can encompass. We shall want to suggest, among other things, that the subcultural styles and epistemological traditions to which particular teaching units subscribe are a powerful determinant of their relationships within and outside the institution, of the curricular patterns which they adopt in their undergraduate programmes, and of the nature of their day-to-day processes of teaching and learning.

Free-standing research units, projects or teams are another species of basic unit (Platt, 1976). They differ in a number of respects from units which have a teaching function, and lie somewhat outside the main pattern of academic activity. Overall, they form only a small proportion of the whole range of basic units. They often depend largely on external funds, and are liable to have a less permanent existence than teaching units; although generally directed by tenured academics, they are predominantly staffed by people on short-term contract; and – symbolically – they are almost invariably located on the periphery of the campus, or even outside it. If their work is successful, they may earn the relevant disciplinary group, and the parent institution as a whole, much credit; but they do not thereby acquire greater political power. They are distributed unevenly as between pure and applied sciences, the social sciences and the arts. Their place in institutions is changing as government sponsorship of research becomes more prescriptive, and as the overall number of tenured posts remains static or declines. But the change is quantitative rather than qualitative.

A third type of unit is that which performs a predominantly service function. Such units include campus-wide computing facilities, counselling provision for students and staff, graduate careers services, and audio-visual resources. University libraries are commonly the largest, and best-regarded, of such service units. But although their operations may be acknowledged as indispensable, such units are not normally treated as on a par with the basic units devoted to teaching and research, and their staff tend to have different terms of employment and a relatively marginal place in institutional decision-making.

Both research and service provision share some of the characteristics of mainstream basic units. Our subsequent discussion will, however, focus on the latter. Although primarily justified in terms of their teaching and research function, a growing number of basic units also provide external services, in one form or another, to industry, the public sector or the community in general – for example, through consultancies, short courses, membership of public committees and the like. The pattern of activity varies considerably from one subject field to another, so it may be useful at this point to consider different broad groupings in turn.

## CATEGORIES OF TEACHING/RESEARCH UNITS

Mainstream basic units may be categorised in a variety of ways. Some universities have faculty structures which combine what are held to be cognate groups of subjects, such as the natural sciences, the social sciences, the humanities and so on. In Britain, the Universities Funding Council describes its allocations through a system of 'cost centres' which comprise a somewhat less coarsely grained set of subject combinations.

Other taxonomies, not very far different from these, are derived from research studies which seek to discover common underlying characteristics between, or patterns within, established academic disciplines. One such classification, which has proved itself to be widely applicable, is derived from the initial work of Biglan (1973a, 1973b) and the later research of Kolb (1981). It divides disciplines into four main clusters, along two dimensions – hard and soft, and pure and applied.

The first distinction is perhaps most readily marked in terms of the apparent clarity of the criteria for establishing or refuting claims to new knowledge. It is also related to the extent to which findings are open to quantification; the extent of reproducibility of results and their cumulative nature; and the degree to which clear causal connections may be identified. The second distinction, between pure and applied, is more familiar; it concerns the degree to which knowledge is expected to be put to practical use.

Within this typology, the hard pure disciplines comprise the natural sciences and mathematics; the hard applied consist of what Kolb (1981) describes as 'the science-based professions' – engineering, medicine and the like. The soft pure grouping brings together the humanities and social sciences; the soft applied designates 'the social professions' – education, social work, law and so forth.

It must be acknowledged that the Biglan–Kolb system of classifying the domains of knowledge glosses over some important points of detail. Thus, for example, economics could be argued to be a predominantly hard pure discipline, at least in comparison with anthropology; physical geography might be held to lie on the hard pure and human geography on the soft pure side of the boundary. Some aspects of medicine — particularly psychiatry – are clearly closer to soft applied than to hard applied knowledge. Indeed, a more detailed scrutiny of different areas of knowledge begins to suggest that disciplines themselves are not by any means homogeneous. The linguistic and philological aspects of language studies are hard in comparison with the critical; the design side of engineering is soft in comparison with its mathematical elements; basic medical science is more pure than applied; and so the catalogue continues.

We shall return later to the issue of internal differences within disciplines: however, the broad brush, hard/pure, soft/applied categorisation will usefully serve our present purposes. Looking at each main grouping in turn, we can broadly characterise their norms and operations.

Basic units concerned with hard pure knowledge are typified by strong peer norms, which are in some cases embodied in prestigious and powerful disciplinary interest groups. Because they deal with collective, cumulative knowledge, research in such basic units is amenable to team work – sometimes on a large scale, sometimes on a small. Their activities – such as defence research or experiments with animals – will in some cases raise ethical issues: whether this is so or not, their work has become more and more subject over time to societal and economic questioning. But the main yardstick for judgement remains that of research excellence as judged by leading practitioners in the field.

In operational terms, hard pure basic units are often heavily dependent on physical resources, and especially laboratories, instrumentation and supplies. In some cases, the size of the investment in plant may determine whether or not a particular research programme will remain viable. Between them, such units may take up a substantial part of the institutional budget – though they may also earn sizeable support in terms of outside grants. Because of the nature of the knowledge with which they are concerned – and particularly its reproducible and cumulative character – their teaching programmes tend to be content-based, and their curricula relatively clearly defined and self-contained.

Hard applied knowledge is associated with somewhat similar basic units, although the emphasis here is on products and skills rather than on concepts and theories. The degree of teamwork tends to be more limited than in hard pure fields, partly because the work is not as strongly cumulative. There are also somewhat weaker academic peer norms and less well-articulated interest groups, though strong links may exist with the wider profession and its own associations. The expected level of accountability to society at large tends to be high. Quality of work is judged as much by external, utilitarian criteria as by internal academic ones.

Operationally, the funding links with industry, or with other outside contractors, are likely to be strong because of the functional nature of much of the unit's research activity. Teaching, although typically very heavily laden in terms of content, also seeks to promote practical professional skills, usually through real-life or simulated job experience.

Turning next to units concerned with soft pure knowledge, one might begin by noting in general terms the extent to which academic activity tends to be individual rather than collective. As a result, although academic interest groups exist, they have in general neither the strength nor the prestige of those in hard pure fields. On the whole, the scale of research is modest and does not call for external justification. The extent of public interest in research findings varies considerably from one discipline to another, and indeed one topic to another, and demands for accountability reflect this variation.

The costs of operation in soft pure units are confined mainly to those of staffing: equipment demands tend to be negligible in comparison with those for hard pure units. There is a relatively limited incidence of outside commissioned work, with the main emphasis on economics and one or two other social science subjects. The pattern of teaching tends to be sharply distinguishable from that in hard pure and hard applied units, particularly in the extent to which students are expected to shape the content of their own learning programmes and to present personal interpretations of phenomena. Academic quality is more contested than in hard pure fields.

Finally, units concerned with soft applied knowledge have some of the normative characteristics of soft pure units, and some of hard applied. They are individualistic in emphasis, and have relatively weak academic peer-group links; but they relate quite strongly to the relevant wider professional groupings. They tend to have a clearer social accountability than soft pure units. There is a significant element of pragmatism in the evaluation of soft applied research.

The units concerned draw for the most part on public sector agencies for research funds. These are relatively modest, in that there is typically no requirement for laboratory or equipment budgets. The teaching pattern is less individualistic than that in soft pure units; there is, as in the case of hard applied subjects, an emphasis on the development of relevant vocational skills, with accompanying scope for professional work placements.

## STATUS AND STABILITY

Taken together, these considerations underline the extent to which the norms and operations of basic units are dependent on the nature of the knowledge fields with which they are concerned. A basic unit's standing within the academic world as a whole, as well as within the host institution, will also be affected by the nature of the knowledge field with which it is concerned. By and large, high academic status is accorded to hard pure subjects, and relatively low to soft applied ones. The reasons may be conjectured. In the first place, pure disciplines tend to have been longer-established than applied ones, and hence to enjoy the plausibility of tradition: their nature is usually more clearly comprehended by the intelligent lay person. In the second place, hard subjects tended to be seen as hard in a different sense: they are well regarded because they appear intellectually demanding in a way that soft subjects do not. They purvey, moreover, a sense of rigour: arguments seem to be clearly right or wrong; they are amenable to proof; they relatively seldom give rise to the kinds of controversies characteristic of soft subjects. This intellectual 'pecking order' – ranging from mathematics and physics at one extreme to nursing and social work training at the other – is, however, liable to be overlaid with a variety of other considerations.

Before the advent of selectivity the emphasis was heavily on academic research as a source of institutional prestige. This was, however, progressively weakened, largely by outside social and political pressures. Even today, basic units which cannot attract a sufficiently large number of applicants for student places to enable them to be moderately selective – that is, to hold out for entry qualifications above the national norm – are liable to lose credibility within their parent institutions. Their bargaining position is weakened still further – however good their research record might be – if they are unable to achieve their collectively agreed undergraduate and postgraduate intake targets.

A further problem may arise in relation to outside service activities. Although some allowance tends to be made in terms of some soft pure disciplines – where it may be difficult to identify what kind of contribution could reasonably be expected – even hard pure basic units may be expected to justify the external relevance of their activities, alongside those of applied subject fields. Again, performance which is seen to be inadequate on this criterion may weaken institutional standing gained through more traditionally defined academic capability.

In institutions which do not operate a conventional academic structure of subject departments, the criteria for establishing the internal status of basic units will necessarily differ from those relating to traditional disciplines. It may indeed be difficult for units based on interdisciplinary themes to identify criteria for judgement of their work, in the absence of anything comparable with an external peer group. However, their activities may none the less be evaluated in relation to their attractiveness for students and their significance for the wider community.

On the whole, units which are not based on well-defined subject fields tend to lack stability, in that they are not dealing with common intellectual currency, and are not part of any clearly recognisable wider academic or professional community. An example may be cited in an interdisciplinary unit dealing with a particular problem in space research. The group – consisting of physicists, chemists, engineers, mathematicians and a computer specialist – had begun to work together satisfactorily when the computer specialist left for another post: the lengthy business of finding a successor and inducting him, or her, into the team's way of thinking and working was a major setback. In a monodisciplinary team, with a commonly established set of intellectual requirements, the replacement would almost certainly have been easier. Both the organisational stability and the academic status of basic units are therefore to a significant extent dependent on the existence of peer groups outside the institution itself; and both have an important bearing on an issue which we shall explore later; namely, the extent to which any basic unit can resist the pressures brought to bear on it by the institution in which it is located.


## THE CURRICULUM MATRIX

At this point, another set of distinctions can usefully be introduced. They are helpful in delineating certain characteristic curricular patterns in higher education, which in their turn influence the nature of basic units and the organisational structure of the institutions in which they are embedded. The first distinction marks the extent to which the boundaries of the subject-matter are strongly defined and guarded, as against the extent to which they are hospitable to considerations outside the strict disciplinary norms (see Bernstein, 1975, on strong and weak classification). A curriculum with closed boundaries is one which firmly rules out the consideration of evidence other than that held to be directly related to the existing disciplinary framework; one which is permeable will allow for the importation of new, but external, ideas.

The second distinction concerns the degree of cohesiveness of subject-matter which is expected within the undergraduate curriculum, as opposed to the extent to which the component elements are permitted to be discrete and not necessarily linked at the conceptual level (see Bernstein, 1975, on strong and weak framing). If the programme as a whole hangs together round a limited number of integrating themes, and there is a clear attempt to achieve intellectual unity, then it can fairly be described as cohesive. If it encompasses a range of separate and apparently unconnected components, where the links, if any, do not seem to be counted as important, then it can be designated as discrete. The two sets of distinctions – the one relating to the permeability of subject boundaries and the other to cohesiveness of content within those boundaries – can be brought together to form a four-cell matrix (Table 6.1).


*Table 6.1*  An outline matrix of curricular patterns

|  |  | Subject boundaries | |
| --- | --- | --- | --- |
|  |  | *Closed* | *Permeable* |
| *Curricular content* | *Cohesive* | 1 | 2 |
|  | *Discrete* | 3 | 4 |

Next, we shall identify the curricular patterns which best correspond with these four different pairs of characteristics. The first cell in the matrix, representing closed boundaries and cohesive content, is easy enough to allocate, since these are the familiar characteristics of single-subject specialist curriculum programmes. The third cell similarly defines a fairly common species of curricular pattern; namely, that in which a number of separate and self-contained thematic topics are pursued simultaneously, but with no special attempt to relate them to one another. Broadly based 'foundation courses', joint honours programmes and unit or modular degree schemes all fit into this pattern. The second cell represents those interdisciplinary courses which are area-based or problem-based rather than related to conventional disciplines (examples would include urban development or European studies). In such courses, a considerable effort is made to develop a sense of unity between the various disciplinary components; but the boundaries of the course remain permeable to new elements, provided only that these have some acceptable degree of relevance to the central theme.

Finally, the fourth cell seems best to correspond to some of the more recent conceptions of open learning, life-long study or *education permanente*. It implies an ability for the student to select individual items of curricular content at will, but not to be subject to the discipline-based restrictions that characterise modular degree programmes. It depends on the notion of cumulative and transferable credit, negotiated in relation to approved pieces of work over a relatively unrestricted time-span. (The Open University in the UK does not provide open learning in this sense; rather, it operates in an interdisciplinary fashion at the foundation level and in a modular fashion at the more advanced levels.)

The completed matrix, with examples of curricular patterns included, emerges as shown in Table 6.2.

*Table 6.2* Some varieties of curricular pattern

|  |  | Boundaries | |
|  |  | Closed | Permeable |
| --- | --- | --- | --- |
| Content | *Cohesive* | Single-subject specialised degrees | Interdisciplinary courses |
|  | *Discrete* | Modular or joint course schemes | Open learning programmes |

It now remains to consider what seem to be the most appropriate organisational frameworks to match these different curricular patterns, and to look briefly at the possible consequences of a mismatch.

## CURRICULAR PATTERNS AND ACADEMIC STRUCTURES

As far as an ideal framework can be found for a single-subject degree, it is surely the traditional specialist department. This offers a complete correspondence of interest between academic organisation and teaching commitment, with the department identified in terms of the specialised subjects it teaches and its staff and students sharing the same clear sense of discipline-based identity.

However, the departmental structure is less appropriate to a modular degree scheme. Individual departments will often tend to compete amongst themselves for student numbers, using a variety of ingenious, but not always educationally productive, tactics. They may also introduce unnecessary rigidities in the system by insisting on a series of prerequisite courses, or complicate matters by keeping to their own marking schemes. In practice, those UK institutions which have gone farthest in the direction of modularising their courses have tended to move to a structure in which course teams provide the organisational basis for teaching and subject groups provide the basis for research. Each course team consists of all the staff involved in teaching a given unit or module. Its success is determined largely by the degree to which the participants work effectively together. An individual member of staff will normally belong to two or three course teams, but in most cases to only one subject group. The course teams often have their own budgets so that they form in effect a basic unit in the terms defined earlier (Watson, 1989).

Just as the traditional academic structure has had to be modified to accommodate modular degrees, so too it has proved clearly unsuitable to interdisciplinarity. The problem stems from the tendency of discipline-based groups to lay unique claim to certain areas of knowledge and to close off attention to what lies beyond their own professional boundaries. This parochialism is exactly what the advocates of interdisciplinary courses set out to avoid. In general, they can only succeed if they manage to bypass or break down the departmental framework. This has commonly been done in UK universities by reorganising the whole structure of the institution in terms of schools of study. These schools are then taken to constitute the basic units within the institution, each devoted to the broad theme which forms the subject-matter of its own degree programme or programmes. Thus one such school might be designated English and American studies, another environmental science, and so on. The sectional interests of particular subject disciplines are, in theory if not always in practice, subjugated to the wider requirements of interdisciplinary teaching and research.

Finally, open learning programmes of the type outlined earlier must clearly call for a much more flexible and open structure than any of those so far discussed. Indeed, they appear almost to transcend traditional notions of structure, much as some modern painting, poetry and music would seem to do. But in practice they involve the creation of relatively informal and shifting networks of co-operating institutions and individuals. Thus, in such a system, a given student might spend six months working full-time on an individual study project on transportation management at Polytechnic A, to earn two credits; work part-time for the ensuing year on a single-credit course on urban geography at University B; follow this after a year's interval by embarking on a two-year part-time programme on advanced network analysis, carrying three credits, at Polytechnic C; and so on. Programmes of this kind represent a new area of academic growth. They are not so much intra-institutional as inter-institutional. Although they may well in the long run modify existing organisational forms at the level of the basic unit, their immediate impact has been on the relationships between different institutions and the structure of the system as a whole (CNAA, 1989).

We have attempted here to show how different curricular patterns call for different types of academic structure, often modifying the way in which an institution's basic units are defined. In terms of our model, a significant change in the predominant values of the peer group leads to a comparable change in the nature of the operating process at the level of the basic unit. This change can conflict with the existing mechanisms at the institutional level and lead to an imbalance between the normative and operational modes. The conflict has eventually to be resolved either by a final refusal on the institution's part to collaborate, or by organisational reform – unless it happens that the institution already has some appropriate mechanism to accommodate structural developments.

## TRANSACTIONS BETWEEN BASIC UNITS

Even at the level of fairly modest transactions between basic units, not involving ambitious modular schemes or interdisciplinary degree programmes, troubles frequently arise from either horizontal or vertical departures from the accepted norm of the single-subject curriculum in our matrix. Horizontally, attempts to open subject boundaries slightly to incorporate materials from other disciplines in the form of 'service' courses run into one particular kind of difficulty. Vertically, moves to widen introductory programmes by pooling an initial intake of students between different basic units run into a different set of snags.

The generally unsatisfactory nature of service courses in higher education is widely acknowledged – that is, courses in which one basic unit is commissioned to provide a limited amount of introductory or remedial teaching for students in another (chemistry for biologists, say, or statistics for sociologists).[1] The main problem derives from differences between the values of the two units involved in such a transaction. The host unit's natural concern is with the integration of the new material into the texture of its own curriculum. It has a largely instrumental view, seeing the exercise as a relatively marginal one in which elementary techniques are to be acquired and basic factual material assimilated by students in the minimum possible amount of time. The guest unit, on the other hand, is generally anxious not to seem to be undermining the integrity of its discipline by portraying it as nothing more than a disconnected set of tools and topics. Its staff show some reluctance in taking on what is seen to be a low-prestige task, and become the more prone to emphasise their disciplinary dignity.

The result of this divergence of emphasis, from integration on the one hand to integrity on the other, is often a course which neither the host nor the guest unit regard as having much value. It will normally, as a necessary chore, be taken on in rotation, if not simply delegated to the most junior members of the guest unit. There will therefore be little continuity of staffing from one year to the next. In any event, the guest staff will tend to be given a sketchy briefing of what is required, and comparably limited academic support, from their colleagues in the host unit. Their own unit will tend to allocate the minimum reasonable amount of preparatory time for the task. There will thus be neither opportunity nor incentive to integrate the outside material with the rest of the curriculum.

In defence of their own and their subject's reputation, the guest staff will be driven to emphasise underlying principles, largely at the cost of applications relevant to the host discipline. They will accordingly demand from students a greater degree of academic commitment than the students (reading the signals emanating from their own units) could realistically be expected to give. The students themselves will usually fail to understand the purpose of the exercise, or its connections with their main programme. They will in many cases soon find themselves out of their depth in coping with an unfamiliar theme, and will withdraw from all but the necessary minimum of involvement.

In contrast with this sequence of mutual failures of adjustment characteristic of service courses, other hazards beset those basic units which combine to provide multi-subject introductory programmes. The common purpose behind such programmes is thoroughly well intentioned – as it is with service courses. It is based on two considerations. The first is that students who are unfamiliar with a broad, general field should have an opportunity at least to sample the range of disciplines it covers before they are required to make a final choice within the field. The second is that even where students have already made such a choice, it is useful for them to be able to see their own specialism against the background of neighbouring areas of enquiry (Squires, 1990).

Programmes based on these considerations usually take the form of first-year or first-semester schemes covering between two and four subjects, the students being expected to select the subject or subjects for specialised study at the end of this period. Normally the time allocation for all subjects is the same within the programme, so that problems of primary and secondary (host and guest) partnership do not arise. Nor is there usually any aspiration towards, or expectation of, framing connections between component elements: the conflict between integration and integrity is also avoided. Each participating unit is of equal standing with the rest and each is expected to devise its own self-contained introductory course.

This very equality of status can create its own problems. When the incoming students are admitted on the basis of primary allegiance to a particular basic unit, that unit will understandably display a possessiveness about its own recruits at the expense of those attached to other units. Special academic or social activities may be laid on, over and above those provided within the framework of the programme. Unit-based activities will be played up, and inter-unit ones played down. This progressive weakening of the original framework will have its effect on students, who will be found to complain that the broadening element at the start of their course fails to fit in with the rest, introduces extraneous and irrelevant material, takes up unnecessary time and deserves to be abolished. Thus schemes of this kind, based on an 'indentured' intake, are liable slowly to atrophy.

Other such schemes are run with 'free' students – that is, ones admitted with a firm expectation that significant numbers of individuals may change their initial preference after completing the introductory programme. Here the endeavour to win the hearts and minds of students can become even more competitive. There is over time a tendency for each participating unit to expect rather more commitment of interest and attention from students than they might devote to the other units, and hence a growing student workload which can eventually lead to disaster. Although in general the competition is kept within decent limits, accepted behaviour being defined by the collective norms of the institution, there can be instances in which one basic unit is deemed by the others participating in the programme to have overstepped the mark. To give one instance, one participating department succeeded in introducing a group project into its part of the scheme, with the predictable result that the students devoted an undue share of their time and effort to working on this. The scheme in question was eventually disbanded as no longer functional.

These examples of relationships between basic units have been considered at some length, because they help to illuminate the way in which normative differences between one unit and another can give rise to operational problems in relation to shared curricular activities.

Similar conflicts of interest, often accompanied by power struggles, can arise in relation to research. There are instances when cognate areas of enquiry begin to overlap and where, as a result, certain tracts of intellectual terrain may be in dispute. Sometimes the situation may be resolved amicably, by a sharing or dividing of the spoils, but in other cases one discipline may succeed in colonising the territory of another. Thus, for example, behavioural psychology in the pre-war and post-war period began to dominate what was previously a largely philosophically based arena of pedagogic research; and in the 1960s and 1970s sociologists largely took over the historically oriented field of science studies. Over time, the basic units concerned generally reflect such changes of disciplinary dominance in terms of a corresponding loss or gain in their status and staffing numbers. Again, the interaction here tends to be one in which normative changes are reflected in the operational mode.

## THE BASIC UNIT AND ACADEMIC AUTONOMY

The autonomy of the basic unit and of the individuals who work in it is arguably a functional necessity in higher education – a necessity arising from the fact that it embodies a cluster of activities which depend strongly on intellectual ability, technical training, individual creativity and the motivation to exercise all of these to the full. This argument, although seldom explicitly developed, is widely taken for granted by practitioners, whether operating individually or as members of a collective with cognate expertise and academic commitment. The case for autonomy rests on the contention that the exercise of creativity by individuals or relatively small collegial groups is the essential socio-technological condition of good academic work; there is an assumption here of a functional link between the nature of the task and the requisite organisation for it.

The opposing case is clearly stated in the Jarratt Report, in which reference is made to

large and powerful academic departments together with individual academics who sometimes see their academic discipline as more important than the long-term well-being of the university which houses them. We stress that in our view universities are first and foremost corporate enterprises to which subsidiary units and individual academics are responsible and accountable. Failure to recognise this will weaken the institution and undermine its long term viability.

(para. 3.41)

None the less, the discretionary content of academic work, whether related to teaching, research or scholarship, can be held to be important enough to render dysfunctional strong controls and management of those tasks from external agencies. Neither advanced research in biophysics nor specialised teaching in medieval history can be sensibly subject to control by outsiders to the fields in question. The nature and range of the external constraints which are in practice imposed upon such tasks will be considered briefly in the following pages. What may be noted here is the deep-seated belief among academics that worthwhile intellectual activity cannot survive in a context in which outside demands begin to exercise a dominating influence over choice and action.

The relationships of the basic unit with the institution and the central authorities manifest these tensions between autonomy and direction from above. As we have seen in Chapters 4 and 5, strong social and economic influences are taken into account at the central and institutional levels, and filter down to the basic units in the form of normative judgements and operational allocations. The basic unit is itself part of the process of transmission of such pressures, in its relations with its individual members.

At the same time, as our model suggests, depending on the nature of its field of knowledge the basic unit is subject to the normative influence of its academic peer group or wider professional body; and it may itself be directly affected by socio-economic developments within the community at large, whether these take the form of normative pressures to adopt certain values or operational pressures to take on particular commitments, in the form of courses, consultancies or pieces of commissioned research.

The tensions to which these varied demands give rise can be seen clearly in the role of the chairperson or head of an academic department or other basic unit. Many such individuals are appointed on mainly academic criteria, but find themselves heavily involved in administration and management. The growing emphasis on conformity with governmental and wider social requirements has added to the traditional expectation that the head should be a leading researcher in the field the need to take on the functions of a line manager (Lockwood and Davies, 1985). This brings with it a growing responsibility for staff appraisal, the generation of external funds, the improvement of student recruitment, the submission of forward proposals for departmental research and teaching and often a part in drawing up institutional plans. Judgements related to how satisfactorily such tasks are carried out are reflected in differential levels of pay.

The time, then, during which academic considerations reigned supreme in the evaluation of basic units and their leaders may have passed. Even so, the case for autonomy in relation to the central core of academic work remains as strong as before, and is unlikely to be directly contested, except at the price of discharging routine teaching functions indistinguishable from post-compulsory education at large.

## THE RESILIENCE OF BASIC UNITS

We noted earlier in this chapter that basic units tend to differ in terms of their calls on institutional resources, according to whether they can be categorised as hard pure, hard applied, soft pure or soft applied; and that the curricular patterns which they espouse may have certain implications for the way their parent institution is organised. But more remains to be said about the relationship of basic units to institutions, particularly in respect of attempts on the part of the institution to influence the values or practices of its basic units.

We have remarked how normative pressures, emanating not only from the institution itself, but also from the central authorities and from society at large, serve to limit the autonomy of the basic units. None the less, one of the noticeable features of higher education, which our model helps to underline, is their resilience in the face of pressure of this kind. The observation should not be altogether surprising, since the basic unit has been defined as the smallest viable grouping in any academic institution, working within its own budget and, to a sizeable extent, its own terms of reference. It may sustain a broadly coherent academic ideology in a way that larger groupings (say, the entire arts faculty) seldom do. It has a key role in the selection of its own members and in determining the curriculum it offers. What is more, the basic unit usually forms part of a wider peer-group network outside the bounds of its parent institution – a network within which individual and collective reputations are established and prospects of mobility and promotion are opened up.

Basic units serve not only as an immediate and direct source of academic identity for individual students and staff, but also as vehicles for the preservation and development of specialist expertise. In this latter respect, they occupy a powerful, though not impregnable, position in the political line-up of the institutions to which they belong. It is not easy for an institution as a whole to call for this or that modification of policy or practice in one of its basic units. In many cases, the unit in question will have the monopoly of relevant specialised knowledge and will be able to respond by rejecting the demand as ill-informed, irrelevant or inappropriate. In a case of conflict it will be more easily able to close its ranks than will the rest of the institution, with its ideologically diverse interest groups. In the last resort, however, the institution can depend on the judgements of those members of staff whose expertise, though different, is closely allied to that of the basic unit in question; or on the views of outside authorities in the same academic field. Where the institution's proposals are upheld, it will have the means of implementing them through its powers to control the unit's budgetary allocations.

Such conflicts between basic units and institutions tend to be confined to cases where the unit has fallen badly out of line both with institutional policy and with contemporary practice in comparable units elsewhere. For the most part, the senior members of the institution can only directly affect the normative mode when a new head of a basic unit is to be appointed; and even in this instance their scope is limited by the need for approval from the wider specialist peer group outside the institution itself.

This characteristic resilience may be weakened in various ways. One phenomenon which manifests itself from time to time is internal conflict. Although, to external view, most disciplines appear reasonably homogeneous, they are, with few exceptions, internally fragmented, and occasionally fissiparous. Sometimes the constituent specialisms may be differentiated in terms of methodology, of technique, or of subject content. In other cases there may be a division of ideology or value. It is perhaps most often the last of these which gives rise to heated argument, though there have been well-documented controversies arising from other sources of difference (see, for example, Crane, 1972; Kemp, 1977). As long as any resulting quarrel remains within the confines of the basic unit, or even its wider disciplinary community, all may be well. However, the situation alters when it becomes public knowledge outside the family circle. Once a particular basic unit becomes identified with dissension and disharmony, its credibility almost inevitably suffers (a notorious case in the early 1980s was the English Faculty at Cambridge, where a young, outspoken, proponent of structuralism was refused tenure: a decision which provoked a considerable and widely publicised outcry). A basic unit which is seen not to have its act together is considered fair game for predators of various kinds; and, in particular, it is readily open to being called to order by its parent institution.

## THE PEER NETWORK AND CONSUMER CHOICE

The position of the basic units is given added strength by the underlying continuities of the academic enterprise. They are protected by the appeal to proper processes of enquiry and the need for validated evidence, as against the use of the superior force of central authorities or institutions. They can trade on the tradition of deferring to expert knowledge as opposed to using arguments from expediency. But above all, they can depend on a separate structure of values and rewards, based on their particular specialist field, which is national, if not international, in scope.

Every such structure, built up round its own particular set of academic concerns, is of its nature protective of its members' interests and conservative of its corporate practice and reputation. It is rarely amenable to rapid change, and thus provides its constituent basic units with a convenient court of appeal in the face of institutional or central demands for reforms in policy and practice.

The series of 'invisible colleges', as they have been called, which define the networks of specialised interest groups throughout the learned world, are no less powerful for being informal in nature (Clark, 1983). Each network does, however, incorporate certain formal elements, whose purpose is to monitor and safeguard standards. Thus, as we have noted in Chapter 4, the systems of academic validation in the UK, based on external examiners (and also, in the case of the maintained sector, on peer-group scrutiny of initial course proposals), can be seen not only as providing public certification but as policing internal practice.

Other visible and formal manifestations of these invisible and informal colleges may include research councils (whose specialist committees are dominated by leading exponents of the relevant discipline), learned societies, and journals which adjudicate acceptability for publication. The offering or withholding of research funds, of membership of prestigious bodies, or of opportunities to publish, are common forms of control exercised by the establishment in any given field over the basic units and individuals in that field.

Peer-group networks, whilst defending the collective interest, can themselves be discriminatory. They are both responsive to, and determinant of, differences of status in the basic units to which they relate. The issue of how that status is determined is a subtle one. The standing of the unit derives in part from the place in the institutional pecking order of its host university or polytechnic, and in part from the collective reputations of its members. But the relationships are reciprocal, in that an institution is judged by the perceived quality of its basic units, and an individual academic's reputation is influenced by that of his or her employing basic unit and institution. In any event, a peer network will usually move more rapidly and decisively to defend the interests of a high- than a low-status unit, or to further its cause. Thus rewards dominated by peer groups (research grants, publication in prestigious journals) are more likely to go to established basic units and individuals than to those outside the favoured circle.

Looked at from one point of view, the principle of mutual judgement by specialists of one another's work is inherently fair and sound. It helps to maintain overall standards; at the same time, by providing basic units with an external frame of reference, it ensures that each unit is more than simply the sum of its individual members. But considered in a less positive light, the powerful position of peer-group networks can be seen to hold certain dangers. In particular, their strong protection of established procedures can have an inhibiting effect on necessary or desirable changes; and the prevailing orthodoxy, as represented in a few influential figures, can systematically penalise the basic unit which – perhaps with good reason – fails to subscribe to the party line. Moreover, the recommendations of outsiders professing a specialist interest can sometimes conflict with the views of those concerned to maintain a balanced development within an institution as a whole.

Were it to rely solely on the device of peer networks for shaping the norms of its basic units, the higher education system could therefore well become inbred. As it happens, however, there is an alternative set of considerations which arise from the outside sources identified in our model – namely, the wider social, economic and cultural values.

The alternative currency to that of academic prestige, as far as basic units are concerned, is the marketability of courses. Although the two are by no means unconnected, they have somewhat independent effects. Thus, for example, although the standing of management studies is not particularly high in the pecking order of learned pursuits, the basic units which provide degree courses in it may gain a certain measure of esteem within their institutions by virtue of the fact that their courses are usually oversubscribed. In a similar way, despite the high scholarly status traditionally granted to the study of Latin and Greek, the absence of any substantial student demand for places in classics departments inevitably affects their power and their credibility inside their parent universities.

The importance of recruitment is strongly reinforced where – as in Britain after 1990 – fees are set at a relatively high level, and thus become a significant element in institutional funding. This accords market power to the consumer in a fairly direct way. The resulting numbers game – the tailoring of teaching programmes to suit the potential customer – can be thought of as a necessary antidote to the otherwise excessive introspection of peer-group monitoring. It is certainly, as we shall see in Chapter 8, a major source of innovative ideas in teaching, learning and curricular design. But it cannot be played with complete disregard for the views of the peer network, any more than the leading members of that network can afford to ignore the influence of market forces. The two currencies are not, as we have already observed, mutually independent. If a basic unit goes in too blatantly for attracting students, at the expense of upholding disciplinary traditions, it risks being cut off from membership of its invisible college, and hence from offering a well-regarded academic qualification; this immediately and drastically reduces the marketability of its courses. Equally, an effective specialist guild or network must be alive to happenings in the schools, in the field of graduate employment and, more generally, in current intellectual fashion. In the effort to defend and improve its standing in society, it has to be ready to take action in its constituents' interests as one political pressure group among many others, without at the same time losing its distinctive academic role.

In any case the fortunes of disciplines fluctuate over time, in accordance with cultural and intellectual fashion. Philosophy, for example, reached a peak in the immediate post-war years, but fell from favour during the 1980s; linguistics rose in esteem during the 1970s but also fell back somewhat in the subsequent decade. Engineering, earlier held in low repute, would seem to be on a rising curve; the same could be unequivocally said of accountancy. The academic stock exchange, in which the wily institutional head will be ready where possible to buy and sell shares in the available academic commodities, has directly discernible effects on the fortunes of basic units. It conditions their resilience to both internal and external pressures no less than some of the other factors already mentioned (such as their degree of internal unity or their standing within the peer group as a whole).

Part of the explanation behind such changes in the values ascribed to various disciplines can be found in the varying balance between the norms of purity and relevance. One might say that, in an idealistic society, purity is given pride of place: academic research is valued for its own sake, and teaching is expected to respond to an untainted desire for knowledge. In an instrumental era, this balance is reversed in favour of relevance: research is expected to serve practical purposes, and teaching is done on a largely contractual basis to meet vocational requirements. In the former context, research tends to be valued above teaching, and the independence of the academy is respected. In the latter, teaching tends to assume greater significance than research, and academic licence is constrained through demands for evaluation and accountability.

An instrumental view of higher education reduces its insulation from external influences and reinforces its links with social agencies and commercial sponsors. The interests of both of these may work against the existing patterns of basic units, favouring a more interdisciplinary, problem-oriented approach in teaching as well as research. This tendency serves to exacerbate a paradox which has always been dormant within the system; namely, that between the inexorable march of specialisation and the perennial demands for broad, generalist undergraduate curricula.

Academic reputations depend, largely if not exclusively, on estimates of capability and originality in research: and originality is most easily established by tackling problems that no one else has tackled. The areas of knowledge that have already been well explored are, for the most part, to be avoided. The best promise for making a reputation lies in hitherto neglected or undeveloped pieces of intellectual territory. Much like frontiersmen in newly discovered lands, academics seek to corner a patch of ground which they can cultivate unmolested by others. This process of identifying one's own specialism helps to account for the fragmentation of disciplinary knowledge domains and the constant emergence of new sub-disciplinary groupings. Here is a clear example of the division of academic labour which Clark (1983) analyses *in extenso*.

But an examination of the clientele for higher education suggests that, as access is widened, student entry criteria become less rather than more specialised. Entrants who have continued to follow a broad curriculum beyond the stage of compulsory schooling, or who return to academic work after a period in employment, are generally hesitant to commit themselves to a narrowly focused programme of study. So the tendency is for institutions wishing to maximise their recruitment to favour breadth at the expense of depth, at least in the early undergraduate years.

The resulting demand for generalist teaching is, on the face of it, at odds with the steady trend towards specialised research. There are two recognisable ways of dealing with the resulting tension; namely, institutional stratification and internal differentiation.

Whilst the UK higher education system has grown, the earlier expectation of comparability of performance standards, in degree examinations as well as in research, has become progressively less realistic, as the historical analysis in Chapter 3 has shown. The introduction of polytechnics as predominantly teaching institutions undermined the close association previously maintained between teaching and research. Subsequent recommendations to create 'teaching only' universities or basic units ineligible for research funding were not specifically adopted; but differential basic unit allocations, based on some form of quality assessment for research activity and on competitive bids for student recruitment, were clearly designed to have a similar long-term effect. Thus the system as a whole has been pointed in the same direction as that historically taken by higher education in the USA; one price of increased access, it would seem, is the creation of an explicit order of academic merit between categories of institutions, between institutions within a category, and by extension between individual basic units in the same field as well as those in the same institution.

In the context of this diversification, basic units concerned to ensure their healthy survival may seek to reconcile highly concentrated research with widely dispersed teaching coverage by allocating the former to one group of staff and the latter to another. Thus, within the framework of a single basic unit, it has become possible to identify two categories of academic – those whose main job expectation is to pursue knowledge and those whose principal task is to purvey it. This internal differentiation is not totally new, though it is more overt than in the past; it is an extreme variant of the informal pattern of activity which has long been in existence: that 'considerable variability' noted by Trow (1976) 'in individual talent, preference and disposition [which] allows people actually to distribute their time and energy very differently among the various functions of the department'.

This latter observation moves in the direction of discussing the relationships between basic units and the individuals, whether staff or students, who belong to them, as well as the roles of those individuals themselves. That is a sufficiently important element of our model to deserve separate consideration, and we shall therefore take it up in the next chapter.

## NOTE

1   An illuminating case study of one such course is given in Fisher, Kapur and McGarvey (1978).

# 7  The individual level

## THE ACADEMIC'S ROLE EXPECTATIONS

In terms of our model, it is possible to consider both students and staff from two aspects – normative and operational – although, as with all other levels of the system, the aspects are closely interconnected (Figure 7.1). The normative elements of the individual level include both the realisation of role expectations – the public component of the academic's world – and the pursuit of personal goals – the private component. We shall begin by considering the former.

The academic is expected, according to circumstance, to perform a variety of roles: those of teacher, of researcher or scholar, of academic manager or administrator, of entrepreneur or service-giver (Clark, 1987b). The teaching role is perhaps familiar enough to need no further explanation. The distinction between research and scholarship is not altogether clear-cut, but scholarly activity usually refers to the accumulation, conceptualisation and reordering of knowledge and research to its generation. Thus, someone dubbed a considerable scholar is expected to have acquired an unusual mastery of his or her field, but not necessarily to have made an original contribution to it. A researcher, in contrast, will normally have made some addition to the stock of knowledge, even if not especially cognisant of the relevant body of knowledge as a whole. Management functions may, in some institutions, be reserved for more senior members of staff, but nearly every academic, however junior, tends to have some administrative obligations – perhaps particularly those arising from teaching, if not from research. The degree of entrepreneurial expectation may vary between one type of basic unit and another, typically being strongest in hard applied fields and weakest in soft pure ones (see Chapter 6). But the performance of service roles – which involve the provision of experience and expertise for the benefit of others outside one's own institution, and often outside the higher education system (such as serving on national

*Figure 7.1* The functions of the individual

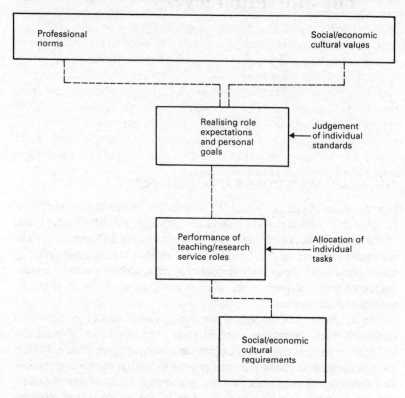

committees or school governing bodies) is less discipline-specific.

There is further variation in the extent to which individuals respond to, and internalise, the demands of their own basic units and institutions, and how far they defer to the norms of the wider profession (a classic paper by Gouldner, 1957, elaborated this distinction in terms of the contrast between 'locals' and 'cosmopolitans'). Current national policies appear to play down the primacy of wider professional values, and to favour the promotion of a direct assimilation by academics of current service norms. There are, as we shall argue, problems in moving too far in this direction. It is none the less the case that academics are influenced – as are people in other walks of life – in more or less direct ways by the wider cultural climate in which they find themselves.

To a significant extent, where an individual places the main emphasis – what balance he or she achieves between these different role requirements and normative points of reference – is a matter of choice. Even in the more dirigiste context of the 1990s, the academic may still be validly portrayed, as in the *laissez-faire* early 1970s, as a one-man or one-woman business (Halsey and Trow, 1971). The options that are taken up in any given case have discernible career implications: they widen or narrow occupational mobility and also affect the direction of professional development.

The opportunity cost of responding to different pressures will, of course, vary from one type of institution to another. Thus, for example, advancement in a polytechnic may be made most readily through an exercise of managerial or administrative or service skills; those who aspire to place their main emphasis on research will find their efforts more fully rewarded in major research universities than in smaller institutions with a stronger emphasis on teaching; and so on.

## REALISING PERSONAL WANTS

The decisions that an individual makes between these various possibilities have a discernible effect on his or her status, both within the system and in society at large. Professional values, broadly defined, impose demands of quality; current social values call for some demonstration of relevance. But the nature of the academic task, as has been argued in Chapter 6, requires a substantial measure of autonomy over content, style and outcome within the limits of available resources.

To understand the ways which personal discretion and choice may be exercised, the most useful starting point is, perhaps, a recognition that the main currency for the academic is not power (as it is for the politician) nor wealth (as it is for the businessman), but reputation. To be held in good esteem by one's colleagues, to earn the intellectual admiration of one's students, to become somebody of consequence in one's subject field – these will tend to be high among the initial hopes of anyone embarking on an academic career. Much, then, of the driving force behind what academics do is concerned with building up, or maintaining, a professional reputation.

Subjected as they are to external pressures – the need to demonstrate teaching quality, to recruit large numbers of students from overseas, to undertake contract work, and so on – academics may well develop other motivations, or may decide at some point in their careers to abandon their initial concern with research in favour of another, quite different one. But the climate of internal values within which they are nurtured, and which they are subsequently expected to sustain, strongly favours the pursuit of a good name in one's particular trade. This in its turn calls for both a creative contribution to a particular field of enquiry and identification with the interests of colleagues engaged in the same activity.

The ingredients of a good reputation vary from subject area to subject area and basic unit to basic unit. The hard pure disciplines of the sciences (see Chapter 6) call for a different set of skills from those in the soft pure domains of the social sciences and humanities; the hard applied technical professions and the soft applied social professions make their own distinctive demands in terms of individual excellence. But when allowance is made for the differences in the way an academic reputation can be earned, the unifying characteristic remains one of a strong identification with a discipline, coupled with a concern to preserve and enhance its public reputation as much as one's own private one.

The exception to this rule is when a group from a particular academic pursuit manages successfully to establish an independent and hitherto undeveloped field of enquiry – as, for example, in the hiving off of research in cognitive studies from linguistics and computer sciences in some universities in the 1980s. In such a case the process is not unlike the resignation of members of a club whose interests have too much diverged from those of the majority of their fellows, leading to the subsequent founding of a rival group. Nor is it altogether different from the secession of a disaffected colony or border territory, leading to the establishment of an independent state (Thompson, 1976).

The possibility of secession itself serves to underline the element of ideology behind the practice of a discipline. From one perspective it would appear that the inherent logic of enquiry, and the lines which it opens up for further exploration, have an independent existence which can somehow control the destinies of those who pursue it. There are cases where whole career patterns have altered, creating sizeable problems of de-skilling. Indeed, this is relatively commonplace in rapidly developing areas of enquiry, or those in which instrumentation periodically becomes outdated (Becher, 1989).

Looked at in another way, internal ideology can operate alongside external manipulation. Disciplines are notoriously subject to fashion. It is those practitioners who are most closely in tune with current trends who hold the main political leadership within the discipline. It would be disingenuous to think that such people do not strive to create new fashions in a direction which further enhances their own prestige.

The argument begins at this point to take the familiar shape of a dispute between the realists and the nominalists: those who wish to maintain that academic knowledge is somehow 'out there' for the finding (for example, see Hirst, 1974; Bhaskar, 1978) and those who suggest that it is no more than a social construct (of whom Bloor, 1976, is one of many examples). The dispute predates Plato and Aristotle and is unlikely to lend itself to brief settlement here. We simply remark that there are occasions when a major breakthrough in understanding transcends all attempts, even by the most strongly established interests, to confine it within the existing barricades of power (Kuhn, 1962).

As far as the issue of disciplinary identity is concerned, there is, however, a fairly clear correlation between intellectual proximity to the existing centres of interest and general academic reputation. The descent is steepest in the more sharply demarcated subjects. For example, a chemist employed in the pathology department of a medical school (and hence not even a 'proper chemist' any longer, however good the quality of his or her work) has to fight very hard to maintain membership of, and status within, the orthodox professional community. Within less tightly bounded disciplines, the slope of the decline is more gradual between reputation and marginality of status. Thus someone specialising in contemporary West African literature or researching into Welsh local history, though manifestly not among those most professionally or publicly visible, would scarcely be disbarred from disciplinary membership as a literature specialist or historian.

The most obvious exception to this general link between orthodoxy and status is provided by the highly inventive academic who works outside the prevailing conventions of his or her discipline. Such an individual must be prepared to take a major reputational gamble, on the possibility of creating a new centre of influence. On rare occasions – as in the case of Albert Einstein or Ludwig Wittgenstein – the gamble comes off. But if it does, there is a tendency to describe the situation as an example of polycentrism rather than marginality, so preserving the integrity of the original claim.

## THE TEACHING ROLE

The occupational quest for reputation, in the sense so far discussed, is not the only source of career advancement. There are significant numbers of academics whose research interests have, as their careers develop, become limited or non-existent, and who respond to other tunes. The incentives, rewards and group values which form the main relationships between individuals and basic units in the normative mode imply that tenured teachers are recruited largely on their records and potential for research: in practice, however, they are primarily employed to teach. But research is none the less the main activity by which, following traditional academic value, they are judged for promotion in the university sector, where additional funding accompanies a high departmental research rating. The paradox is less clear-cut in colleges and polytechnics. Indeed, whilst universities serve in some respects as role models for the rest of higher education, teaching has become a less private activity in polytechnics and colleges as a result of their stronger emphasis on team teaching and the susceptibility of their staff to external scrutiny by HM Inspectorate.

It is too much to say that teaching provides no pay-offs. Some academics find their teaching duties internally satisfying and rewarding and un-reservedly accept their professional obligations to students; and some institutions – including a number with high research reputations – put a premium on excellence in curriculum planning and in classroom com-munication. Nevertheless, considering the central part that it plays in the operational aspects of academic institutions, and the extent to which the funding of those institutions is justified in terms of the numbers of students they attract, the teaching function of the individual member of staff is in general undervalued (Hewton *et al.*, 1986). This appears obdurately to remain the case despite the pressures exercised by the central authorities and symbolised in such exercises as the Jarratt (1985) and Reynolds (1986) inquiries referred to in Chapter 4.

There seem to be two main reasons for the relatively low valuation of teaching. The first has already been indirectly considered. We have noted that subject loyalties within academia tend to be enduring, and that the academic's related concern with reputation is focused on the fulfilment of the expectation that one should contribute to and promote one's chosen discipline. The leading practitioners – those who set the standards which others seek to follow – usually reach their key positions because of the energies which they put into earning a reputation in these terms. Few of them have a similar degree of creative energy to spare for undergraduate teaching, and thus do not portray it as an activity of comparable signifi-cance. The influential members of the peer group, in other words, give no strong lead in the direction of regarding teaching as a serious intellectual task.  The second reason relates to the institutional conditions under which teaching activities normally take place. By long tradition (broken only by the occasional co-operative venture in course development or team teach-ing), the quality of the interaction between a member of staff and his or her students is regarded as an essentially personal matter. In universities in particular, teaching problems are not a generally accepted topic of dis-cussion among colleagues, and the practicalities of giving lectures or tutor-ials, or running seminars or laboratory classes, have not until recently been thought to need any explicit preparation. Like sex amongst the British, teaching has remained in the realm of the private, the unspoken and the amateur. So competence as a teacher is not easily assessed, especially in contrast with research (or consultancy, or scholarship) whose processes are often visible to colleagues and whose products are usually within the public domain.

There is, accordingly, no commonly established means by which individual excellence in devising a course, in putting across ideas or in helping students to explore ideas of their own can be identified – and hence no standard mechanism by which such competence can be rewarded. The continuing pressure exerted by the central authorities may eventually succeed in changing this state of affairs. In particular, the requirement for regular staff appraisal may bring teaching issues into the open; an emphasis on staff development could provide opportunities for individuals to acquire new techniques and fresh ideas; the introduction of system-wide as well as institution-wide procedures for the evaluation of teaching quality could give added significance to staff–student interactions; and the move towards consumerism adumbrated in earlier chapters may strengthen the concern of basic units, having to compete for student numbers, to acquire a good name for the quality of their courses in terms of both content and delivery.

However, such pressures, deriving ultimately from the wider social and economic context, have to compete with the inherent characteristics of higher education. Where the academic's fundamental loyalty remains – as it will in many cases – with the advancement of knowledge, and where there is no evident career reward in putting major effort into the improvement of teaching, the latter will not be treated as a matter of prime importance. This view has inevitable consequences for the students' perspective on their academic experience and on their relationships with the basic unit to which they belong.

## THE PERFORMANCE OF ACADEMIC ROLES

The individual academic's freedom of choice is (as we have argued in Chapter 6) a fundamental requirement stemming from the socio-technology of higher education. But the exercise of that choice is commonly constrained by the requirements of collective activity as well as the limitation of resources. In many cases, as Hardy *et al.* (1984) demonstrate, the adjustment between personal autonomy and organisational constraint is made by a process of 'pigeon-holing' – by creating a set of standard categories. These categories set broad expectations on the activities being pursued, and offer a reasonable alternative to administratively imposed systems of co-ordination. In terms of teaching, for example,

> The reason why individual professors are trusted to make their own decisions ... is that their skills and knowledge have been standardised through long years of training.... Thus a professor teaching physics to engineering students need not spend a great deal of time co-ordinating

his or her efforts with another teaching calculus to the same students: the former has been trained to know what to expect in a standard calculus course. The necessary co-ordination between the two can be effected almost automatically.

(Hardy *et al.*, 1984: 352–3)

Within any such broad category or pigeonhole, as long as the boundaries are not transgressed, the individual can find adequate room to exercise creativity or to develop personal interpretations in terms of teaching method, intellectual approach, course content and the like. It may be noted, incidentally, that the best teachers are referred to as gifted and stimulating rather than as dutiful or observant of external prescriptions.

A similar compromise can be found in many collaborative research exercises, where individuals may be given responsibility for one particular aspect, or a series of different aspects, of the work – again within a system of mutually understood categories, which help to ensure overall coherence while allowing personal discretion. Even in areas where research follows a strongly individualistic tradition (as, for example, in most historical enquiry), the study of the available research literature is regarded as essential, and the work done is expected to be set within that general frame of reference – so here, too, creative interpretation has to be exercised inside the boundaries of collective understanding.

Resource limitations impose a different set of boundaries. In some costly areas – such as, for example, particle physics or space research – no individual can reasonably expect to command access to the necessary experimental apparatus, except through participation in a national or international programme. At the other extreme, someone engaged in philosophical enquiry may need no facilities at all, except perhaps a reasonable personal library. In between, there are research topics, even of a relatively inexpensive kind, which are out of the reach of particular individuals because of an absence of sufficiently well-equipped laboratories or adequately stocked institutional libraries. Where a career move to another, better-favoured institution is not possible, the only alternative is to choose a different research topic for which the necessary facilities exist. But here again, subject to the constraints imposed, the discretion to carry out the research in one's own way still remains.

If autonomy is accorded within limits to academics in their teaching and research, that autonomy also extends to the scholarship which many feed into both. But what can be said of the other economically and socially derived obligations which individuals may be called upon to meet? A distinction was earlier made between management and administration and the performance of entrepreneurial or service obligations. In the case of the first pair, few academics are likely, in terms of their general training, to be content with a purely mechanical observance of instructions from above: they may not be particularly gifted managers or administrators (though quite a few prove to be so), but they would normally expect to exercise their own judgement and discretion to a significant degree. The same is also true of the service and entrepreneurial roles: in responding to requirements outside the institution, the academic would see himself or herself as deploying a special expertise, and hence as making a particular contribution to debate or development. Those external agencies who contract a piece of research may wish to specify more or less closely the ends to be achieved, but, if they consider themselves to be sufficiently knowledgeable about the means to reach those ends, it is questionable whether they should be seeking academic expertise in the first place. On the whole, academic researchers – particularly those in applied fields – do not regard themselves as unduly constrained by taking on commissioned research, in spite of the fact that they may be held more directly accountable than in the case of grant-supported work for reaching a predetermined outcome. Their common complaint is, rather, about the amount of their time which has to be spent in pursuing external sources of funds, to the detriment of their other activities.

## THE ACADEMIC AND THE OUTSIDE WORLD

We have already noted that academics are amenable to outside influences impinging on their beliefs and values in the normative mode and conditioning their activities and practices in the operational mode. The external normative dimension includes professional norms as well as social, economic and cultural forces. As far as the former are concerned, little remains to add to what has already been said. The wider academic or professional community is seen as a legitimate source of guidance and an appropriate mechanism for the appraisal of quality. It helps to inform the individual about the corpus of current ideas and to connect him or her with those pursuing cognate interests. It provides a context for career development as well as for influencing the views of colleagues. It may discriminate somewhat unfairly between those who have acquired positions of prestige and those who have not; but its collective judgements are not easily gainsaid.

The normative pressures from outside the academic and professional fraternity are less predictable and seemingly more inexorable. The social, economic and cultural requirements to which individual academics are exposed may at times appear ill-informed and unjustified. However, it could also be remarked that academics have in the past tended to pay little attention to promoting good public relations, regarding their other commitments as calling for a higher priority. In consequence, it could be inferred that the higher education system as a whole, its constituent institutions and basic units, and not least its individual members, were not sufficiently concerned with accountability to the taxpaying public for the significant sums spent on keeping the enterprise going. In such a situation, the opportunities for political intervention were evident, and were duly seized, in the decade culminating in the 1988 Education Reform Act. The net result has been both to focus and to amplify the demands made on those working in universities, polytechnics and colleges in the name of enhanced social and economic responsibility.

The operational counterpart of this change in normative expectations has taken the form of a significant increase in the impact of market forces. These forces operate in two main directions. The first relates to funding for research and development and the second to student recruitment.

The problem of funding affects some – but not all – disciplinary areas; namely, those in which academic work at the individual or basic unit level is to some degree dependent on the support of public bodies, commercial agencies or private benefactors. Such funding organisations may have their own budgets suddenly reduced by a sharp decline in economic growth; or they may decide, for one reason or another, to develop new policy initiatives outside the area in question. The net result in either case is likely to be a reduction in the level of active large-scale research or development.

The second manifestation of market forces – namely, the ability of basic units to recruit students – is indiscriminate in its effects, and is liable to affect any and every subject field. Here the vagaries of the economy may be reinforced by the inevitability of demographic patterns to produce a situation demanding significant structural change. Paradoxically, the individuals in a discipline which is much in demand may find themselves with heavy teaching commitments and relatively little time for advancing their own professional careers, though the necessary supporting resources may be adequate enough; those in a subject whose lack of student numbers allows them ample time to pursue their own academic interest may be hindered from doing so through lack of funds and facilities. Good institutional management may seek to equalise the balance over time, but such adjustment may be relatively slow to take effect.

These external pressures are themselves part of the setting within which the central authorities make decisions. The responses which they make may be both material and symbolic, leading not only to changes in allocations of resources but also to status rewards and appointments which favour leading individuals and so signal strong support for a particular field of activity. Governmental patronage may thus provide a direct and immediate link between the contemporary social climate and a limited number of leading academics.

It is relevant here to recall the argument in Chapter 4 that the academic peer system is co-opted by the central authorities into both the normative and operational modes, and that this serves to protect basic units and individuals against purely administrative decisions. The effectiveness of this co-optation process has in recent years been considerably weakened, as a matter of deliberate central policy, so that academics are put under pressure to respond to institutional management as well as to peer-group requirements. Be that as it may, an appropriate accommodation has to be reached between the academic ambitions of individuals on the one hand and the demands for qualified manpower and for efficient management by central authorities on the other. We return to the point that every academic is expected to exercise his or her own sense of integrity even when working in collaboration with other colleagues: the limitations are not so much those of command from higher authority as of negotiation between the individual's saleable expertise and the supporting facilities and resources afforded by the market and the state.

Changes in the external environment can thus be seen to impinge in a variety of ways on individual academics. They may give rise to normative shifts at the central authority level, which are then operationalised by adjusting the pattern of resource allocations to institutions and (less directly) basic units and individuals. These operational changes may in due course lead individuals to modify their own norms, and collectively to adjust the norms of the basic unit. But new economic and social pressures can also impinge directly on academics as members of the wider society, and cause them to change their own sense of priorities. The values of academics, viewed in this wider context, are clearly not as self-contained as some of the protagonists – or some of the detractors – of the doctrine of academic freedom have been inclined to suggest.

Taken as a whole, such values are only partially represented in the financial and status rewards available at the individual level. In universities in particular, the paths to academic virtue vary in their length, steepness and navigability. The most admired and influential publications lead not only to promotion or employment in the more esteemed institutions, or both; they also produce rewards for the home institution, which may pass some of it on to the basic unit and to the individual through yet further salary enhancement. Individuals who secure research grants also contribute towards basic unit research gradings and bring in overheads from the relevant funding councils: they too may be rewarded in the promotion stakes or through benefiting from part of the overheads they have generated.

Consultancies and contract research are less highly valued in the peer review system, but may carry financial rewards, either direct or through the basic unit, from fees or overheads. Undergraduate teaching carries none of these forms of financial bonus, though work on externally funded short courses and the like may do so. However, the bidding procedures put pressure on basic units and individuals to consider the time costs of additions to their teaching load. A system intent on differential recognition for good performance cannot avoid rewarding those individuals who in consequence will bear greatly increased teaching and administrative burdens. The conscientious or gifted teacher has traditionally enjoyed only the relatively less prestigious prospect of appointment to a senior lectureship. The reward system has differed in the polytechnics and colleges in that they have had less easy access to the research councils and private foundations, if not to commercial sponsors. But here, as elsewhere, there is increased convergence between the two sectors.

## OTHER CATEGORIES OF STAFF

There is a subgroup of academic staff who escape any conflict of priorities between teaching and research, by virtue of the fact that they are employed as full-time researchers. The differences between staff in this category and their colleagues who have been appointed as teachers are numerous, and serve to underline some of the major adjustments which would need to be made to the model in Chapter 2 if it were to relate specifically to the research component in higher education.

In the first place – aside from a very few prestigious individuals, usually designated as Professorial Research Fellows or Research Professors – the large majority of research-based appointments are temporary, because most funded research is conducted on the basis of short-term projects relying on 'soft money'. Accordingly, those in research posts do not enjoy the same privileges of assured employment as teaching staff, and are usually on limited contracts. Individuals may continue to work on this basis as part of a kind of itinerant labour force, for substantial periods – though in the end most appear to succumb to the growing pressures on them to take up some permanent post (whether inside academia, in some independent research body, in industry or in the public services). As temporary inhabitants of any particular academic scene, they enjoy few of the privileges of staff membership. In particular, they seldom achieve any foothold within the political structure of their institution – nor are they likely to be entrusted with, or burdened by, administrative responsibilities outside their own research units.

Second, while tenured academics have – at least in theory – a free range of choice over their research topics, professional researchers are explicitly contracted to work on a defined project under the authority of a named research director. They may choose whether or not to apply for a given job, but once appointed they forfeit most of the discretion that their teaching-based counterparts take for granted. Pursuing this distinction further, a member of teaching staff works largely within a collegial relationship in his or her basic unit, even if one which is ultimately dependent on the head of the unit for resources, operational tasks and recommendations for pro-motion. In contrast, the relationship of a director of research with a member of the team on contract is virtually that of a manager to a subordinate, no matter what the style of work may be. In the central structure of the academic institution, accountability is blurred. In a research unit it is quite clear: the director is professionally accountable to the funding agency (usually outside the institution, and often outside the central authorities responsible for higher education); the contracted staff are in their turn accountable for all their work to the director.

The common observation that, in most institutions of higher education, research enjoys greater prestige than teaching seems then to be falsified by a closer examination of funded projects and their comparatively weak integration within the institutional structure (Platt, 1976). The explanation which suggests itself for this contradictory state of affairs has been hinted at earlier. It depends on the distinction drawn in our model in Chapter 2 between the normative and the operational modes. It is clear that, norm-atively, both the individual academic and the basic unit are prone to regard research as a primary activity and teaching only as a secondary one; even at the level of the institution and the central authorities, its significance is far from negligible. But operationally, research is subsidiary to the teaching programme. Money, manpower and materials are determined in large part by student numbers. Individual attitudes are shaped accordingly: tenured teaching staff are aware that, operationally, they owe their post first and foremost to teaching; untenured research staff must often feel themselves, in operational terms, to be defined by their conditions of service as second-class citizens.

The numbers of non-tenured, full-time researchers have increased as institutions have sought to limit their long-term budgetary commitments in a context of financial uncertainty, and to avoid the inflexibility to which permanent appointments give rise. Another institutional strategy has been to employ teaching staff, full-time or part-time, on short-term contracts. Typically, such contracts allow little or no scope for other activities. Those who enter into temporary teaching arrangements may do so, as many contract researchers do, in the hope of subsequently obtaining a permanent post. The chances that their hopes may be realised depend in large part on the state of the academic labour market: recent years have offered few opportunities for members of either group to escape from the treadmill. Their situation is exacerbated by the difficulty many of them have in building up a substantial publication list: the temporary researchers, because their names are commonly listed as junior authors, with the research director enjoying the main credit; the temporary teachers, because their substantial time commitment to the teaching function may allow little leeway for research. There is thus a signficant underclass of academics, often on unfavourable salary scales and with unsatisfactory conditions of service, whose existence helps substantially to underpin the day-to-day functioning of the system, but whose work enjoys little recognition from the more favoured, fully fledged members of the academic world.

Both these groups will usually share the values of their colleagues on permanent appointments, even if they participate only to a limited extent in the operational mode (in that the temporary teachers may do little research; the contract researchers may do little teaching; neither may be much involved in academic administration or service activities). But there are two further categories of employee whose norms and operations do not at all closely relate to those discussed earlier in this chapter; namely, the administrators and ancillary staff.

Administrators have their own, quite independent, career structures. As a group they respond to almost the direct inverse of the essential academic values. Where academics value their basic units above the institution, it is the latter with whose interests the administrators identify. They are called upon to promote a reliable, responsive institution, enjoying favourable relationships and a sound reputation with the central authorities in general and the funding bodies in particular. In the external context, academics pay more attention to the wider peer group or the related professional network than to the needs of society at large; for administrators, the opposite is true. The institution's public image, and that of its component units, has to be fostered both with the local community and in the national arena – a requirement which the administration is expected to meet with such partial and partisan help as it can muster from those who populate the basic units. In operational terms, too, the administrators are responsible for reducing the diverse interests and activities of academic staff into coherent lines of policy and practice (see the discussion in Chapter 5). One might say that, where the latter have a perpetual tendency, both normatively and operationally, to diverge and fragment, the former typically seek convergence and cohesion.

There is also in every institution a sizeable body of other employees – the common term 'ancillary staff' is indicative of how they are viewed –

who perform a variety of essential operational functions. They include technicians, secretaries, clerks, porters, telephonists, catering staff, maintenance and ground staff and the like. Many of them have long periods of service; many identify strongly with their employing institution, in spite of scales of pay which compare unfavourably with their opposite numbers in private sector establishments. Their work is largely taken for granted, its importance for the institution only being generally recognised on the rare occasions when they go on strike. The members of this group are not normally given an opportunity to contribute actively to the policy of the institution or its basic units, except in relation to staff welfare and conditions of service. If they too are marginal elements at the individual level, it is a different form of marginality from that of administrators and different again from those of temporary researchers and teachers.

## STUDENTS' ROLES AND THE NORMATIVE MODE

At this point we turn to another important but often neglected group of individuals within the higher education system. It is not easy to generalise about the characteristics of students in UK universities, polytechnics and colleges, particularly as, at the undergraduate level, the pattern is no longer a relatively uniform one of 18-year-old English school leavers, the majority coming from middle-class home backgrounds. But even though students are of differing ages, nationalities and (to a lesser extent) social backgrounds, there are nevertheless certain constant features of their behaviour and a shared predictability about their attitudes which it may be useful to examine in the context of our model.

There is, to begin with, an ambivalence about how they perceive themselves, and how they are perceived by their teachers, in relation to the higher education system. In one obvious sense, they comprise its clients: a role which is perhaps at its most evident when they are potential students, exercising some measure of choice about the university, polytechnic or college in which to seek acceptance. The national policy of raising fee levels has underlined the power of students as consumers and has increased the need for institutions to compete for their allegiance, a process reinforced by the funding councils' bidding procedures. Other roles, operative at various times and in various settings, emphasise the aspect of membership of the academic body. At times, students may adopt the stance of partners in the enterprise, seeking to exercise a relatively direct say in the policy and practice of their basic units and institutions. This notion came strongly to the fore in the late 1960s and early 1970s but has since remained less prominent. Another characteristic view is of students as acolytes, junior members of the academic body in a relation of dependency with their mentors, on whose professional altruism they must rely.

But, however strongly students of all ages and stages may be inclined to take academics as their role models, the value sets of the former remain significantly different from those of the latter (Startup, 1979). In particular, although they do not necessarily choose courses for their vocational relevance – a consideration which does not loom large in soft pure knowledge areas, or even in a number of courses in hard pure domains – students are none the less closely conscious of subsequent job opportunities. A survey by Boys *et al.* (1988) suggested that the concern to obtain a good degree was stronger – because of its labour-market implications – than a concern with knowledge for its own sake. Students were also found to give a higher priority than academic staff to work-related elements in the degree programme. These divergencies serve to underline the multivalue nature of higher education, at the individual as much as at other levels. But it should be added that the same survey made it plain that staff take student opinion about courses seriously; that students correspondingly consider that their needs are taken into account; and that for the most part students also consider their courses to be well taught, and express a general satisfaction with the quality and standard of their degree programmes.

In considering the process, as against the context, of learning, various psychologists have suggested that learning styles can be located along a number of closely related continua. Thus Bruner *et al.* (1956) refer to a 'focussing/scanning' antithesis; Getzels and Jackson (1962) to 'convergence' and 'divergence'; Marton and Saljö (1976) to 'something that happens to you' versus 'something you do'; and Pask (1976) to 'serialist' and 'holist' strategies. One might, at some risk of oversimplification, relate these categories to common-sense notions of active and passive learning. A passive approach suggests treating pieces of knowledge as separate entities to be acquired in a serial fashion; an active approach implies synthesis, the bringing together of apparently distinct pieces of information so as to develop some sort of structure or pattern.

Kolb (1984) maintains that there is a clear connection between the value contrasts implicit in this spectrum of learning styles and the characteristic cultures of different knowledge domains. Bereiter and Freedman (1962) had earlier speculated 'whether this is because individuals are shaped by the fields they enter or because of selection/evaluation processes that put people into and out of disciplines'. Kolb's work suggests that both considerations interact: a view that would be consistent with our own arguments.

A further common feature of the student estate is the basic currency in terms of which most academic activities are evaluated and most future plans assessed. Much as academic staff are guided by the wish to maintain and enhance their scholarly reputations, so students understandably seek to optimise their credit in their final degree assessment. The personal as well as the occupational sanctions of failure are usually perceived as severe, and this reinforces the students' sense of anxiety to 'make the grade'. Much of this anxiety focuses on the assessment system, and especially on attempts to unravel its complexities, understand its processes and identify the relative weightings of the different components (see Becker *at al.*, 1968; Marris, 1964; Snyder, 1971).

One interesting study of the phenomenon of assessment suggests that students fall into three groups (Miller and Parlett, 1974). The first, labelled 'cue seekers', quite deliberately set themselves to find out as much as possible (by picking up hints in lectures, asking staff leading questions, scanning previous examination papers, and so on) about their assessment tasks. The second, designated as 'cue conscious', do not themselves take active steps to glean such information but are sensitive to any hints that may be dropped. The third, referred to as 'cue deaf', consider everything that they are taught to be of uniform importance, and set themselves to be assessed on all of it. In the study in question, there was a close correlation between the cue seekers and those awarded first-class degrees, the cue conscious and those who got seconds, and the cue deaf and those who got thirds or worse.

The students' concern with 'earning marks' is often deplored by staff whose common tendency is to discourage them from playing the numbers game. The divergence of value on this point can, if it becomes pronounced, give rise to problems. One frequent cause of contention is the confidentiality of marks and of examination board discussions. The main fear by staff is that too much knowledge of what happens could lead to unjustified but damaging litigation by disappointed candidates. The common concern of students is that apparently arbitrary and unfair decisions might remain unchallenged. A means of ameliorating this problem by formalising accountability arrangements for the examination process was part of the code of practice proposed for the university sector in the Reynolds Report (1986).

Another identifiable characteristic of most students' careers seems to be a sequential change of attitudes, abilities and anxieties over time. Perhaps understandably, in the early stages of their courses in higher education, students are beset by a good deal of uncertainty over norms and expectations. They find it difficult to establish, for example, what is considered in their particular field to be a reasonable amount of work for a week; how long their essays should be; how many set exercises they should tackle; what standard of performance is viewed by staff as reasonable for a first-year student; and so on. They are also liable to sense a certain amount of confusion about the nature and identity of their subject field. A characteristic pattern in the middle stages of the course is that, with these questions resolved, students experience a falling-off of enthusiasm and develop a perception of their work as being somewhat routine-bound. Their heavy initial dependence on staff can, in some cases, be overcompensated by a deliberate distancing as they attempt to establish their own independence and identity. But it is usually not until the final stages of the undergraduate course – and sometimes not until after it has ended – that students acquire some sense of mastery of their subject field, a confidence in their own abilities to understand its underlying methods and principles, and a full sense of autonomy as people who can guide their own learning (Perry, 1970).

## STUDENTS' RELATIONSHIPS AND THE OPERATIONAL MODE

Some general features can be noted of students' relationships with one another. The milieu in which they work tends to be one of competition rather than co-operation (certain basic units strive to counteract this in the structure of their undergraduate programmes, but even in their case, the classified degree system imposes strong competitive strains). As a result, the operational pattern of students' work is in general individualistic: corporate activities are rare, and in many instances (helping friends with, or asking friends' help on, assignments) are discouraged. In this competitive atmosphere, students commonly admit to a reluctance to seem foolish in front of their peers: and this leads to their hesitating to ask staff for clarification of points they have failed to understand. The consequence can be a situation in which large numbers of students are floundering, whilst each of them thinks all the others have managed to keep their heads above water, and their teacher assumes that none at all is out of his or her depth (Bliss and Ogborn, 1977; Zinberg, 1976).

Particular problems can arise in courses with a significant proportion of atypical students – for example, those from overseas or entering at mature age, often with unorthodox qualifications. Overseas undergraduates, depending on their country of origin, may suffer from linguistic handicaps and from the difficulties of adjustment to an unfamiliar culture and an alien educational tradition. Their presence in a group is sometimes resented as slowing down the pace of learning and as calling for a disproportionate share of tutorial attention. Mature students present a different set of difficulties. They tend to be more anxious than recent school leavers about their academic performance and potentiality, and are liable to take up substantial amounts of staff time in seeking reassurance that they are doing what is required of them. As against this, they are usually more confident in social terms than most students straight from school, and their relatively easy relationships with academics can also cause resentment. So can their attitudes to younger members of the course, which are often perceived as patronising (Challis, 1976). The internal tensions which result within heterogeneous student groups of this kind are seldom serious enough to come into the open, but it does not follow that they have a negligible effect on the quality of learning.

Within the system as a whole, relations between students and staff vary considerably. However, the structure of academic institutions promotes the tendency towards an 'us and them' division: a discernible psychological barrier between teachers and taught (Parlett *et al.*, 1976). This is at least to some extent inherent in the basic educational contract between someone who has knowledge and someone who does not. Assessment is another obvious factor in promoting social distance. Other incidental ones may include difference in age, income, occupational status and leisure interests. However, given that some sort of barrier is probably unavoidable, its height and solidity can be adjusted by changes in the ethos of basic units and the attitudes of individuals within them.

There is good evidence to suggest that the context in which students learn – the pattern of their relationships within the basic unit whose programmes they are following – can have a direct effect on their efficiency as learners. In those situations in which the atmosphere is formal and impersonal, students comment (not perhaps surprisingly) that they feel alienated and inhibited. In those which encourage a direct and personal contact between teachers and taught, they feel more easily able to ask for help over their difficulties. What has been called 'the hidden curriculum' can have an impact on a student's learning experience which is none the less powerful for remaining inexplicit and unexamined (Snyder, 1971, Parlett, 1977). There is also a somewhat less direct link between staff–student relationships and the quality of teaching. In any given course, the teacher will have certain conscious or unconscious expectations about connections which will be made, analogies which will be understood, crucial points which will be noted by those he or she teaches. In nearly all cases where a member of staff decides at the end of the course to put such assumptions directly to the test by questioning students about how the message came across, or how the intentions worked out in practice, he or she will admit to having made a number of surprising discoveries. The finding that some particular aspect of the teaching has not worked as it was intended to will usually lead to some attempt to put it right – and so, with any luck, to a positive improvement when the course is next given. But where the divide between staff and students is too wide to allow for the kind of honest reporting which such exercises demand, the teachers in question are denied at least one important means of checking that their courses are being interpreted in the way they expect. The likelihood is that, over time, they will build up a good many erroneous assumptions about what can be taken as learned, and that their students will become progressively more alienated and confused.

In many institutions students' unions are closely involved in the relationship of students to staff, and students to other students. They offer a social base, as well as counselling and recreational facilities, sometimes in competition with basic units or with the institution as a whole. Within the union itself, the characteristics of student individualism to which we have already referred are maintained – so that, for example, elections for office can be fiercely fought no matter how much solidarity may be created on particular issues.

Those who take an active part in student-union affairs become members of a reward system not dependent on staff evaluations. Student leaders have access to property, funds and power; regardless of academic performance, they may become leading campus personalities with whom negotiations must be conducted. The unions thus have their own patterns of deference, dependency and resource allocation in those contexts in which they have achieved full political viability.

## POSTGRADUATES AT THE PERIPHERY

Postgraduates are another group who, although they apparently enjoy at least the limited participatory rights of students, are marginal to the enterprise in much the way that we have observed full-time contract researchers to be. There is a distinction to be made here between students on taught master's degree courses, who are often treated as if they were more mature undergraduates, and those on doctoral programmes.

With few exceptions, the institutional provision for doctoral students is more limited than that for undergraduates. On the arts and social science side, such students may complain of a sense of isolation, since their academic contact with the institution is largely confined to a single supervisor (who, because often a busy senior academic, may prove difficult to see regularly). On the science and technology side, far from being isolated, doctoral students often have to work in an overcrowded laboratory, and may only be entrusted with intellectually somewhat limited tasks whose completion none the less promises them the doctoral reward they seek. Both categories of student may perhaps, near the end of their programmes, be offered modest teaching assignments (for example, as tutors to first-year undergraduates or as laboratory demonstrators) but are rarely given initial help on how to teach.

This state of affairs is a relic from the time when the proportion of postgraduates in the total student population was small, and any special arrangements would arguably have been uneconomic. However, in many universities (less so in public sector institutions) this proportion has risen steadily to 25 per cent or more; so it is on the face of it puzzling that the postgraduate's marginal status remains virtually unchanged. By way of explanation, it can be postulated that the institution sees its doctoral postgraduates – and indeed that many of them see themselves – as initiates to academia. So it is understandable that a rite of passage should be devised – in the doctoral dissertation – which is deliberately given the features of an ordeal. To make things too easy would be to fail to put disciplinary devotion to a proper test.

Recent studies of postgraduate education (Kogan and Henkel, forthcoming; Becher, forthcoming) confirm that the standards of recruitment and the level of quality required for a doctoral dissertation remain very demanding. At the same time, the disincentives (including income forgone, adverse study conditions, poor prospects of obtaining an academic post, and limited enhancement of employment opportunities in the general labour market) ensure that only those strongly committed to the study of their chosen subject are willing to apply for doctoral degrees. Many more masters' students, in contrast, will have vocational ends in view, and will regard their qualification as a means of career advancement.

The situation of UK doctoral candidates may be contrasted with that of their US counterparts, who are strongly supported by their membership of often sizeable and prestigious graduate schools. The greater measure of recognition they are accorded stems in part from the much larger average size of American institutions geared to awarding higher degrees. This makes it possible to organise provision in specialised graduate schools for large groups of research students, in contrast with the very small numbers typical of most UK universities and polytechnics.

It may be noted that Ph.D. students provide perhaps the most unequivocal example of internalist norms and operations. In the normative mode, they identify strongly with their own academic peer group, but seem hardly at all affected by wider social, economic or cultural considerations. Operationally, except in the few cases in which they are engaged on an industrial or other externally funded contract, they work largely within the confines of their own basic unit. Despite this relatively sheltered environment, their situation would seem to be the least enviable of all the categories of individual reviewed in the present chapter.

# 8   Initiating and adapting to change

## THE PLACE OF CHANGE IN THE MODEL

This chapter and its successor mark a shift of emphasis from the four which have preceded it. Chapters 4 to 7 have been concerned with exploring the characteristic norms and operations of each level of the system in turn. Chapters 8 and 9, in contrast, aim respectively to characterise the relationships between one mode and another and one level and another. The difference in purpose necessarily brings with it a shift of both content and style. The argument becomes illustrative rather than analytic; the complex of interconnections between components in the model is less firmly delineated than the components themselves have been; more emphasis is given to particular instances of general processes.

Ways of explaining change are numerous and diverse. A review of some of them will follow a brief initial consideration of the innovation process as represented in our model. As far as the latter is concerned, it was suggested in Chapter 2 that the links between the internal normative and the internal operational modes should be taken to represent a state of dynamic equilibrium. When norms and operations become, for whatever reason, significantly out of phase, this will usually give rise to changes in belief or practice designed to restore normal functioning. Once the necessary degree of congruence has been re-established, the system reverts to equilibrium once more.

The appropriateness of the notion of equilibrium remains to be established, and that will be one of the aims of the subsequent discussion. For the present, it should be noted that the metaphor embodies the assumption that academic life requires a reasonable continuity of values, an organic accretion of knowledge, and patterns of power and authority which allow both. This explains the striving of academics towards equilibrium following periods of normative or operational change. There is, however, no implication here that the origins of change are necessarily internal and parochial. On the contrary, as the model itself implies, innovative pressures may derive from a diversity of sources. They may be normative or operational, external or internal. They may stem from the peer group at large, or the wider social environment, or they may originate from within the system itself.

## EXPLORING THE NATURE OF CHANGE

There are two main problems inherent in any discussion of change as a phenomenon. The first arises from its protean character: to speak of change is not to denote a simple, neatly defined concept, but rather one which appears in a whole variety of contexts and guises. Modifications in the terrestrial landscape have little in common with shifts in clothing fashions or alterations in the political balance, except that they mark some difference from the status quo ante. The second difficulty derives from the general unpredictability, especially in many social situations, of the direction which future changes may take. There are seldom any clear prescriptions for bringing about a desired state of affairs, and it is generally unwise to proceed as if they exist.

It is therefore scarcely surprising that there is no single, generally accepted theory to explain the change process, nor any well-validated prescription for bringing about change. Instead, several competing accounts have been put forward of what change comprises and how it can best be implemented. No one of these is comprehensive in its coverage, though some have pretensions to be.

One might usefully begin by noting some main dimensions along which the analysis of the notion of change in higher education can be carried out. There are, first, differences of context. Some accounts are internalist, dealing with innovations within a closely bounded area (for example, Bailey, 1977) and others externalist, dealing with forces operating from outside any such boundary (for example, Davies, 1987). Others, closely related, explore the contrast between 'top down' and 'bottom up' innovation (Elmore, 1979, 1985; Sabatier 1987). Others, again, focus on the dichotomy between planned and unintended or inexorable change (Braybrooke and Lindblom, 1963). And there are wide-ranging theories, dealing with the phenomenon at large, or at any rate across a broad spectrum of human activity, as against those which relate specifically to the academic scene. The distinction between macro-sociology and macro-politics and micro-sociology and micro-politics is relevant here.

Differences in scale and time-span are to some extent subsumed in the contextual category. But one may wish to differentiate between large-scale or radical and minor or limited changes within a given context, as well as to mark off those which are the result of incremental drift from those which fall within a tightly scheduled plan. Finally, in focusing on the mechanisms which can be used for implementing or bringing about change, a distinction can be made between coercion, manipulation, and persuasion or conversion.

We shall return to a number of these distinctions in the subsequent discussion. At this point, however, three main types of theoretical framework may be identified, relating to research on innovation *per se*, to organisation theory and to policy studies respectively.

Approaches which examine innovation as a phenomenon in its own right have little direct relevance to our present concerns. They tend on the whole to be prescriptive rather than explanatory, offering guidelines to the would-be innovator (often designated as a 'change agent') and portraying the process of bringing about change as predominantly rational, sequential and instrumental. Thus, although writers such as Havelock (1969), Bennis *et al.* (1969) and Zaltman *et al.* (1977) distinguish, in their different ways, between coercive, rational and persuasive strategies, their perspective is predominantly one in which change is instigated and carried out according to a deliberately pre-ordained plan by an identified agent on a designated recipient group. Procedures of this kind assume a system which is tightly coupled, in which new policies and practices can be straightforwardly decreed from the top and implemented in a linear managerial sequence. Insofar as higher education, as argued in Chapter 1, is loosely coupled, this assumption is inappropriate. However, the early work in this genre by Lewin (1952), later applied by Ostergren and Berg (1977) to innovations in higher education, has a much closer intellectual kinship with our own approach.

The study of types of organisation, and their nature and characteristics, offers some potentially useful material. In particular, the discussion of exchange relationships within and across institutional boundaries, and how they affect organisational dynamics, associated particularly with Blau's work (Blau, 1964, 1974), and elaborated by Archer (1979) in relation to educational systems, helps to illuminate some key aspects of the process of bargaining and compromise, to which we shall subsequently draw attention. Again, within this framework of organisation theory, Clark's (1983) work throws light on the way in which structures affect the adaptive capacities of systems, institutions and basic units, and suggests how the existing cultural climate exercises its own imperatives.

Policy studies derive from a different heritage, and exemplify a distinctive approach. Their origins lie in the more general field of political theory, which tends to give them a particular emphasis on the way in which policy is formulated: how that policy, once defined, is put into practice has tended until relatively recently to be regarded as unproblematic. Thus, the early and influential developments by Easton of his 'political system' model gave close attention to how 'policy inputs' were converted into 'policy outputs', but ignored any discrepancies there might be between what was eventually promulgated as policy and what, if anything, happened as a result to change the status quo (Easton, 1965). Lindblom had earlier contested the rationalism implicit in such approaches (Braybrooke and Lindblom, 1963), but it was not until some years later that Pressman and Wildavsky (1973) focused attention on the question of policy implementation. The subsequent emphasis on this issue on the part of policy analysts has produced a number of ideas relevant to our concern to explore the relationship between norms (which might be said to embody policy intentions) and operations (which can be seen as offering the main source of evidence about the outcomes of those intentions).

Another strand of argument in the political sciences has explored the notion of a pluralism of interests: this has been developed by Premfors (1984) in the context of higher education into a detailed account of the relationships and tensions between the academic oligarchy, the state, the market and society at large. The conflicts engendered by pluralism can also be related to notions of the division of academic labour. Clark (1983) writes of the constant upheaval and reordering brought about by the contradictory purposes of the academic understructure and the organisational superstructure; Metzger (1987) shows how constant differentiation is the outcome of the inexorable march of academic specialisation. Such accounts, too, have direct relevance to the discussion of change as set out in our model.

## THE CONTEXT OF CHANGE

In approaching the phenomenon of innovation in higher education, as it relates to our earlier account, a preliminary distinction needs to be made between those minor, incremental modifications at any given level in the system which have little or no impact on the prevailing value configuration or the overall operating pattern – which may be referred to as organic changes – and those more significant revisions – which could be termed radical changes – demanding a noticeable shift in existing normative assumptions or established practice or both. An example of the former would be the removal of Latin as a matriculation requirement in British universities – an evolution of thinking about what skills undergraduates need to master before beginning their courses – and of the latter, a rapid switch from deficiency grants to contract funding, or a sudden determination to make academics justify their work by a formal process of accounting for their activities.

Organic changes, it is generally agreed, are frequent and numerous, causing the fabric of academic life to be subject to continuous, but not easily visible, internal adjustment. Clark (1983) ascribes this bias towards small-scale changes to the 'bottom-heavy' nature of the higher education system, which promotes 'grass-roots innovation'. He goes on to remark that 'Incremental adjustment is the pervasive and characteristic form of change. Since tasks and powers are so extensively divided, global change is very difficult to effect.' It should be noted that this pattern of constant adjustment is not incompatible with the notion of equilibrium embodied in our model; it merely serves to emphasise that the equilibrium is dynamic rather than static.

Many incremental changes of this kind are a direct consequence of the role of higher education in the advancement and transmission of knowledge. Every new discovery, every fresh insight, is liable in some way or other to affect the current apprehension of the field to which it relates; and that modified apprehension in turn may occasion alterations to the content and structure of the curriculum through which an understanding of the field is purveyed.

During a period of organic development, higher education continues its work of redefining and modifying the curriculum as changes in knowledge or teaching techniques are assimilated, and adding to the stock of knowledge through research and scholarship. Changes in higher education's second-order characteristics of management and the like will also occur, partly as a consequence of academic developments and partly as managers get wiser about new techniques of management and accounting technology. Control is likely to be professional and academic; academics have an implicit mandate to continue to make progress according to the rhythms of their own disciplinary and peer-group development and to assimilate external pressures on largely their own terms. During such times, the system can produce well, because there is relative security and lack of conflict; energies can be devoted to issues of research, scholarship and teaching rather than to those concerning the distribution of power and resources.

There are also – though more rarely – quite dramatic reconfigurations in the current map of knowledge arising from what Kuhn (1962) labelled as major paradigm shifts. What is perhaps the majority of far-reaching changes come, however, from sources outside the pursuit of knowledge as such: many of them are occasioned by pressures from the outer framework rather than the inner core of our model (see Figure 2.1, p. 11 and the subsequent discussion in Chapter 3). It is such large-scale innovations – those which have the effect of calling into question, and demanding changes in, the prevailing values and activities in the academic world – which are most liable to arouse controversy and to give rise to defensive reactions. But in due time, the changes enforced from outside are either absorbed or rejected by the academics concerned, who then move again to a period of relative stability, a normative steady state, but with a changed framework and mandate.

As the discussion in Chapter 5 implied, the institutional head can sometimes play a crucial role in transforming what from one perspective appears as a radical change into an organic process. One significant leadership skill, indeed, lies in the ability not only to understand the values of the relevant constituency, and to identify the values inherent in a proposed innovation, but also to mediate successfully between the two. The exercise is not unlike an educational activity, in which the starting point is where the learners currently are, but where the end point leads them well beyond this. It has none the less to be acknowledged that a number of vice-chancellors and polytechnic directors adopt a more strongly authoritative, if not authoritarian, stance.

The processes of both organic and radical change (elaborated for school education by Wirt, 1981) can be observed as involving disequilibrium between the normative and operational modes and their subsequent realignment within a new equilibrium, as described in Chapter 2. The pattern may indeed be seen, as Wirt argues, as a cyclical one, in which periods of external intervention alternate with phases of internal consolidation. Which is the dominant mode can only be determined in relation to a specific time and place.

In relation to this general discussion, the empirical study by Cerych and Sabatier (1986) of a variety of innovations in higher education in European countries suggests that it is not the most wide-ranging and fundamental reforms that are the most effective. Writing in a different context, Elmore (1979) and Weatherley (1979) argue that 'bottom-up' change is more readily implemented than 'top-down' reform. Clark (1983) in his turn writes that 'many centrally announced reforms have no lasting deposit because internal constituencies are not effectively summoned to support them. When a system is bottom-heavy, groups at the grass-roots are key participants in implementing policies and reforms.'

## RESISTANCE TO CHANGE

What is commonly seen as academic conservatism – the hostile reaction of academics, individually and collectively, to top-down pressures for root and branch reform – can also be viewed in a different light. The individuals concerned may well have invested many years and much intellectual capital in the acquisition of a particular body of ideas, and the development of an associated strategy of research, scholarship and teaching. Anything which can be seen as threatening to devalue this professional investment will naturally be resisted; its eventual acceptance will depend on overcoming the initial resistance by one strategy or another.

There is much here which is common to cultural innovation in general. As Bailey (1973) observes in relation to his anthropological study of an Alpine village, 'innovation ... is necessarily a social process ... to a degree varying according to the extent and nature of its ramifying connections, [it] is likely to become the subject of political activities', and hence to involve bargaining, trade-offs and compromise.

The institution itself may be a strong defender of established academic values. But the basic unit is, of the different levels in our model, perhaps the most substantial barrier against externally imposed innovations, and the one within whose protective walls the individual academic can most effectively shelter from any unwelcome winds of change. It may be able to call a range of political allies to its defence: not only similarly threatened basic units in its own or other institutions, but also at times the parent institution and the relevant wider peer group. Where the field includes members who practise their profession in society at large (such as medicine, law or engineering) the range of potential allies is even more extensive.

Bailey's point about the political characteristics of innovation can be seen as relevant here. It is the securely established departments in prestigious institutions and fields which enjoy generally high status which are best placed to survive drastic attempts at reform. As the recent study by Boys *et al.* (1988) underlines, weaker academic groupings – particularly if they are located in low-status subjects and relatively marginal institutions – are more readily susceptible to wholesale reorganisation, if not to virtual elimination from the academic scene. They are also more liable to trade off their professional credibility against what they perceive to be a greater degree of social acceptance. From a somewhat similar perspective, the constant concern of individuals, basic units and institutions to improve their standing in the hierarchy of esteem can be seen as a potent force for change – often in response to external stimuli. In terms of our model, one might say that basic units in a politically disadvantageous position are by the same token more permeable to external social influences, whether it be operationally, in response to commissions from outside agencies, or normatively, in response to changes in wider social, economic and cultural values.

## THE PROCESS OF CHANGE

A consideration of how change may be resisted leads on to the question of the way in which it may be brought about. According to Lewin's (1952) analysis, the precondition for any change process is that – as a result of one or other form of 'driving force' – an existing system should begin to show 'cracks'. Impulses from the environment then flow into these cracks, causing the system to 'unfreeze', and hence creating a potential for movement. In terms of our own account, the initial opening-up of any particular level of the higher education system to change may occur either in the normative or in the operational mode; but the process remains incomplete and ineffective until the necessary adjustments have taken place in both modes.

A distinction needs to be made here between what is often referred to as 'planned change' and change which is in some sense unplanned but inexorable. The latter notion embraces that type of adjustment which the system, or its institutions or basic units or individuals, find themselves forced to make in their pattern of everyday activity as a result of external forces which are largely or entirely beyond their control. One example at the institutional level would be the way in which the overall pattern of teaching demands to be reshaped in response to major changes in upper-school curricula and examinations; an example at the level of the system as a whole would be the changing recruitment pattern, age distribution of students and course structure resulting from the demographic decline in the early 1990s. Inexorable change may result, for instance, from fluctuations in perceived disciplinary status at the level of the basic unit. Such innovations tend to be viewed in somewhat the same way as minor natural disasters; that is to say, they are accepted in a fatalistic spirit rather than actively resented. They may have only a negligible, or at most an indirect and gradual, effect on individual or collective norms: but even where the old values remain intact they will be played out in a very different way in the operational mode. There is no contesting the effectiveness of this kind of change: it is change for survival.

By way of contrast, those innovations which originate in planned changes based on deliberate coercion are more likely to arouse conflict or contention. They typically stem from a higher level within the system itself, commonly in response to environmental pressures which operate strongly at that level. They may comprise operational changes (as in the case of devolution of institutional budgets to groupings of basic units designated as 'cost centres'), or changes in the normative mode (as instanced in the changed accountability arrangements at the individual level consequent on the abolition of tenure), or a combination of both (as in centrally inspired attempts to exercise selectivity among the basic units in a particular field). The central authorities have become increasingly prone to the introduction of coercive reforms along these lines.

It may be observed that there are some coercive changes which, without necessarily being framed with such an intent in view, offer opportunity for differential exploitation at various levels in the system. Individuals, basic units or institutions alike, in what is an inherently competitive environment, may seize the opportunity of a new requirement or procedure to gain advantage for themselves over their competitors. For the politically astute, a change hailed as disadvantageous by the majority may be operated so as to yield positive results.

Coercive changes, particularly when they conflict with strongly held internal norms, are inherently unstable. They are implemented, if at all, under a sense of duress, with its attendant overtones of resentment, rejection and, in some cases moral outrage. Operational compliance may consist in no more than 'going through the motions', if not of deliberate subversion. Unless there is an eventual acceptance in the normative mode that the change is in some genuine sense justifiable, the operational procedures which embody the prescription are likely in the longer term to be regarded as of no real significance and to be bypassed or tacitly ignored.

Even if those directly affected have, as Marris (1974) puts it,

> little part in the decisions which determine the policy of the organisation ... collectively, they have great power to subvert, constrain or ignore changes they do not accept because, after all, they do the work. If innovation is imposed on them, without the chance to assimilate it to their experience, to argue it out, adapt it to their own interpretation of their working lives, they will do their best to fend it off.

In contrast, manipulative changes can be characterised as those which, whether internal or external, normative or operational, depend on the offer of some form of incentive to those who carry them out. Examples would include the provision by central authorities of special funding for desired types of research activity, or the sponsorship by industrial or professional agencies of a particular form of course provision. Innovations based on a manipulative strategy are liable to be viewed with cynicism rather than with hostility, particularly when – as is usually the case – the element of manipulation is easy to discern. If an incentive for change is put forward on a 'take-it-or-leave-it' basis, the temptation may be to derive maximum advantage from the offer in return for the minimum acceptable level of disruption. Operations may be nominally modified – that is, without any significant accompanying normative shift; or norms may be symbolically adjusted – that is, without any significant instantiation in operational practice. However, where there is some element of negotiation involved, and a mutually acceptable bargain is struck, both partners are likely to consider themselves under an obligation to carry out the terms of the arrangement in reasonably good faith.

There may also be cases in which normative changes are successfully achieved by a process of persuasion and conversion – and hence where the acceptance of the need for a new policy is established – without any steps being taken for implementation at the operational level. Such changes are in a literal sense inconsequential, since there is nothing to show for them. The institutionalisation of a policy – its internalisation in the governing values and its embodiment in the day-to-day functions of the organisations and individuals to which it is designed to apply – can only occur when implementation and acceptance are both fully in place. And once this institutionalisation has been brought about, the system is ready, in Lewin's parlance, for 're-freezing'.

The business of institutionalising change is thus a complex one. Marris (1974) draws a sustained and interesting parallel with personal loss and bereavement, arguing that significant innovations necessarily give rise to internal tensions which have to be 'relived and worked out through collective action.... They merge into political action, but are also expressions of mourning, in the sense that they give meaningful structure to a process of transition whose outcome is still clouded by ambivalence'. He is emphatic that however reasonable the proposed changes, the process of implementing them must still allow the impulse of rejection to play itself out. Those affected by an innovation

> cannot reconcile themselves to the loss of familiar attachments in terms of some impersonal utilitarian calculation of the common good. Hence the reformers must listen as well as explain, continually accommodating their design to other purposes, other kinds of experience, modifying and negotiating, long after they would like to believe that their conception was finished. If they impatiently cut this process short, their reforms are likely to be abortive.

In the end, acceptance of a change will often be brought about, Marris suggests, by 'understanding that what must be given up is not, after all, vital'. Bailey (1973) makes a similar point, suggesting that successful institutionalisation is

> likely to happen when the innovation is revealed as being in conformity with some transcending value and thus not 'really', once it is got 'into perspective' a change; rather it is an innovation in the strict sense – something perceived as a new and more effective means towards an already accepted end.

These considerations are strongly reinforced by writers such as Weatherley and Lipsky (1977) and Elmore (1985), whose researches were carried out in a different intellectual tradition. Insofar as they are appropriate to innovation in general, they are perhaps especially so in the context of higher education where the working lives of individuals are liable to be closely bound up with their personal values, so that what they do has a very direct connection with what they stand for.

In terms of our earlier analysis, it can be argued that the most effective – because ultimately the most stable – changes depend on an alignment between normative and operational modes, the one having interacted with the other to achieve a state of equilibrium. Further, we suggested that significant normative change depends on a process of adjustment (comparable, Marris suggests, with coming to terms with bereavement) in which the new norms (as Bailey remarks) can be seen to have some continuity with, or bear some discernible relationship to, existing ones. It is here, as noted earlier, that the skills of academic leadership are likely to prove particularly important: it is one of the characteristics of a successful leader that he or she is able to identify and draw out the links between traditional, widely established and strongly held values at any particular level in the system and those new norms whose adoption at that level may be desirable or expedient – or perhaps even essential to survival at a particular point in history.

It is, however, one thing to argue that the model we have put forward, insofar as it incorporates the notion of change, is consistent with at least some of the writings of others on the subject; it is quite another to show that it matches reality. The next step must be to explore how far our analysis is able to accommodate to actual changes which have taken place, or innovations which have proved unsuccessful, at various levels in the system.

## CHANGES TO THE SYSTEM AS A WHOLE

The central authorities in higher education are expected to ensure that the system as a whole appears adequately to meet the needs of society and the economy, and that proper institutional standards are maintained. In performing the first (external) task, they have to find means of influencing the activities of the basic units, who are not readily persuaded to abandon their strongly established professional loyalties in favour of demands from the centre. In satisfying the second (internal) requirement (the maintenance of institutional standards), the only obvious form of reward and punishment they can mete out is through the use of their power to allocate resources.

Accordingly, there is no easy way for central authorities to attempt to correct an imbalance between their normative and operational modes – that is to say, when resource commitments and the pattern of course provision move out of line with national policy, however defined. One common strategy is some measure of structural reform, so designed as to affect the pattern of institutional power and to promote activities seen as more educationally desirable or more economically worthwhile than those which already exist.

It is possible for drastic changes to be brought about by unilateral action of the central authorities in both the normative and operational modes. To publish judgements that some university departments are 'below average', as the UGC first did in its 1985 grading exercise, may plainly unsettle the existing normative climate and lead to operational consequences such as the closure of departments or the radical alteration of undergraduate courses. To divest a university of 40 per cent of its funds, as in the case of Salford in the UGC allocations in 1981, may result not only in major operational disruptions but in the necessity radically to rethink institutional norms. Such interventions are outside the patterns of gradual and organic change and have long-term implications for both morale and practice, the costs and benefits of which are not easy to calculate.

In addition to their allocative powers and their (relatively circumscribed) scope for introducing legislation, such as that, in 1989, relating to student loans, the central authorities also have more subtle ways of bringing about system-wide change through the manipulation of the current political climate and through the deliberate use of symbolism to alter that climate. But the effects of such activities are not always easy to trace, because they are in their very nature both elusive and diffuse.

We shall at this point briefly examine a number of familiar changes in the category of structural reform in British higher education, and consider with the wisdom of hindsight the degree to which they might be regarded as successful. The first case in point is the establishment of the new universities, as part of the wave of expansion heralded by the Robbins Report in the early 1960s. One of the hopes behind the creation of new institutions, as opposed to the further enlargement of existing ones, was that they would provide a better opportunity for trying out new educational ideas. The initial claims of those who founded them were ambitious: a much-quoted phrase referred to 'drawing a new map of learning' (Briggs, 1964).

In retrospect, it would be fair to claim that the new universities succeeded in introducing certain modifications to the existing maps without significantly altering the landscape. A number of them made genuine attempts to break out of the straitjacket of established academic disciplines. It was only when the staff they recruited began applying for posts in more conventional universities that the real problem was laid bare. Given the choice between a historian and a member of a school of European studies, most history departments will go for the former. However sound the latter's credentials in history might be, his membership of the club is questionable and his loyalty suspect. So there will be an inevitable tendency for academics working in interdisciplinary contexts to reassert their original disciplinary identities.

An underground network of departments based on traditional subjects can therefore be discerned in many of the institutions dedicated to interdisciplinary teaching and research (Boys *et al.*, 1988). A change in a system of currency cannot be brought about unilaterally by a minority group – and that is in part what the new universities were expected to do.

The second example is also related to the expansion of degree-level teaching. In this case, rather than extending the range of university-based provision, the attempt was made to provide an alternative to it. (A fuller account is given in Chapter 3). The creation of a separate, rival sector of higher education (and the laying down of an imaginary boundary, the binary line, to protect it from falling into the academic trap of the universities) took place even before the last of the new universities, Ulster, had been given its charter. New institutions, designated as polytechnics, were developed from those technical colleges which had an established record of advanced work. Their remit – first spelled out in a speech by Anthony Crosland at Woolwich in 1965 – was to concentrate on teaching largely to the exclusion of basic research, to emphasise vocationally relevant degree programmes, to provide social mobility for students and to be 'directly responsive to social needs', especially in relation to the local setting. The consequent redefinition of the student clientele – involving the acceptance of larger numbers of working-class, adult and part-time applicants – was seen as one important potential source of a shift in both norms and operations.

In the event, none of these ambitions has been fully realised. The basic units in the polytechnics, no less than those in the universities, respond to peer-group norms associated with their disciplines. Their academic staff by and large look outside the institutional structure for their professional identity. Since academic reputation rests on published papers, the opportunity to do research and to conduct scholarly enquiry is claimed as a right. Vocational relevance is not discouraged in degree programmes, but the differences in this respect from university provision are moderate. As for achieving a higher intake of working-class students, the polytechnics are as much in competition for the best-qualified applicants as are the universities. This meant that they did not, in the initial stages of their existence, recruit a significantly larger proportion of those from working-class backgrounds than the universities succeeded in doing (Whitburn *et al.*, 1976). For the same reason, their catchment – at least for full-time students – has tended to be national as well as local: they have sought to attract students from all parts of the UK and overseas. Their local ties are therefore relatively weak (except insofar as they recruit a proportion of part-time students who are necessarily based within commuting distance, and mature students who tend to be so).

This, again, seems a case in which the original intentions of central authority were powerless when set against the resilience of values in the system (Burgess and Pratt, 1974). When institutions compete for prestige and the ability range of students is relatively narrow, it would appear naïve to set up a separate and rival structure and pronounce it to be 'equal but different'. Only a few years after the polytechnics came into existence, some were openly aspiring to university status and, somewhat later, conferring professorial titles on senior staff: the rest, perhaps more hesitant at abandoning the very principles on which they were founded, none the less seemed anxious to divest themselves of local control and to devise some alternative formula for becoming 'equal and similar'.

In terms of the model, one might argue that both types of newly created institution – the new universities and the polytechnics – represented operational changes, prompted by external demands for an increase in the number of graduates produced by the system, which did not significantly change the internal norms of the academic world. In the former case, the institutions concerned became, over time, hardly distinguishable from the older universities whose values they had attempted to call into question. But in the latter case, the position remained unstable over a lengthy period.

This very instability, created by the disjunction between the operational requirements first imposed on the polytechnics and colleges and the norms of the system in which they were placed, provides an interesting further example of the process of change. In this instance, it is possible to see clearly – since it was public and protracted – the process of bargaining between the system and its external environment which led to a mutually accepted outcome. The polytechnics were, in the first instance, accountable to local government: a source, as we noted earlier, of some frustration in both normative and operational terms. But other constraints were also imposed on them: their courses had to be approved as operationally viable by Regional Advisory Councils, and validated in terms of their academic acceptability by the CNAA. Subsequently, the problem of cost control also arose, when economic cutbacks made it difficult to defend the 'pooling' system (under which all local authorities were required to make pro rata contributions to a potentially limitless fund from which the costs of the public sector institutions were met). But once the decision was taken to 'cap the pool' (a curious metaphor used at the time to denote the placing of cost limits on overall expenditure), a more systematic and coherent allocative mechanism had to be devised. The establishment of the NAB illustrates the process of political compromise (Nixon, 1987). It allowed the local authorities a further period of influence over national higher education policy as well as nominal control over the polytechnics and colleges. At the same time, however, it progressively superseded the cumbersome Regional Advisory Council mechanism for course approval, and helped promote the devolution of much of the responsibility for course validation from the CNAA to the institutions themselves.

By the time the Education Reform Act was drawn up in 1988, central government was looking for ways in which to play down and marginalise the influence of the local authorities. At the same time, the polytechnics welcomed the opportunity to rid themselves of what many had continued to see as the irksome burden of local control. The Act conferred incorporated status on the polytechnics and some other public sector institutions. The proposal, embodied in the Act, to dismantle the NAB and to place public sector institutions of higher education under the direct central authority of a new Polytechnics and Colleges Funding Council provided a satisfactory harmonisation of the system's norms with those current in the wider context. It also served to reinforce the streamlining of operational procedures, enabling the public sector more readily to meet external demands for vocational courses and industrial contracts. The simultaneous creation of a Universities Funding Council to replace the UGC, though considerably less welcome to the university sector, none the less brought the two hitherto uncomfortably disjointed parts of the British higher education system more closely into alignment and prepared the ground for a possible unification.

## CHANGES AT THE INSTITUTIONAL LEVEL

We now turn to consider the nature and effectiveness of innovations at the institutional level. We shall review three main types of change in this category, reflecting the different sources of pressure on the norms and operations of academic institutions identified in our model: those responding to external social, cultural and economic values; those which stem primarily from the operational requirements of the external market; and those which are consequent on changes at other levels in the inner core of the system itself. The majority of our examples will be of the creation, for one reason or another, of new basic units. Much as the main scope for change at the central level has rested in the establishment of new institutions or the disestablishment of existing ones (whether to meet external operational or normative requirements or both), so innovation at the institutional level commonly takes the form of promoting the emergence or, more rarely, sanctioning the closure of particular subject groupings.

The pressures generated by external socio-cultural changes can be illustrated by taking two contrasting cases from a time when the policy system was less pressing in its demands; namely, biological sciences and computing. In the former instance strong intellectual arguments were marshalled in the 1950s and early 1960s for amalgamating existing departments of botany and zoology to reflect the newly emergent concepts of a unified study of living matter, embracing genetics, cell biology and ecology. The operational barriers in the way of achieving this intellectual objective were, in many institutions, considerable. Nevertheless, in a majority of cases the change happened, and schools of biological science have become a more familiar feature of the academic scene than the old pattern of separate botany and zoology departments. Metzger's account of 'affiliation' (Metzger, 1987) refers to a somewhat similar process.

In contrast with this case of fusion of two existing basic units, our next example illustrates what is perhaps the more common process of the fission of one basic unit to produce two. In the early years of the development of the computer, the mathematics department seemed the natural base for those teaching and researching into its applications. However, as computing reached a state of academic maturity, in the sense both of resting on a substantial body of specialist knowledge and of generating intellectually important and socially useful applications, the case for independence became strong. Computer scientists had already established their own peer network, separate from that of any of the existing branches of mathematics; they had their own identifiable research interests; they had enough conceptual material to justify teaching a distinct degree programme and enough candidates to allow for viable recruitment. In short, they had all the prerequisites for forming self-sufficient basic units independent of their parent departments of mathematics. Again, the necessary organisational changes were made, often with some practical difficulty but seldom with any strong intellectual opposition. (What we have here labelled as fission is denoted by Blume, 1985, as differentiation, and by Metzger, 1987, as parturition.)

A contrasting set of attempts to innovate at the institutional level, again in response to social and cultural considerations in the outer framework, represents a general failure to satisfy internal academic norms. Extrinsic pressures for the introduction of 'socially relevant' interdisciplinary groupings such as those concerned with peace studies, black studies or women's studies have generally come up against objections based on academic credibility and intellectual coherence. As Clark (1983) observes 'Such new fields "make it" to the extent they are able to form a legitimacy, using events and whatever influence they can muster to educate others to new perceptions and definitions.' Metzger describes the same process as 'dignification'. In general, even in the relatively few cases in which innovative basic units of this kind are given an operational existence, their normative credibility remains precarious. They tend to find themselves with few political allies within the inner core of the system, and are thus readily susceptible to closure at any sign of trouble within their parent institution.

Alongside such examples of external normative demands, it is possible to identify cases in which innovations are first instigated in the operational mode as a result of external market requirements. The vogue for establishing 'science parks', to which commercial firms are attracted by the offer of possible research collaboration with relevant academic groupings within the associated institution, offers one instance of this process. It may, however, be noted that the success and stability of the arrangement depend to a considerable extent on how far institutional norms are modified to match the resulting operational procedures: unless those within the institutions are amenable to an appropriate change in research emphasis, the arrangement can prove to be a largely symbolic and nominal one (Dalton, 1987).

Other illustrations of the same phenomenon can be found in the emergence of a new source of potential student recruitment and eventual employment. Where such a market opens up, provided that the subject-matter can be regarded as academically respectable, there is a strong temptation (particularly in institutions in search of additional student numbers) to establish a new basic unit and offer an appropriate degree programme. This tendency seems to be particularly marked in relation to courses leading to a professional qualification; the explanation may lie in the normative reinforcement offered in such cases by the existence of organised external interest groups (see also Blume, 1985, on the process of professionalisation). Two instances which come readily to mind are accounting and nursing studies, where the interest groups concerned have been generally successful in persuading institutions of higher education to offer graduate status to potential entrants to the profession and to create chairs in the subjects. Although such innovations are liable to be viewed with greater suspicion than conventional academic developments, they can be readily enough accommodated in most institutions, provided that they establish their promise in terms of student recruitment and their acceptability in terms of intellectual substance.

The third type of change at the institutional level, namely, that stemming from demands made by other levels within the system, offers a somewhat different range of cases. In the early 1970s, it was as a result of normative pressures from below – themselves reflecting a prevailing sentiment for participation within the wider society – that junior academics and students were given a recognised place within the decision-making structures of the institution of which they were members. In the case of the students, the concession proved relatively ineffective: except in the short term, 'student power' was not strong enough to override entrenched academic norms. However, the erosion by non-professorial staff of the dominance of the professoriate had more lasting effects in many institutions. Perhaps because it chimed in with traditional notions of collegiality, the movement for democratisation was able successfully to challenge the established hierarchical values and procedures. A tangible result, in many parts of the system, was that the headship of the basic unit ceased to be a permanent appointment, but rotated between senior members at specific intervals (often five-yearly); in some instances the appointment was by election and did not demand professorial or equivalent rank (Moodie, 1986; Middlehurst, 1989).

Attempts at 'top-down' normative change include the Enterprise Initiative promoted by the central authorities under the auspices of the Training Agency (MSC, 1987). This provides a clear instance of innovation by manipulation. Institutions were offered substantial additional sums over and above their normal budgets in return for undertakings to gear their curricula towards entrepreneurial values. The extent to which new norms were firmly reflected in the resulting modifications to their operational activities remains open to debate.

The procedures adopted by funding councils in making allocations to institutions, following the creation of the UFC and PCFC in 1989, provide a further example of top-down pressures exercised by the central authorities. Both councils adjudicate between costed bids in allocating student places; in addition, the UFC distributes funds to universities partly in accordance with the ratings awarded as a result of research grading exercises. In consequence of the former process, the previous negotiated pattern of student place allocation has been superseded by a stronger measure of institutional prescription; the latter is accompanied by an expectation that universities should reward the more successful research groups and reduce the funds available to the less successful. In both cases, the result has been to change the relationship between the basic units and the institutions. Here as in some other cases, operational changes have resulted in significant normative consequences.

## CHANGES AFFECTING THE BASIC UNIT

At the basic unit level our model suggests four main sets of pressures for change: those in the normative mode which derive from the wider social context; those which stem from changes in professional norms outside the basic unit itself; those which arise from external operational demands; and those which are generated at other levels within the system's inner core.

The first type of change has already been touched on in Chapter 6. It usually arises from a major shift in values in the external environment of higher education – a shift which may not only call into question the established assumptions which lie behind a given basic unit's work, but also jeopardise its existence by reducing its attractiveness to students. There can, for example, be no denying the steady modification in intellectual climate over the past century which has demoted divinity schools and departments of theology from a major to a marginal role in university affairs. In consequence, many such units have chosen to reappraise their own internal norms, and to extend their function from the traditional one of training future members of the clergy to the provision of broadly based comparative courses on world religions, with few if any vocational implications. This form of innovation is the more powerful for impinging simultaneously on the normative and the operational modes of the basic units affected by it; the more inexorable for giving rise not merely to changes in curricular provision but also to a search for a new ideology and *raison d'être*.

In more subtle ways, the same process can be seen to operate across the whole spectrum of basic unit provision. In Chapter 6 the shifts in external credibility and market currency of different subject areas were likened to the operation of a cultural stock exchange. Such externally generated changes in disciplinary fortune have predictable repercussions – in terms of levels of research support and demands for student places – on the norms and operations of the units concerned.

It is the task of the peer group as a whole to promote and defend the interests of its subject field, whether that group is mainly defined in terms of an academic constituency (as in the case of subjects such as history, physics or sociology) or whether it also embraces practitioners in the wider community (the obvious examples would be professional groupings such as medicine, law or teaching). But it is also through the peer group that significant normative changes in the conception of the subject itself are promulgated, representing the second of the four characteristic sources of innovation at the basic unit level. What is in view here is not the straightforward accretion of new findings, materials and interpretations which constitute the everyday task of research and scholarship, and which duly find their way into the currency of the undergraduate curriculum; it is, rather, that more remarkable process referred to by Kuhn (1962) as a change of paradigm: a substitution, in our terms, of a substantially new element for a significant part of the existing norms of a whole academic peer group. Changes in this category are closely comparable with the broader realignment, at the institutional level, of basic units such as biological sciences and computing to which we referred in the previous section.

Conceptual revolutions which involve the wholesale reappraisal of an academic subject area are rare: those involving a particular sub-specialism within a broad field are relatively more commonplace. There are also, however, more gradual changes which result in a noticeable modification in paradigm, or set of disciplinary norms. One such example can be found in economics, where the earlier emphasis on according qualitative attention to political factors has given place to a highly mathematically biased approach. This has occasioned significant changes in course provision – changes reminiscent of earlier, though more limited, influences on physics from the establishment of relativity theory and the uncertainty principle and on social history from the importation of the techniques of demographic analysis. Such changes might be claimed to constitute the essence of the academic enterprise, even though they involve a limited range of components of the system as a whole. The process characteristically starts in the operational mode with new patterns of research, whose findings in their turn affect peer-group norms in the wider scholarly community. Once the new norms are sufficiently established at the level of the basic unit, they begin to be translated back into the operational mode in terms of innovations in the nature and content of courses.

The norms of basic units in vocational subjects may be further affected by changing external professional expectations, often strongly reinforced by the outside body responsible for maintaining professional standards. One example would be the inclusion in engineering curricula of a component which is meant to relate functional competence to an understanding of the social and economic context in which technological developments take place. The obligation to introduce 'engineering in society' courses was strongly pressed by the professional engineering institutions, but it reflected a wider demand on the part of employers that graduate engineers should have certain qualities beyond narrowly vocational skills and a narrowly technocratic outlook. The effect, in terms of our model, has been for a new element in the norms of the wider peer group to lead to a comparable reshaping of the norms of the basic unit, and thence to shifts in curricular emphasis in the operational mode.

So far we have considered changes in the formation of basic unit values – and hence, indirectly, in operational practice – brought about by external normative demands in the wider society or in the relevant professional groups. A further set of innovations, this time manifesting themselves first in the operational mode, are generated by external operational requirements, and perhaps especially by market pressures on recruitment. They characteristically affect newly established teaching programmes and also some courses in institutions which have relatively low status within the system. The problem confronting the basic unit involved in such forms of provision is to compete effectively with rival offerings which are of long standing, or situated within prestigious institutions. The solution involves seeking some special means of attracting students, often by drastically reshaping the conventional degree programme. Leaving aside examples of this strategy at the level of the institution as a whole (interdisciplinary courses in a number of colleges of higher education; modular degree programmes at some polytechnics and universities; 'sandwich' courses interweaving academic study with work experience at several technologically oriented institutions), instances at the level of the basic unit would include language programmes which abandon classical literature for an emphasis on practical competence and an awareness of contemporary social and economic developments; and the adoption of a 'systemic' integrated approach to medical training, alongside an early introduction of clinical work, in some of the recently established medical schools. The range of innovative enterprises of this kind at the basic unit level is constrained by institutional regulation as well as by the risk of disapproval from the wider peer group. Nevertheless, the need for survival in a competitive market can generate powerful internal norms within the basic unit, leading to the successful institutionalisation of the change as more than a passing aberration. Such internal norm changes may be accelerated by the introduction of competitive cost bidding for student places: a development which does not necessarily favour well-established institutions with relatively high staffing costs.

Finally, there is a miscellaneous category of innovations triggered off by internal pressures within the system, whether from the bottom up or from the top down. Changes initiated from below – from the individual level – are typically those pedagogic innovations which affect the operations of the basic unit, in whole or in part, rather than those which are amenable to individual staff initiative. Examples would include the adoption of project work as a significant component of the undergraduate curriculum, the exploitation of small group techniques in place of lectures, the development of independent learning schemes, or the introduction of substantial elements of 'concentrated study' in which one particular topic is pursued exclusively – that is, with no other competing courses – for a sizeable block of time.

Very often, the origins of such developments can be put down to serendipity, and their justification to improvements in the quality of life. That is to say, the staff of one basic unit may pick up an apparently interesting idea through contact with the staff of another unit – or have it imported through the arrival of a new faculty member at a fairly senior level – and may eventually agree to put it into effect. The (relatively minor) adjustment in group values will often be achieved by the argument that the change in question will result in a significant improvement in current practice, and thus enhance student motivation as well as increasing the job satisfaction of the teachers concerned. From that point, it remains to put the new norms into operational effect (a step which, while it may in some cases call for a sizeable investment of staff effort, is usually undertaken with some enthusiasm once the conviction is there).

An example of a significant top-down innovation, that relating to staff appraisal and promotion procedures, may be argued to fall into the category of internal changes relating primarily to the basic unit, although its explanation in terms of our model is more complex than those which have been advanced in previous instances. There has long been a disjunction within the system between the centrality of undergraduate teaching, viewed in operational terms, and its marginality in terms of career rewards and incentives. This accords with the arguments advanced at the beginning of this chapter, as a case in which the internal norms of the basic unit, influenced strongly by external professional values, tend to value research more highly than teaching; while at the same time, external operational requirements ensure that few units can survive unless they devote a substantial part of their time and effort to the provision of courses attractive to potential applicants.

The resulting imbalance between norms and operations calls for some form of equilibration. Within the context of British universities (though for a variety of reasons the phenomenon is less marked in public sector institutions), this instability has persisted while the system as a whole has moved from an elitist to a mass form of provision. However, through the insistence of the central authorities (reflecting, it might be supposed, concerns within the community at large), a mandatory requirement for the annual appraisal of staff was introduced at the end of the 1980s, with the expectation that this would embrace teaching as well as research activities. Although not directly linked with promotion, appraisal procedures were expected to stimulate the provision of departmental and institutional programmes of staff development, and by this means to exert pressure on basic units to give greater allowance for teaching competence in their recommendations for career development.

It is too early to judge how far this strategy will succeed, although a further expansion in the direction of a universal, market-driven system would be likely to accelerate the tendency towards giving quality of teaching a greater prominence in the norms of many basic units. The value shift could well be further reinforced if – as seems highly probable – increased student numbers were accompanied by a more marked selectivity in research funding. In that event, all except the relatively well-favoured basic units in prestigious universities with a strong research tradition would have reason to play down the currently dominant role of research excellence as a criterion for professional advancement. But as the example of US higher education demonstrates, such an outcome would not necessarily result in the abandonment of internationally competitive research.

These various considerations suggest that basic units can be subject to internal as well as external pressures. Such pressures will in some cases generate a major change in both normative and operational modes; in others the effect will be discernible largely or exclusively in the operational mode (representing an accommodation to an external threat rather than a fundamental shift in values).

We have put forward no examples of changes which impinge only on the normative mode and leave the operational mode unaffected. This should not be surprising in the light of the earlier discussion of the general nature of innovation in higher education. If the collective values of a particular basic unit change, the need to give tangible expression to those values constitutes a powerful incentive for a commensurate change in practice. The only effective hindrance is likely to come either from the external peer group (which is liable in the end to have its way, if it cannot be converted or divided) or from the institution.

## INNOVATION AND THE INDIVIDUAL

Even though a basic unit, or an institution, or the whole higher education system, is somewhat more than the sum of its parts, it is none the less largely dependent on the co-operation of those parts. And if one is to avoid the trap of reifying organisational entities, it has to be remembered that individuals, in one role or another, go to make up not only the various basic units in an institution but also the institution itself, and a discernible part of the network of central authorities as well. There is a sense in which all reference to innovation in higher education *ipso facto* involves a reference to academic teachers. Nevertheless, there is a clear distinction between talking about a given staff member *qua* head of department or member of a planning committee or chairman of a subcommittee of the Science and Engineering Research Council, and that same staff member when functioning as a teacher on such and such courses or as a researcher in such and such a project team.

In the present discussion, we shall concentrate on the second case; namely, that in which teachers are viewed in their role as particular persons. This is not because we want to belittle the importance of the other functions which they may fulfil, but because most of what can usefully be said about them is already implicit in our earlier account of changes at the levels of the system, institution and basic unit.

There are a number of factors which limit the scope of what the individual can do, how far he or she can depart from established practice, and how far he or she can bring about collective change. Among the most powerful of the external constraints, as suggested in our model, are the peer-group norms which map out, for the members of any given basic unit, the acceptable range of professional beliefs and the expected style of conduct for those at different levels of seniority. Changes deriving from this source are likely to affect individual perceptions of the nature of the field in which the academics in question are engaged. They may result in consequent operational changes in teaching emphasis or research direction or both.

Academics are members, not only of their professional community and their own basic unit and institution, but also of the society in which they live. As our model emphasises, they cannot remain entirely independent of the values of that wider society. Extrinsic social expectations of what academics are and ought to be impinge subtly, if not directly, on their ideas and on their practice. Even those intellectuals who see it as their obligation to be critical and questioning of some of the currently fashionable assumptions of their own period and environment are nevertheless susceptible to other such assumptions. That is to say, no academic – man or woman – is an island, but only at most a peninsula: there is always some set of external norms which even the most independent-minded individuals can be seen to have internalised, and adopted as their own. Such norms in their turn may exercise a powerful effect: perhaps particularly on individuals' self-conception of their credibility and status outside the institution, on their sense of autonomy, and less directly on the ways in which they go about their everyday professional tasks. If external normative pressures can bring about normative changes at the individual level, and at a further remove affect operational practice, the reverse may be said of those pressures which stem primarily from external operational requirements. In their case, the immediate impact is on working practice; though significant modifications here may lead on to subsequent adjustments to individual norms. Thus, for example, where an academic may be commissioned, in his or her own right, to undertake an outside research consultancy or to meet an external training or lecturing commitment, this may not only serve to modify existing work patterns but may also affect the perceptions of the individual concerned about the very nature of the field in question. One particular instance, cited in Youll (1988), is the way in which academic physicists' involvement in industrial applications (such as materials science and laser optics) has succeeded in influencing both the actual content of teaching and research and the conception of the subject itself.

Other constraints on individual autonomy derive from internal normative demands of accountability to the basic unit, or internal operational requirements, such as quasi-contractual obligations to undertake a certain minimum of teaching hours. But despite these curbs on individual action, even the most junior academics retain a fair degree of liberty to determine how they will present the required curriculum content within a pre-determined structure, and to decide how they will direct their energies in relation to scholarship and research. Insofar as the choices call for departures from established practice, personal and educational values are likely to be crucial components in the effectiveness of the consequent change.

There are also questions of personal value judgements to be considered. Individual academics necessarily have personal preferences as between one kind of activity and another, and their own particular ideas of what it means to be doing a worthwhile and rewarding job. These various considerations colour their judgement of any new and unfamiliar proposal. Thus, for instance, an academic strongly committed to research and relatively uninterested in teaching is likely to show little enthusiasm for developing a programme of 'skill sessions' in undergraduate physics practicals which promise to be time-consuming to work out. Similarly, a teacher who believes strongly in preserving the authority of staff members will be reluctant to embark on the democratic procedures inherent in some forms of seminar activity.

A comparable contrast can be marked at the level of the individual between those who, explicitly or implicitly, see teaching issues in terms of developing an appropriate technology (which implies the existence of discrete entities, absolute values and clear-cut causal conditions for change) and those who, consciously or unconsciously, emphasise the organic nature of the educational process (which carries with it the notion that learning is complex, contextually sensitive and essentially unquantifiable). The former view gives little weight to the educational milieu; the latter regards it as extremely important, and holds that phenomena which are abstracted from it will lose many of their crucial characteristics.

Differences in basic educational value of this kind generate quite different responses to various types of curricular innovation. For example, those who take a holistic perspective are unlikely to look kindly on courses with a tightly programmed structure based on closely defined behavioural objectives, or to favour a modular curriculum pattern. In contrast, those who take an aggregative view of knowledge will tend to have little sympathy with the psychodynamic overtones of small group learning, or with the integrative aspirations of interdisciplinary degrees.

Given the complexity of the relationships between each academic's personal, educational and professional values on the one hand, and the demands made by different forms of pedagogic and curricular innovation on the other, it may seem surprising that change ever happens. Two considerations help to explain why it does. First, it is inherent in the notion of the academic community that mutual accommodations and working compromises should be sought even where they are not accompanied by any significant shift in value position. (Were this not so, it would make adequate teaching provision virtually impossible: any curriculum must have at least some sense of convergence, and in the majority of cases it has to be achieved by negotiation between individuals with different priorities.) The second consideration stems from the relative success which most people have in matching themselves to their environment. When a new member of staff is appointed (or a new student enrolled) to a basic unit, it is usually as a result of a skilful, though unacknowledged, process of mutual choice. So it is much less common than it would be by random selection to find a maverick individual whose values are strongly at odds with those of his immediate academic colleagues. Indeed, one might go further than this to observe that the main constraints on change are social, not psychological: they depend more on the way the system operates than on the particular stand that its individual members choose to adopt.

Those who write on innovation often appear to make the prior assumption that change is inherently desirable. There is, however, no reason why academics any more than other people should embrace novelty for the sake of novelty. If a particular course is attracting a large surplus of good, well-qualified applicants, and the teachers and students involved in that course are well satisfied with it, then there would seem no good reason to tinker with it merely at the behest of a self-instruction enthusiast or a devotee of interdisciplinary enquiry, any more than most of us would change our jobs merely on the advocacy of an employment bureau, or sell up our homes solely on the urging of an estate agent. We noted earlier in this chapter that institutions and basic units sometimes introduce major curricular reforms in response to the need to attract students to newly established programmes or courses which are relatively low in the pecking order of recruitment. The other side of the same coin is that the higher up the ladder of disciplinary prestige a particular group of teachers may be, and the more reputable their institution, the less likely they are to want to institute any far-reaching innovations in curricula or teaching methods.

Nevertheless, the historical perspective of Chapter 3 should serve as a reminder that times change faster than institutions, and that, outside the world of higher education, political fashions and economic climates come and go with little regard for the well-being of academia. The problems with which the system and its constituent institutions and basic units are now expected to contend are almost unrecognisably different from those which faced the much smaller and more insulated network of universities in the immediate post-war years. The degree of autonomy which they assumed, and the strong sense of freehold which individual academics felt able to enjoy, have had few parallels in contemporary higher education. The present-day system is called upon to defend its legitimacies and demonstrate its responsiveness to market pressures in a way which would have then seemed unimaginable. But whether or not externally derived innovation is thought to be a good thing, it is arguable that it has always been an endemic feature of the relationship between higher education and its wider environment.

# 9 Evaluation, accountability and the allocation of resources

## THE NATURE OF EVALUATION

In this chapter we shall be considering the contrasting sets of horizontal links in the model; namely, those evaluative functions in the normative mode which we have labelled as being concerned with judgement, and those in the operational mode which we have designated as having an allocative purpose. Both evaluation and allocation are ingredients of accountability.

Evaluation and accountability have been serious concerns in higher education for over a decade. In the 1980s anxiety was expressed by political leaders if not by academics or employers (Roizen and Jepson, 1985) about the standards of work being achieved in higher education. Reports concerned with both universities and polytechnics (Lindop Report, 1985; Reynolds Report, 1986; and CNAA, 1989) proposed procedures for the monitoring of standards, and these were followed by the installation of performance measures by the UGC, the NAB and their successors. In part, these anxieties can be construed as a direct consequence of expansion, for such measures would have been considered unnecessary in the elite university system in the 1950s and 1960s. More comprehensive and stringent evaluation could to some extent legitimise an expanded system with its more open access.

In terms of our model, two changes can be noted. First, the link between the allocation of resources and evaluation became stronger and more explicit. The bottom and top halves of our model came closer. Second, changes in the locus of allocative power towards the central authorities were accompanied by changes in control over the modes and amounts of evaluation. This control shifted decisively from being the preserve of academic and professional peer groups towards becoming a function of system and institutional management. At the same time, however, because of the increased convergence of the two sectors, the CNAA moved to allow polytechnics and colleges to validate their own courses so that the large majority of them now do so. The increased power of internal peer groups to evaluate was reinforced by their links with the outside world.

The nature of evaluation might be described in various ways. Evaluation can be used as a basis for reward and control; achievements may lead to preferential allocations to those with good track records in the expectation that they will perform even better. Such an evaluation is summative rather than formative (Scriven, 1967). In summative evaluation, an independent evaluator renders a judgement based on accumulated evidence about performance. In formative evaluation, an evaluator collects and reports data and judgements to assist the development of an activity. In its formative mode, evaluation is a tracking mechanism enabling the innovation itself to be redirected in the light of progress.

A further distinction rests on whether the evaluation is directed at judgements on the quality of the process or of the product (Stufflebeam, 1969). Where education is seen to produce outcomes which are not easily measured or defined, evaluation may be more meaningfully directed towards process, so that the satisfaction enjoyed, the experiences received, and the style used become more directly relevant. It is, however, possible to evaluate both process and product.

These distinctions between the different purposes of evaluation also denote differences in style. Formative evaluation is more likely than summative to be interactive, and the evaluation of process to be more humanistic than the evaluation of discernible products.

## MODES OF EVALUATION

Evaluation can be characterised by its modes and mechanisms. Different modes of evaluation imply different considerations against which a particular judgement may be made. The nature of the comparisons implied by an evaluation is not simply a technical matter but entails issues of value and power. A distinction may be noted between criterion-referencing and norm-referencing. If an evaluation is criterion-referenced it refers to objective and ideal standards. Where it is possible to set up a priori standards in this way, the operational advantages are considerable. Judgements can be ranked and allocations and decisions in the operational mode can follow on an explicitly justified basis.

The extent to which evaluation in higher education is amenable to criterion-referencing varies according to its subject. Ultimately all academics concede a degree of relativity in the judgements they make on one another's work, and this accords with the assumption that knowledge is provisional. But there are more limited skills in all subjects – the precise use of language, or the ability to use accepted formulae, for example – where standards can be applied absolutely.

Norm-referencing, in contrast, makes comparisons not against assumed ideals but against the general pattern of performance to be found in the type of activity being evaluated. Performances are thus ranked in relation to one another rather than judged in absolute terms. Like need only be compared with like; for example, business studies could be ranked without reference to the norms applicable to economics, or nursing studies matched against other paramedical studies rather than with, say, biology. Such an approach tends to be favourable to those subjects whose reference groups are client- and practitioner-based as much as academic.

Finally, self-evaluation refers to the inner universe of the values and operations of the unit being evaluated. It is likely to give weight to context and the quality of process as much as of product. It is, accordingly, the mode favoured by those concerned with the evaluation of the less tangible and predictable features of the higher education system, and who have doubts and reservations about the impact of imposed external criteria. We shall return to it later.

## PERFORMANCE INDICATORS

Evaluative mechanisms are either quantitative (for example, performance indicators) or qualitative (peer review or inspection, self-evaluation and student evaluation). Although there are no unbreakable and certain links, mechanisms can be matched to the modes of evaluation and to the levels of the system to which they are applied. It is the quantitative mechanisms which have predominated in recent years.

Quantifiable measures are employed to assess the performance of the system and its components. There is a tendency to use them summatively to make authoritative judgements on past and present performance. Decisions can then be made for managerial purposes. Yet they could, in principle, be used formatively for self-evaluation and development in conjunction with peer review.

Performance indicators can be defined as authoritative measures, usually in quantitative form, of an attribute of a higher education activity (Cave *et al.*, 1988). One of their apparent advantages is to translate difficult judgements into figures. Figures are manipulable, whilst verbal evaluations are less so: 'words are fatter than numbers, and usually have multiple meanings' (Miles and Huberman, 1984). Using them makes it easier to compare the performance of one unit against another.

The process of compiling indicators requires agreement about what constitute good inputs, processes and outputs of performance. Indicators thus raise questions about objectives which cannot be shirked if one is going to put a quantity on them. But to the extent that the compilation of indicators avoids the resolution of such questions whilst maintaining an appearance of objectivity, they may be harmful. It is argued in their favour that they are unaffected by the received reputations which dominate academic currency. At the same time, however, they cannot reflect fully the contexts within which academic activity takes place. It is generally agreed that they need to be used in conjunction with less cut-and-dried forms of evaluation, including peer review; that they are more effective in raising questions than in providing answers.

Several operational problems arise in using indicators. They cannot be safeguarded from, and may encourage, 'strategic' behaviour on the part of the entity being appraised. Basic units or institutions have considerable scope for determining their inputs or their outputs, and in many cases academics themselves decide the 'quality' of their output by determining degree classes or the completion rate of research degrees, no matter how assiduous external examiners and accrediting bodies may be. More important, because of their partial nature, performance indicators often provide misleading impressions of productivity since they make no distinction between the significant and the trivial. At the end of the assessment process, to reward those with 'good' indicator scores may fail to take heed of the fact that resources applied at the margin may have a greater effect on a basic unit whose performance is unimpressive, than on one working well.

A critical appraisal of the literature and current policy proposals for performance indicators (Cave *et al.*, 1988) has suggested criteria against which performance indicators may themselves be evaluated. They include type of indicator (input, process, output, productivity of final outcome, for example); relevance (does the indicator measure true underlying performance?); ambiguity (is, for instance, a high staffing ratio 'good' or 'bad'?); degree of proof against cheating; cost of collection; level of aggregation; and relation to other indicators. If they are able to pass this battery of tests, performance indicators offer a mechanism for making judgements within the normative mode which translate conveniently into decisions about allocations in the operational mode.

On the face of it, quantitative measures are best used for the evaluation of aggregates of performance at the level of the system, institution and, to some extent, the basic unit. They do not seem well suited to the judgement of individual performance (Miller, 1986). In practice, however, such indicators as citation indices and publication records are used to evaluate both basic units and individuals.

## PEER REVIEW

Elements of peer review cannot be avoided in any of the evaluative mechanisms used in higher education. Even performance indicators use data originating from it. For example, data about contracts negotiated and grants received, or the results of citation indices, use data originating in the judgements of peers.

Peer review has long informed the decisions made by central authorities, who use academics to evaluate departments, courses and research proposals; their judgements thus underpin allocative decisions. Peer review in these cases is used summatively, because the object is to make allocative judgements of either resources or status: it is not directed primarily at the formative function of helping basic units or institutions to improve themselves. External examiners, too, are mainly concerned with attesting to standards rather than with providing feedback to the academics whose work they evaluate; although, increasingly, they are expected to make reports to the heads of institutions which may not only be fed back to those concerned but also used to ensure accountability for standards (Reynolds Report, 1986). Perhaps the most comprehensive and sustained system for assessing curriculum and teaching programmes has been that of the CNAA in the polytechnics and colleges.

The operation of peer review goes beyond academic scrutiny by peers from the invisible college of their own subject area. Henkel (1986) notes the extent to which reviewers may fail to display the empathy to be expected from equals in the same field. The assumption that peer review will be subjective, interactive and to some degree formative, is contestable – particularly as such policies as contraction and selectivity will inevitably colour the operation of any form of external review. The extent to which reviewers are or are not colleagues in closely related areas affects their authority. Peer review generally emerges as summative and authoritative, rather than as interactive or in any way 'soft'. Indeed, interactive and formative evaluation may often involve non-academic as well as academic participants. For example, departments or faculties may have visiting committees which, alongside their peers, include employers relevant to the courses of studies offered. These lay members are invited to work with academics in assessing their objectives and outcomes with a view to securing improvement.

As we have noted, it is mistaken to associate peer review too exclusively with the appraisal of individuals. Evaluation is, however, an important aspect of the normative interactions between basic units and their constituent members of staff. In the past comparatively few evaluations occurred in the career of the average UK academic. For the most part, appraisals were confined to initial selection for membership of the unit; the granting of tenured status to recent entrants to the profession; the decision to award some form of approved status (as in cases where an 'efficiency bar' operated for salary increases); and specific proposals for promotion from one level to another.

There were also numerous occasions when some informal – perhaps not even explicit – evaluation of individual strengths and weaknesses was made. Many such evaluations related to the allocation of tasks in either the teaching or the research domain; others involved selection for some activity outside the basic unit (such as an institution-wide committee or some conference involving the wider professional network); others again led to decisions about the granting of special facilities (leaves of absence, secondment, extra resources for research, and the like). The procedures for reaching judgements of this informal kind were seldom constitutionally defined. Their nature depended largely on how any given basic unit was organised: the relationship of the unit with the individual could lie any-where on the range between a collegial appraisal (approximating to the process of wider peer-group assessment) and a hierarchical and authoritarian judgement by the head of the unit.

Moving beyond the basic unit to the wider scholarly community and the external environment, we have already remarked in Chapter 6 on the influence of 'invisible colleges' and special interest groups in certain academic domains. For example, a chemist who is awarded a Fellowship of the Royal Society on the basis of judgement by eminent fellow chemists is thereby certified in the eyes of academia at large to have scaled the higher reaches of his profession. If any doubts existed about his competence on the part of the colleagues in his basic unit, this judgement would be deemed to override them, and even to cast doubt on the academic competence of such colleagues.

More recently, largely on the insistence of the central authorities, annual appraisal of individual performance has become part of the evaluative scene. Appraisal is of research, scholarship and teaching, administration and the capacity to earn external funds. To some extent the evaluations gathered in the course of annual appraisals enter into the judgements on promotions and other forms of preferment, as well as on decisions whether members of staff should be encouraged to take early retirement.

Her Majesty's Inspectors provide a particular form of quasi-peer review, but one whose coverage is limited. Two problems arise from their work within higher education. First, HMIs are drawn mainly from the ranks of competent teachers, few of whom have engaged in research or teaching in research-directed higher education institutions. The range of their subject competence is, moreover, not coterminous with that of higher education. There is thus an issue of competence.

Second, HMIs are bound to take heed of government's assumptions about what is socially useful; in consequence their concerns are as much managerial as professional. In principle, peer review is conducted by those who are amenable to similar evaluation procedures. The same cannot be said of HMIs who possess external authority rather than the authority of being part of the peer system.

HMIs have access to polytechnics and colleges and to teacher training departments in universities to enable them to assess teaching quality. In default of universal coverage by HMI of teaching quality, which would constitute a massive task, various outcome measures have been proposed. The 1987 White Paper (DES, 1987a) suggested that standards could be raised by systematic arrangements for staff training and development, staff appraisal, evaluation of the results achieved (including analysis of external examiners' reports), scrutiny of students' employment patterns, the involvement of professional practitioners in vocational courses, and feedback from students. The universities have followed these suggestions by creating a unit (Committee of Vice-Chancellors and Principals, 1990) to evaluate the procedures by which institutions themselves promote and assess teaching quality.

## SELF-EVALUATION

The self-evaluation of institutions or basic units is generally conceived as being formative and developmental rather than summative and managerial in purpose. The very process of self-scrutiny in terms of identifying goals, considering working methods and analysing present and potential performance is held to enhance self-development and to lead to improvement. Swedish experiments have emphasised that self-evaluation is designed to stimulate critical self-study and that it should not be prescribed or ordered from above (Furumark, 1981). But self-evaluation could also provide information about milieu and context which might then be matched by some form of external judgement. One UK experiment (Sizer and Frost, 1985) tested a procedure enabling departments to develop a profile of research and scholarship. The project was intended to encourage the departments in question to evaluate their own research by keeping an up-to-date record of both the nature of the research and the types of outputs, benefits and impacts it produced. It was found that peer review worked best in relation to particular projects and within a single subject area, rather than at the level of the basic unit as a whole.

It is to the polytechnics and colleges in the UK that we must turn for the strongest examples of institutional self-evaluation. In 1979, the CNAA took note of the growing strength of institutions within its remit and announced a policy of 'partnership in validation'. Validation was to take greater account of the institutional context of courses, the strengths and weaknesses of institutional structures and their bearing on an institution's capacity to take greater responsibility for maintaining academic standards. This led to the growth of internal systems of monitoring and validating courses.

Other proposals for institutional performance assessment (for example, Sizer, 1987a) have sought to assist institutions to be responsive to the needs of a complex and changing society. A portfolio approach has been designed to enable the institution to make clear distinctions between existing and emerging growth areas, consolidation areas, and withdrawal and redeployment areas.

In the USA, institutional evaluation has long been undertaken by state governments, by the voluntary peer-accreditation system, and by the institutions themselves. Stress has been placed (Kells, 1986) on the importance of building consensus within institutions and overcoming the behavioural problems surrounding institutional self-evaluation.

## REVIEW BY STUDENTS

Review by students is more frequently practised and more highly developed in the USA than in the UK. Questionnaires are typically used to record students' judgements of their courses (Miller, 1986). The Reynolds Report (1986) advocated their development in UK institutions.

In Britain, the origins of systematic appraisal of courses by undergraduates, as of many other academic reforms, rest in the radical movement of the late 1960s. At that time, a number of student unions organised 'underground prospectuses', each offering some form of consumers' guide to the courses available in their own institution. These were predictably condemned by the proper authorities as dangerous and irresponsible; but on careful scrutiny, some at least were found to be reasonable, balanced and helpful in advising new applicants (Parlett *et al.*, 1976). The idea eventually gained ground that students – who were among other things expected (and sometimes explicitly trained) to develop sound judgement – were in fact capable of exercising that competence in commenting on their own academic fare.

The case for such critical appraisals of curricula can be supported on grounds of general principle. Even where all the teachers on a given degree programme try carefully to co-ordinate what they are doing (which is by no means a universal practice) they are not able either individually or collectively to know at first hand what the course as a whole comprises. They cannot know this, because each only sees directly that part of the course which he or she teaches. The actuality of what colleagues do has to be inferred indirectly from discussions about syllabus, comments from students and the like. In contrast, the students, individually and collectively, experience all or nearly all the separate components as a complete entity. It is only they – or the rare members of staff who take the role of students and sit in on colleagues' teaching – who are actually in a position to aggregate the components and to say whether they fit together in a sensible and coherent way. On this argument, then, students more than anyone else have the opportunity of assessing whether the degree programme is the meaningful entity which its planners and providers intend it to be.

In the event, judgements of this kind by individual students of the basic unit's curricular provision are collected in a variety of ways – for example, by routine questionnaire on the completion of each course, by detailed interviews of a sample of students each year, or by requests for reflective essays from recent graduates. In most cases the purpose is to inform the basic unit of possible or necessary improvements. The proportion of cases in which the resulting information is acted upon is less easy to determine. Students' judgements are clearly individualistic. They are not normally in a position to compare the courses they have taken with provision on other degree programmes in their own, let alone in another, subject area. Few of them would have the confidence to claim access to a set of external and objective standards in terms of which teaching programmes could be definitively assessed. At best, they can aspire to a personal response to a unique experience.

## DIFFERENT MODES AND MECHANISMS AT DIFFERENT LEVELS

On a commonsense view, the individual academic and the basic unit could best be subjected to self- and peer-evaluation whilst the institution and the system, concerned as they are with aggregates of performance, could best be evaluated by a combination of quantitative measures with qualitative judgements. But in current practice, the classic and autonomous mode jostles with managerialist and market perspectives of government. This has rendered individuals and basic units subject to quantitative measures, especially performance indicators, at the same time as peer review is used summatively to denote research ratings. The evaluation of institutions and of the central authorities remains more patchy and less determined in either mechanism or mode.

Even if changes in government policies were not a complicating factor, evaluation in higher education has always been complex because so many of the key functions are carried out by self-directed individuals called upon to perform multiple and potentially conflicting roles. Those required to act as arbiters will normally have quite other obligations (which seem in certain cases to be inconsistent with, or at odds with, the evaluative function). Many internal examiners are simply course teachers and tutors in a new and temporary guise; equally, those who sit on today's tenure and promotions committees are yesterday's and tomorrow's friends and colleagues. Even at the level of the institution and the central authorities, as the discussion in Chapters 4 and 5 makes plain, individual academics are co-opted to help reach decisions which may affect colleagues in their own basic units, whether for better or for worse. The requirement for some academics (and especially the more senior, experienced and established ones) to adopt a series of different roles at different levels in the system is an inevitable consequence of the high value placed on specialised academic knowledge in this context, as opposed to many other areas of public policy. It means that a straightforwardly hierarchical system of management, with evaluative decisions flowing from the centre through the institutional elements to the individual, is in conflict with the operational assumptions of the academic world.

Taking the multiple evaluations of individuals first, the new emphasis on managerial appraisal accords with general demands for efficiency in higher education which are themselves related to the notion that what is 'productive' about the individual is also efficient. The use of indicators represents a shift from the power of the invisible college, which tends to be more concerned with individual quality, to the power of management, which has been compelled by the centre to regard productivity as the norm. By creating data about individuals in partly quantifiable or ordinal rating form the system has moved from the academic to the administrative and managerial elements within institutions. Performance Indicators (PIs) have been described as 'a substitute for trust' (Trow, 1989). They can be identified with broader concerns about the social audit of academe in terms of not only its academic task but also its responsiveness to access and labour market pressures. Miller (1986) draws attention to the dangers: judgements can be acted on too hastily; it seems wrong to subordinate individualistic activity to evaluative formulas; excessive reliance on quantification can be detrimental.

Many institutions claim to use individual evaluation for staff development rather than for managerial purposes. In practice, however, it seems difficult to dissociate the two in a climate in which the emphasis is laid on performance as the way to institutional and individual rewards.

Before the specific evaluative systems of the 1980s were installed, basic units were already subject to several forms of external evaluation. The funding bodies (UGC and NAB) made judgements through specialist visiting committees which contributed, at least at the general level, to decisions about funding. The CNAA made explicit judgements on the quality of course design. These were essentially peer judgements, although the numbers of students recruited and their level of entry qualification were quantitative elements brought into the evaluation.

The 1981 and 1986 UGC exercises were vigorously criticised (for example, Kogan and Kogan, 1983, and Smith, 1987) on the grounds that the peer-review process was incompetently administered and the quantitative criteria haphazard or inappropriate. The funding bodies have since created more comprehensive forms of review, to include both summative peer judgement and more carefully worked out performance indicators.

More complex considerations apply to the evaluation of institutions. For the most part, the 'outcomes' of higher education are attributed to the individuals who undertake research and scholarship, and the basic units who provide the corporate base for these activities. It is their products that have to meet the criteria against which institutions as a whole can be judged and which legitimise the placing of the institution within the hierarchy of esteem. It would be virtually unthinkable to conceive of a 'good' institution in which its main constituents are 'bad'.

Inasmuch as an institution can be evaluated, the criteria will be second order and not directed primarily to the basic tasks of higher education. For example, an institution can encourage, discourage or perhaps even require the basic units to adopt particular policies on access for different groups of students within the community, or to divert attention from traditional functions of research and scholarship towards more market-orientated activities (profitable short courses and consultancies, for example), or to ensure that their curriculum is infused with the spirit of enterprise and conditioned by close attention to the views of employers. It would be possible for external bodies such as the PCFC or the UFC to attempt to see how far the institution has sponsored such policies and to assess the extent to which it is successful in persuading or otherwise guiding basic units to adopt them. Nearer higher education's main tasks is the requirement that institutions will operate procedures for the judgement of teaching quality. Some of the criteria are susceptible to quantitative evaluation – the first destinations of students, for example, or the proportions of drop-outs.

Other aspects of evaluation, more explicitly concerned with the institution as such and the quality of its management, are less easy to capture, and for a simple reason: administrative performance measures have proved difficult to assemble because the 'outcome' of administration is little over and above the outcomes of the academic activities of a higher education institution (Seldin, 1988). Tracing the connection between administrative activity and academic outcomes would be a difficult and artificial task. However, it is clearly possible to determine administrative costs as a ratio of the whole range of costs of an institution. No doubt it would also be possible (but would prove difficult) to establish criteria for administrative performance such as the quality of academic plans produced by an institution; we have remarked on how the UGC has passed judgement on universities' reports on their research selectivity exercises.

If the different levels in the institution are thus subject to different evaluative modes and mechanisms, and if, indeed, each level might be evaluated in more than one way, there is a problem of aggregation. Judgements cannot be competently added together to produce a holistic assessment.

The evaluation of the central authorities is even less well developed. In constitutional theory, the central authorities are accountable to Parliament and its institutions: the Public Accounts Committee, the Specialist Committees, Parliamentary Questions and debates should ensure that policy is devised and administered under critical gaze. Government departments are subject to review in particular cases and on specific issues by the Parliamentary Commissioner and the National Audit Office. Individual civil servants operate under rigorous evaluation by their superiors. The central intermediary bodies can be disbanded if they fail to meet ministerial wishes. But, taken as a whole, the central authorities are required to face only sporadic and non-analytic critique of their actions, from the press and some academic groups who may hold them up to scrutiny.

## THE NATURE OF ACCOUNTABILITY

If evaluation involves the making of judgements about performance or behaviour, accountability entails using such judgements for the allocation of rewards or punishment or resources.

Although evaluation and accountability are closely interrelated, the relationship is not symmetrical. That is to say, accountability presupposes evaluation but evaluation does not necessarily imply accountability. It would be not merely odd but positively unacceptable to hold individuals or institutions to account for what they have done or failed to do without first trying to make an informed judgement of the merits of their performance. But it is quite common to make judgements of performance which are not then used to call individuals, or basic units, or institutions, or the system as a whole, to account. The differences lie in the degree and type of authority imputed to the evaluation.

The notion of accountability entails some procedure for action in relation to those who are judged to have fallen below acceptable standards, a matter which has been the subject of concern in both UK sectors (Lindop Report, 1985; Reynolds Report, 1986). It may be seen as a means of translating the results of an evaluation process into practical effect – perhaps by refusing approval or recognition, perhaps by withholding resources or changing the conditions of their availability, or possibly by making public the relevant details about inadequate performance (Becher and Maclure, 1978; Kogan, 1988).

In describing modes of evaluation in higher education we have shown how the central authorities, mainly through the operation of their intermediaries, make judgements of institutions and units through a variety of mechanisms ranging from the use of performance indicators through peer review to the use of inspectorates. The institutions evaluate the procedures and outcomes of the basic units which themselves have varying control over the standards of their members.

These evaluations then convert themselves into the operational domain in which the different levels, taking account of social, economic and cultural demands and requirements, consider how best to optimise the resources available to the system and thence to sponsor developments. Thus the central authorities allocate the power to provide courses and give funding for them. Institutions maintain themselves, engage in forward planning and allocate budgets to units and programmes. And the basic units provide places for students and programme teaching and research through the allocation of individual tasks.

## MODES OF ACCOUNTABILITY

There are several potentially conflicting modes of accountability. In education in general, we can identify (Kogan, 1988) the public contractual and managerial mode which informs different levels of government; the professional mode in which the academic collegia and hierarchies operate; and the consumerist modes of accountability in which different proxies for a market are present. In the 1980s higher education became subject to all three. In the managerial mode different levels are held together by the strongest form of relationship; namely, that of subordinates to superiors. Subsystems are committed to the pursuit of collective objectives set down for the system by the centre. Performance is rewarded and punished according to the degree of success in achieving the collective goals. Such a system seems remote from the tradition of higher education in western Europe, but it is not absent from the higher education of totalitarian systems or from those areas of training and education in which technical and disciplinary conformity obtains – for example, in training for the military, the police or, to a lesser extent, nursing. In such cases, there is assumed to be no conflict of value, a high degree of conformity about requisite technical content, and a clear programme of tasks that must be performed, albeit with differences over the priorities to be allocated to some of them.

An ambiguity in usage should here be noted. We have just described a model of accountability in which the values of managerial structure and power are strong. But this should not be confused with the more neutral connotations of 'management', which is essential to the good working of any form of organisation, and which concerns the organisation and pro-gramming of the use of resources in terms of agreed goals. Management in this sense need incorporate no judgment about who determines the goals.

The second mode, professional accountability, assumes that the practi-tioners set the standards; that exogenous criteria are subservient to those of inherent quality and to the ability to adapt expert knowledge to the indiv-idual nature of the task to be performed. Thus medical practitioners have freedom to prescribe almost entirely according to their sense of what the patient needs. Equally, the academic satisfies autonomous normative cri-teria in teaching methods and content and in formulating and carrying out a research programme. In some respects, the more strikingly individual the academic performance, the more highly rated the individual academic might be.

In the professional mode of accountability, there is regard only for second-order objectives concerned with observing due academic process, standards of integrity in the achievement and presentation of scientific results, and relationships with students. The perceived problem of pro-fessional accountability is that it lacks deference to social and public needs, and a machinery for establishing them. Not surprisingly, professional accountability has been linked with modes of self-evaluation (for example, Sockett, 1976).

The third model, the consumerist, has been scarcely discernible until recently in higher education in most countries except the USA. It assumes that the Welfare State model of provision for higher education is not sufficient to ensure good performance and an adequate return on resources to those who fund its activities. Whereas the Welfare State model embodied the view that the academic enterprise produced undisputed benefits and should be funded accordingly, the consumerist or market model insists that academics must demonstrate their utility to society by placing themselves on an open market. They must accordingly compete for students whose fees will provide the bulk of that core funding which until recently was given as a deficiency grant by the central authorities. Similarly, if academic research is worthwhile, it can stand up in a more rigorous competition for the limited funds made available by research councils or, because of its 'strategic' quality, will be funded for its utilitarian worth. The good institution will be entrepreneurial and will, perforce, have its objectives set not by the academy alone, nor by central government, but by the negotiations and quid pro quos set in a competition which is fed by public funds but which operates as a market.

## MECHANISMS OF ACCOUNTABILITY

If the modes of accountability are managerial, consumerist and professional they may be related to mechanisms of hierarchy, the market and the collegium.

Hierarchy has been defined as a mechanism for distributing responsibility for work according to capacity, and this gives a clue to the difficulty of applying it to the more important working relationships in higher education. Stratification into a multilevel hierarchy is an improbable mechanism when individual quality and accountability for it are the key assumptions. The ablest workers are to be found practising their art aside from, or at the bottom of, structures designed to deal with the non-academic aspects of higher education's functioning. Similarly, the powerful institutions making up the higher education system more plausibly form part of a polyarchy (Dahl, 1971) than a hierarchy.

As we have noted in Chapter 5, hierarchy is present in higher education. The non-academic sides of institutions are headed by managers with their own hierarchies. Heads of basic units have always operated with different degrees of managerial power, which may include the distribution of resources and work, and making recommendations on promotion or leave.

The mechanisms of the market are not of themselves incompatible with either hierarchy or collegium, although their explicit introduction may lead to distinctive behaviour. If hierarchy gives authority to cause others to behave in particular ways by virtue of structural position, the market creates inducements to act by virtue of rewards, usually of resources. The market has a double meaning in higher education. In the first meaning, basic units and individuals have services to sell; short courses, consultancy and research, market-related degree programmes and the like. Money might also be earned by recruiting more students, a process to be encouraged by the bidding procedures installed in the 1990s. A secondary sense is that in which reputation is the currency operating in a non-monetary market. It is generated by good performance and may be transmuted into real resources because it is those with good reputations who get the most resources and the best jobs.

Finally, there is the collegium. A collegium is a non-hierarchical structure whose members convene for the minimal purposes of admitting newcomers, of maintaining admission and membership standards and of making decisions about the use of collegial resources. It invites maximum individual autonomy and in this respect is different from a collective, which assumes shared objectives.

## ACCOUNTABILITY IN PRACTICE

The three modes of accountability coexist. Central government may set down, virtually in a managerial mode, explicit objectives for funding councils. The central authorities also require institutions to set up managerial modes in which individual academics will be in line hierarchy with heads of departments, deans and heads of institutions under councils and boards of governors which are to emulate as closely as possible the model of the commercial board of directors. The central authorities may interact with institutions through relationships deemed to be contractual or market-led, in the sense that specific returns are required for specific allocations of resources. They also, however, support normative judgements of quality through performance measures and systematic peer review.

At the same time as the managerial joins the professional approach to governance, the insistence on consumerism and its power to correct weakness and reinforce strength becomes strong. These mixed economies of higher education are not special to the UK alone. They are being promoted in, for example, Holland and West Germany (van Vught, 1988; Frackmann, 1987).

What might be the impact of these different modes on the individual teacher, a level of the system almost wholly ignored in the flow of prescriptive literature (for example, Jarratt Report, 1985, and Croham, 1987), which has conveyed the new dispensations to higher education institutions? The typical academic has been acculturated to respect a combination of individualism with deference to the growing knowledge and testing procedures of his or her subject field. Deference to the tradition of a discipline and immersion in its knowledge are the basic qualifying requirements for admission to the academic profession; the display of creativity, critique and originality distinguishes the able academic from the merely competent one. Such an individual has not been encouraged to pursue material rewards in the form of institutional power or a high salary, but rather to seek reputation in the larger and cosmopolitan world of academia.

An emphasis on the formulation of shared objectives through academic plans and the like, and on deference to market forces, serves to complicate the accountability of the academic. At one time it would have been the quality of research and scholarship, and to a lesser extent of teaching, that mattered. In the present climate, performance as an administrator and as a money earner must be taken into account, and not only in the more vulnerable institutions. Academics have therefore to consider carefully the opportunity costs of everything they do. The accountability is both more explicit and more diffuse than before.

## RESOURCE ALLOCATION

Finally, it remains to link evaluation and accountability with resource allocation. At this point it will be appropriate to remind ourselves of the connections between them. In our model, evaluation links the levels of the system as it operates in its normative mode. The judgements then made may be used – but we have stressed that not all evaluations are so used – for two main purposes. In the one case evaluation will be the basis on which accountability may be exacted. In the other case evaluation will provide the judgemental data upon which allocations of resources or status may be made. It is such allocations which provide the horizontal links between the different levels in the operational mode.

The central authorities seek to optimise the use of public resources and to sponsor appropriate developments by allocating funds and by distributing courses and other activities to institutions. The institutions allocate resources and programmes to basic units – and so on through the system (Morris and Sizer, 1982; Shattock and Rigby, 1983). In each case there is an evaluation, whether explicit or not, of the likely performance of those receiving the allocation, and they will subsequently be held to account for its use.

The modes of resource allocation can be typified as rational, internal market, external market and political. To allocate rationally would mean to determine the ends of resource use and then to specify appropriate means. The determination of ends, or goals or objectives would entail making an a priori judgement about the preferred scope of activities and would thus require holistic or synoptic planning. Such is the intention behind requiring each institution to submit an academic plan, with annual updating. On the basis of these plans, the assumption is that the central authorities are able to see whether institutions and their components will meet the social and economic expectations and demands which the allocations are intended to satisfy.

The essential difficulty of the rational model is that premier academic work is individually rather than socially driven, and that where individuals are capable of stating objectives with any predictive force these are virtually impossible to aggregate, except in shopping-list form, let alone to put into a meaningful plan. Institutions and basic units have been required by the UGC and UFC to submit research plans. These may be effective in causing some individuals and units to state more explicitly what they intend to do. They are, however, unlikely to be meaningful blueprints of further action.

Yet academics cannot survive in a weight-free and solipsistic universe. They seek and receive resources as the result of a process that is institutional and social. For the most part they have operated in a private, non-monetary academic market. The bulk of the resources have come to institutions *en bloc*, as the result of largely reputational judgements made by the central authorities. Both between the central authorities and the institutions, and within institutions, there has then been an internal market in which the currency of academic reputation is encashed for real resources in terms of staffing, buildings, equipment and money.

As we have already observed in discussing the mechanisms for accountability, the external market, in which academics offer services in return for resources, is proposed as a key mechanism which will make them more responsive to social needs and enable the more active entrepreneurs to secure freedom through fund-raising. In such a system allocations are likely to follow success in this regard: allocating bodies will then have to determine how to combine the rational, internal and external market mechanisms into a convincing whole. The operation of the market is likely to reduce allocative bodies' power, as is the government's intention.

Finally, the political model of allocation also remains important, although increasingly supplanted by both the rational and the external market. It is not antithetical to the notion of the academically determined internal market, but as described by Baldridge and others (1978), assumes that academics make alliances and seek support from one another. The system within which these activities take place is seen primarily as a micro-polity, in which persuasion, promises and threats have their place. In making alliances, academic reputations as well as the ability to bargain about resources or to create consensus will be part of the exchange process. The political pressures may become regularised into accepted procedures and constitutional structures.

## MULTIPLE FRAMES

To establish how each of these patterns operates at the different levels, we must begin by noting that several allocative, evaluative and accountability models are now in contention. The central authorities continue to act in a primarily political mode in which both normative and operational procedures are determined by what is seen as acceptable to the distant electorate or the closer centres of political power. They none the less increasingly use the language of the rational mode. At other levels all modes of accountability are in contention. The institutions and basic units do their best to steer between them, wondering, for example, whether to go for success in the external market or to continue to assert the need for academic distinction. The individual academic, too, is uncertain about which behaviour will produce the most favourable allocation, although, for the most part, academic reputation remains the prime reward, and the internal market the battle ground on which it is won or lost.

# 10 Managerialism and the market

## THE MODEL REVISITED

In this final chapter, we consider the changing balance between the components of the model. In doing so, we remain confident that the model itself is a usable heuristic device: in particular, connections between the normative and the operational modes of working as they evince themselves at, and between, the different levels seem to be permanent characteristics of the higher education system, as do the evaluative and allocative links between the levels.

The substantive components of each level of the system, too, remain stable; but their historical setting has changed to a degree that could hardly have been predicted even a decade ago. If the basic unit remains paramount in any reasoned description of how higher education can and should work, government has done its best to ensure that both the market and the strengthening of management objectives will more confidently challenge the power of the professional academic at the base of the system. This has in recent years been a policy applied to all professions.

In Chapter 1 we contrasted mass systems, associated with strong central control, with universal systems governed primarily by market considerations. The review in Chapter 3 of the evolution of higher education in Great Britain noted how strongly the 'command model' of centralised direction and planning had insinuated itself towards the end of the 1980s, and how this was advanced against the still strong elements of academic autonomy. But quite quickly there were signs that the centralist phase had begun to give way to a very different policy approach, based on the predominance of market modes over managerial planning.

There has always existed, in the field of higher education, as in other areas of public policy, tension between organic growth and imposed radical change; examples of their interplay were cited in Chapter 3 and explored further in Chapter 8. The recent emphasis on management and accountability in the British system is not an unprecedented phenomenon. Similar trends can be seen in other contemporary systems, each responding to their different contexts. Thus both the Dutch (van Vught, 1988) and the West German (Frackmann, 1987) systems have moved from detailed control by the state to the assumed disciplines of the market, whereas British higher education has developed from an emphasis on largely autonomous institutions operating in the internal academic market through a phase of strong central management and only subsequently onto the external market.

At any one time there will be tension and accommodation, too, between social norms as voiced, or at least interpreted most directly, by central government, and academic values as represented by self-determining institutions, basic units and individuals. But there are cycles of dominance: one approach gains ascendancy for a time over the other, and there are transitional states when the two are in uneasy coexistence. Boundaries are continuously changing and being negotiated. Britain's higher education system was in such a transitional state as it moved into the last decade of the twentieth century.

There is a quadrilateral of interests, each emphasising their own value positions, with which higher education must negotiate, and within which it must find its own path. One group of values is professional and derives from academic norms and aspirations. Another is governmental and is concerned with the demands of the state, which can range in different times from those of theocracy to those of the economy. A third is that of the market as it seeks particular skills in its workforce and particular forms of knowledge for conversion into wealth production. And, finally, there is that of public and social utility at large, whose interests may lie both in increased educational opportunities and in the maintenance and enhancement of a civilised society.

Such forces, pushing and pulling as they do in most forms of public policy, are further elaborated by changes in the very content of higher education. The explosion of knowledge and the ways of packaging and conveying it have caused any brief monopoly of learning that higher education enjoyed to be diffused and complicated into a knowledge polyarchy within which the universities and polytechnics may as easily follow as lead the developments made in a particular field.

## PROFESSIONAL VALUES

The classic and autonomous ideal of the government of higher education is one which has never been fully realised in any but a few prestigious universities, let alone in the whole range of British higher education institutions. We have associated it with the small and elite system that obtained before the large expansion of higher education in the 1960s. Its components, however, still remain recognisable and are regarded by many academics as denoting a value system and pattern of behaviour conducive to the most prized outcomes of higher education.

The beau ideal was that of the self-governing institution. An essential prerequisite of self-governance was independence from resource constraints. Before the ending of the quinquennial grant system in the early 1970s, the universities were virtually free from financial pressure; the polytechnics, too, though on far shorter rations, were increasingly moving towards independence from local authorities, whose grip was in any case weakened by the operation of the national pooling system. Either through the guarantee of grants by a benevolent state, or through private endowment, or both, the autonomous institution could set its own objectives and create its own programmes of research, scholarship, teaching and relationships with the outside world.

The autonomy was made legitimate because it seemed consistent with the nature of the higher education task. In its purest form, higher education was there to ensure the generation of knowledge which was essentially a pursuit for individuals, even when they worked in quite large teams. And the more individualistic, indeed the more deviant at a certain level, the more the academic could test received knowledge and create more and better of the same. There was, therefore, what has earlier been referred to as a socio-technological defence of these values. Social or organisational arrangements were predicated upon assumptions about the nature of the task to be performed.

In this conception, it is hardly appropriate to talk about the setting of objectives other than in terms of the inner psyche, or at most in terms of a limited set of role expectations. The motive force is not that of pre-stated social consideration, but rather that of the disinterested and often unpredictable pursuit of the truth. It follows that the unit which makes decisions about what to do is not the state, even if it gives the money. It is not the institution, even if it protects and enables the academic to keep at work. Authority is not imposed by hierarchy working through managerial systems. It is modelled on Polanyi's 'Republic of Science' (1962), in which rules of knowledge and their application and testing contribute towards a science which is both coherent and pluralist. Exchanges are made, and the values placed upon the exchanges are derived from the quality of the work. Authority derived from society and the market is a weaker value.

In its purest form, the organisational basis of this model is, therefore, not managerial but collegial. Managerial hierarchies maximise collective force through stratifying power and authority according to assumed function and ability. By contrast, the collegium is a minimum organisation convening itself to admit new members, to establish minimum standards, usually through its admission rules, and to apportion the common resources. The strongest academic institutions do not require shared objectives or common working patterns. Their members act collectively when they have to and compensate, perhaps, for their displays of autonomy by eating together and joining together in occasional rituals.

In Britain important components of this value system have persisted, but on a steep sliding scale according to the status of the institution. During the great period of expansion it was allowed to run because it was assumed that the interests of society and of the academy coincided. The academy was trusted to educate and train a functioning elite and to deliver the knowledge that would sustain the economy and society at large. It, too, could read off social needs as well as people in Whitehall or in industry, but it treated social imperatives on its own terms. That serendipitous notion of convergence became weaker as higher education failed to convince governments of its undisputed claim to do good by doing what academics wanted to do.

## THE VALUES OF MANAGEMENT

The traditional ideology of autonomy may be contrasted with that of accountable management. Whilst many, of the shining examples of development in higher education depended on securing freedom from government, many, too, have been quite strongly dependent on state initiation or support; such examples include the *grande écôle* in France and the Humboldtian university in Prussia.

Management values in higher education are thus not intrinsically hostile to professional values. A particular strand of governmental ideology, however – that which promotes such values above those of the academic enterprise which management is meant to serve – is in conflict with academic norms. In examining the ways in which higher education governance has undergone change it will be necessary to remind ourselves of those constituents of the management–governmental corner of the quadrilateral which are essential to the good running of higher education systems and institutions before noting the pathological obtrusion of management values that can be called the managerialist ideology.

In Chapter 5 we outlined the essential tasks of institutional management. One main element is to hold the institution together through the maintenance of common rules and procedures. A second is to find and account for resources. A further task is the development of the overall portfolio of the institution. Before facing the question of who should control the management it will be appropriate to see what these functions involve, in terms of both their value and their operating content.

First, management concerns the creation and administration of collective rules. For example, academics determine criteria for student admission and for assessment, but the rules must be consistently administered across the institution and contracts made and kept. Rules cannot be individualistic but, by definition, are collective. They thus embody values of control and coherence.

Second, the getting, spending and accounting for the institution's resources require negotiation with funding bodies, the creation of procedures for their distribution to cost centres and the maintenance of systems that pay out and account for spending. Accountability is a strong value component here.

Institutional development is a function in which contending values may emerge. Academics may start an individual process of development, but the development of the portfolio of the whole institution is a management task. The stronger the basic units, the stronger the need to set the development within the wider framework of the equitable allocation of resources, fairness between competing constituents and concern for those interests which the institution is not yet meeting. The leadership of the institution must also take a view of what activities might be allowed to disappear and what might replace them.

Financial control and rule setting, and planning in a developmental sense, are thus key elements of the task of institutional management. They have their own value base: they are concerned with systems maintenance on the lines of equity and probity and constitutionality – a respect for evenhandedness and due process.

Other tasks that fall to management, and which are hardly the concern of the academics and the basic units, include the maintenance of the physical arrangements: buildings and catering, residential accommodation, the provision for student lettings and the like. But from our point of view, the key functions of management are those whose control might be contested between professional administrators and academic staff.

The setting of the curriculum, of the research agenda, of the appropriate forms of academic activity are plainly decisions that belong to the basic units and individuals. Institutional leaders and administrators can reasonably criticise and seek to influence courses and research plans which seem inadequate or capable of improvement. But if they attempt to dominate decision-making on those core issues they risk producing the mediocrity that comes from compliance. In aggregate the basic unit's decisions constitute the mission which institutions are increasingly required to make explicit.

Management is a second-order set of activities, but an important pre-requisite to the successful achievement of institutional purposes – and indeed an essential adjunct to good academic work. In contrast, managerialism in higher education attempts to pre-empt the process of academic decision-making. It assumes that the institution and the system to which it becomes subordinate can specify objectives under which those of the basic units can be subsumed. A non-managerialist approach will concern itself rather with general goals – with reaching consensual understandings of a broad framework of priorities – than with laying down prescriptions.

The Jarratt Report (1985) attempted to promote management into a self-justifying activity and allowed that it might take on imperatives of its own – with the implication that they could be endorsed separately from higher education's primary objectives, and could be distributed hierarchically. As we saw in Chapter 6, the Report complained about 'large and powerful academic departments together with individual academics who sometimes see their academic discipline as more important than the long-term well-being of the university which houses them', and put its weight behind universities as corporate enterprises to which the component units and individuals should be subordinate.

The alternative view, seriously held at other times and in other places, is that the institution is important insofar as it promotes and ensures the quality of work of the academics in its membership; that the essentials of such work must count for more than those of overarching policy-making, which only takes on meaning and outcome in terms of individual academic activity.

The Jarratt Report, translating the (admittedly idealised) role of the vice-chancellor as leading scholar and *primus inter pares* into 'the style of Chief Executive', reinforces this by identifying the head of department as holding a 'middle management' role. His or her duties, responsibilities and reporting lines are to be made clear. But there is no corresponding analysis of duties at the primary production level of individual teachers and researchers. No picture is given of what they are supposed to do, apart from having to be accountable and to fulfil the institution's purpose.

It is a curiosity that the corresponding document for the polytechnics and colleges, issued two years after Jarratt (NAB, 1987), adopts a different tone. One might have expected, since most of the institutions had their origins in the more hierarchical milieu of colleges of education, further education and technology, that the message of triumphal managerialism would have been at least as firmly enunciated. But instead, the National Advisory Body's Good Management Practice Group (NAB, 1987) were clear in their assertion that 'people work best if they are not only committed to what they are doing but also have control over the resources and activities involved'. (There are interesting echoes here of Edmund Burke's widely quoted dictum that 'to be attached to the sub-division, to love the little platoon we belong to in society, is the first principle of public affections'.)

Perhaps it is only to be expected that, despite some strongly coercive measures subsequently adopted by the central authorities (and notably the UGC itself) to ensure that universities should implement the Jarratt proposals in full, the evidence that they have done so remains patchy and open to debate. There may be some vice-chancellors alongside some polytechnic directors and college principals who have eagerly embraced the Chief Executive concept, and some senior career administrators who have, under the Report's dispensation, taken to themselves decision-making powers in excess of those normally accorded to those working in professionally rather than commercially or bureaucratically dominated institutions. But there still appear to be many who, despite a prudent level of lip-service to the simplistic rationalism of the Jarratt doctrines, have managed to maintain a more traditional balance between central and individual initiatives in the framing of purposes and the allocation of tasks.

The Jarratt Committee commented adversely on the fact that university objectives and aims were defined only in very broad terms. This failed to acknowledge that higher education is essentially concerned with the development and transmission of specialist knowledge at the expert level. It addresses problems spanning a range of human experience too vast for holistic objectives usefully to cover. Knowledge creation is primarily individualistic or even idiosyncratic rather than collective in its nature.

Two issues are provoked by managerialism along these lines. The first is the nature of objectives setting, and the second the ownership of the institution and its management. The objectives issue is whether higher education's tasks should be derived from broad aims which must then be disaggregated into academic activities, or whether the institution should, rather, see itself as advancing multiple states of knowledge generation and dissemination, within a broadly indicative frame of social objectives. In some societies, objectives imposed by the economy and government might be necessary. A country with no tradition of higher education, for example, may need, or be able to afford, no more than to train its elites and provide rudimentary applied research for the economy. But that is unlikely to apply to a developed country. Even if the institution takes the lead in setting objectives, that still leaves over the question of which actors are the institution for this purpose. Objectives might be set through consensus rather than by the unilateral action of the institutional leadership.

The Croham review of the University Grants Committee (Croham, 1987) was in line with Jarratt in its implication that academic outcomes ought to be determined and judged in terms of social rather than intellectual criteria. Its recommendations on membership of the funding body reinforced higher education's role as part of the economic machine. It represented the question of who should run the institution – the academics or the leadership and its management group – as primarily a matter of political choice.

## MARKET VALUES

The managerialist movement symbolised by Jarratt could be represented as no more than a passing phase, another in the series of administrative fashions which come and go with reassuring regularity. For hard on its heels could be discerned the emergence of a very different set of strategies, those of the market, strongly promoted by a radically right-wing government.

Some contrasting ingredients of the market and of managerialism are displayed in Table 10.1. Market values underpin two distinct modes of operation. A 'market' run by the funding bodies will require institutions to bid for allocations, at what they must estimate to be competitive prices. In the more familiar usage of market operations, however, institutions will secure funds by selling their services, including undergraduate teaching and research, on an open market. Both market modes are designed to privatise what some would consider an over-protected sector of public activity and to force its activities into open commercial competition. The motivation to do so might have been political in its origins, but the formal justification rested on social and economic arguments. Developments in the labour market, fuelled by the growth of high technology, were creating new needs and opportunities for highly educated manpower, of a kind which higher education existed to provide. There was therefore a strong economic case – leaving aside any more nebulous arguments in support of social equity – for a further rapid expansion in graduate output. The costs of such expansion could not, without unacceptable rises in the levels of government expenditure, be met from the public purse. Some level of privatisation must be the inevitable solution. The system must be broken of its heavy dependence on taxpayers' money, and forced to sell itself to its immediate clients, the intending students and the employers of graduates.

The notion that higher education should be subject to market forces has several distinguishable elements. There is the recurrent demand that it should be relevant and well tuned to the needs of the economy. As noted earlier, this is separate from two other linked propositions, that institutions should vigorously market their wares on priced market lines and that they should act as entrepreneurs within a market created artificially by funding councils for students and other providers of resources.

*Table 10.1* Managerial and market rhetorics

| Managerial (planned) | Market (competitive) |
| --- | --- |
| 'European' control model | 'American' consumerist model |
| Central authority as holding company | Central authority as merchant bank |
| Comparability and 'gold standard' degrees | Contrast and 'ecological niches' |
| Institutional accountability and central planning | Financial frameworks and market forces |
| Subject numbers determined by national need (manpower planning) | Subject numbers determined by (rigged?) consumer choice |
| Student grants | Sponsorship, loans |
| Standard, specified fees | Locally and subject differentiated fees |
| Uniform salary scales | Performance-related individual pay bargaining |
| Formula funding (includes research base) | Competitive bidding (teaching and research separately funded) |
| Critical size, economies of scale Concentration, selectivity Mergers and closures Subject reviews | Natural selection, survival of the fittest |
| Quality control and departmental grading | Quality assurance and self-accreditation |
| Managerial hierarchy and institutional control of finance | Departmental autonomy and devolved budgeting |
| Forward planning and objectives | Entrepreneurialism and serendipity (with mission statements) |
| Management | Leadership |

The connection between higher education and the economy, whether or not it is reinforced by government action, has many positive elements which might be occluded by enforced relationships. Private industry and commerce may provide the testing ground for the knowledge produced by institutions. It may take the lead in producing the knowledge that is needed to solve its own problems. In such areas higher education follows industry rather than the other way round, and must make sure that the knowledge and skills which it hands on are somebody else's state of the art. This has long been so in such areas of public sector training as medicine, teaching and social work.

The assumption that higher education should behave entrepreneurially is not intrinsically antipathetic to academics. Within the system itself, as the discussion in Chapter 9 has indicated, there has always been a strong internal market, and something of an external one as well. Although the currency has not hitherto been one of money, but of reputation, there has always been a place for the individual entrepreneur. The element of competition is endemic in the system: students compete to get the best degree results; individuals jostle with one another to get the largest grants, solve the most significant problems, produce the best or most prolific publications, win the most prestigious chairs and earn the most coveted honours. Even in relation to the outside world, which has no part in the internal battles, there is a discernible strand of competitiveness. Professional notoriety, or the grudging envy of colleagues, accompanies the high public visibility of those academics who write best-selling popular works, or who display their talents to a wider audience through their appearance on television or more generally in the media.

The competitive urge is not confined to the level of the individual. Basic units contend vigorously with their rivals in the same field, and with their neighbours in the same institution, to win greater prestige, recruit better-qualified staff and students, and earn the most resources. Institutions, in more or less subtle ways, continue to promote their own standing at the expense of others. The university sector and the polytechnics and colleges do battle for the largest share of political favour and public esteem.

What most clearly differentiates the market emphasis of the 1990s from that of the 1980s and before is its implication that the predominant values must be set by the customers rather than by those who generate the goals. There is no such thing as a free market in higher education or anywhere else: any market is bound to be rigged to a greater or lesser extent. The question then arises of who will do the rigging. The main contenders must be the academics, the government as the surrogate for the wider society, and the clients – that is, the students and their eventual employers. Each has a part to play in creating both supply and demand, and each can put a price on the products once the planned economy approach to costing gives way to market forms of pricing.

Until recently, it could be argued, the suppliers, the academics, have been able to assume a fixed price, fixed profit system in which the other parties have had no say, except inasmuch as government might have somewhat tentatively challenged the arithmetic. Because the bulk of resources came by way of deficiency grants, institutions were not under pressure to charge full costs, let alone to make true profits. Operations in the free market were marginal and brought in marginal resources. Under such circumstances it was alleged that there was insufficient regard to the needs of the economy for certain kinds of skills; and further, that applied research and development suffered because the abler academics engaged in more prestigious but less 'useful' theoretical research which none the less continued to be funded by the public purse. To open the academy to market forces would be to provide a stimulating challenge to the more traditional academic reward system.

Free market assumptions have been held to suffer from two principal faults. The first is the objection of potential sponsors, particularly in the private sector, to providing resources for work which they believe should be supported from the taxation they already pay. This has been the response of industry to attempts to enforce payment for any but the most directly appropriate research and development.

Employers, if they have acute needs for graduate labour, may be persuaded to enter sponsorship arrangements for certain categories of student. Such arrangements cannot, however, be expected to account for a very substantial proportion of the student population, given that more narrowly focused in-house vocational training is likely in many cases to be a more attractive economic proposition.

The second objection is based on the nature of work in higher education. It is maintained that good research and teaching require continuity, and therefore a degree of institutional protection from the episodic demands that might be made by sponsors with specific and time-limited needs. Moreover, the needs of the economy, as represented by those who might be able to afford to sponsor research or teaching, are not isomorphic to the whole range of work that constitutes a good higher education system, incorporating as it does the humanities, the critical social sciences and the theoretical bases of science and technology.

## SOCIAL UTILITY

The fourth value position set up by higher education can be associated with concepts of social utility and the doctrines of the post-war Welfare State. (Our four value positions constitute two linked pairs: the concepts of professional and management control are about governance; the concepts of market and welfarism are concerned with the destination of ultimate outcomes.) Such an approach is concerned with advancing such values as citizens' rights, equality, participation, and social and not simply economic usefulness. In principle, it need not be in opposition to professional values; its advent in such schemes as those following the Swedish U68 reforms coincided with a growth of management, if only because it entailed an enlarged system, but its priorities are somewhat different from either. It would be vigorously opposed to market principles which emphasise outputs and de-emphasise socially determined objectives and processes.

The social utility perspective of higher education contains several linked premises, and these have dominated the post-war expansion of higher education in western Europe and the USA. The first is that the state has a responsibility for furnishing the economy with trained and qualified human resources, and that this burden is not to be handed over to particular economic or social interests for its fulfilment. In so doing, it is likely to advance a broad rather than narrow view of what the economy needs, which would certainly include the human resource needs of the public service. This would be a driving force behind wider access policies, the advancement of continuing education and the opening up of higher education facilities for non-specialist and cultural activities. Second, it addresses citizens' rights to individual self-development and employment to the highest possible level, without hindrance due to inability to fund their own higher education. Third, it looks to higher education to help develop the sense of community and social cohesion which might result from a wider diffusion of the common culture and of shared moral and social beliefs.

This value position – which is emphasised differently according to political and social affiliations – is the justification for deficiency funding through which the state makes up the shortfall between what higher education can earn and what it needs to meet objectives which go beyond those advanced by the market.

## PRESERVING THE ACADEMIC CORE

All these approaches accept the premises that higher education is required to advance knowledge and understanding and to make them available to society at large, particularly in the form of applied research and development and programmes of advanced education and training. The problems of potential mismatch between expectation and performance are that research does not necessarily progress in a way congruent with the needs of the wider society and that not all worthwhile academic activities are *ipso facto* justifiable in external – and particularly in utilitarian – terms.

Good intellectual work, in whatever domain it may occur, deserves a measure of society's nourishment and support. The case may be that an esoteric subject contains insights into the history or the culture of a society that would otherwise be lost to humanity's memory. Or it may be argued that learning to decode a difficult inflected language or to operate with difficult philosophical concepts helps preserve a watermark of good thinking and powers of expression against which the more utilitarian subjects can measure themselves. Or the claim may be that trained minds can be put to other more instrumental uses. If such contentions are granted in principle, the judgement of what is good enough may not be within the outside world's capacity to decide. The closer the work is to the frontiers of knowledge, the fewer there are in a position to assess it. So, it must follow, the academic world as a whole has in many such cases to be trusted to certify the quality of the activities in which it is engaged.

Therein lies the strength of the twin academic traditions of autonomy and a highly competitive environment. Within whatever external constraints exist, individual teachers and researchers need to be able to exercise discretion over the content, style and outcomes of what is produced, for that is the precondition of creativity. The safeguard against the abuse of that privilege is, however, the knowledge that what they do will be judged by the highly critical eyes of their competitors in the field.

For the most part work of quality cannot be done under control from above. But as we have argued earlier, this does not mean that all programmatic and commissioned work is detrimental to higher education. Knowledge systems outside higher education are one of its important resources, and social and industrial problem-solving has produced good and enduring research alongside the *ad hoc* and ephemeral. Nor does it remove the argument for lay scrutiny and critique of objectives and utility which are not necessarily inimical to the exercise of discretion by basic units and academics.

## THE MODEL REVISITED

In terms of our model, the balance of control has shifted from the inner core to the outer framework. In the 1980s, external expectations and requirements had largely been mediated by the central authorities, which then passed directives through the system. However, once serious attempts were made to pass on a noticeable share of the costs to the client body, the role of the centre necessarily changed to one of less close control. The market still required to be regulated; limiting frameworks had to be set; sizeable amounts of central resources still had to be distributed. But some of the initiative passed to the mechanisms of consumer choice, and external demands bore more directly upon the institutions and the basic units themselves.

In one sense, this could be seen as a reversion to the earlier 'autonomous' state of the system, when the central authorities exercised their guidance with a light touch, and the strength of the system lay in the basic units. But there were two important differences. First, the institutions had become stronger during the managerial phase and retained that strength as the main co-ordinators and testers of the current market, identifying the niches into which their collective activities might best fit, and promulgating appropriate statements of their mission. Second, as already noted, the advent of the 'market' stage of evolution largely substituted external values for the internal values which characterised the heyday of autonomy. The long-term consequences of this latest change of state remain to be worked through. Whether society will succeed in preserving the best features of the old elitist system in conditions of near open access remains to be seen. If the US experience is anything to go by – and its culture is very different from the European – one might expect to see a much wider spectrum of quality emerging, with a few highly prestigious institutions maintaining high standards of academic excellence, but with many others serving more mundane and functional needs. In such a system, the binary line between the polytechnics and the universities would cease to serve even the symbolic function it was first invoked to perform: the market would be a common one, with a single regulatory body. But it will take a massive cultural and economic shift to make institutions as open to the free market as are their American counterparts. Higher education in the UK has no donors or political supporters that would make that likely. It seems more probable that the four sets of values explored in this chapter – those of the autonomous professional, of management, of the market and of society – will continue to coexist in different mixes in different institutions and for different functions. The model deployed in this book, with its differentiation between the normative and operational modes at the different levels of the system, provides a framework for monitoring the continuing interplay over time of these contending forces.

# References

This bibliography contains the works to which we refer in the text and other principal authorities we have consulted. It is not an attempt to give an exhaustive bibliography of the literature on British higher education, let alone that of other countries.

## JOURNALS

*Higher Education*, Elsevier.
*The Higher Education Review*, Cornmarket Press.
*Higher Education Quarterly*, Blackwell, (formerly *New Universities Quarterly*).
*International Journal of Institutional Management in Higher Education*, xxx.
*Minerva*, The International Council on the Future of the University.
*Studies in Higher Education*, Carfax.

## SERIES OF PUBLICATIONS

Carnegie Council on Policy Studies in Higher Education (1980) *A Summary of Reports and Recommendations* (Jossey-Bass). A large-scale series of studies, mainly, but not exclusively, about the USA.

Society for Research into Higher Education/Leverhulme, *Programme of Study into the Future of Higher Education*. A set of publications between 1981 and 1983, edited by G. Williams and T. Blackstone, based on papers given at invitational conferences.

Organisation for Economic Co-operation and Development, Country Reviews of Education. A series beginning in 1961, most of which refer to current policies and problems in higher education in the different member-countries.

## OFFICIAL REPORTS (IN DATE ORDER)

University Grants Committee (UGC) (1948) *University Development 1935–1947*, HMSO.
—— (1953) *University Development 1947–1952*, Cmd 8875, HMSO.
—— (1958) *University Development 1952–1957*, Cmd 534, HMSO.

—— (1968) *University Development 1962–1967*, Cmd 3820, HMSO.

Percy Committee (1945) *Higher Technological Education, Ministry of Education*, HMSO.

Barlow Report (May 1946) *Report of the Committee on Scientific Manpower*, Cmd 6824, HMSO.

Robbins Report (1963) *Higher Education*, Report of the Committee Appointed by the Prime Minister under the Chairmanship of Lord Robbins 1961–1963, Cmd 2154, HMSO.

Department of Education and Science (DES) (1965) *A Plan for Polytechnics and Other Colleges*, Cmd 300, HMSO.

Brynmor Jones Report (1965) *Audio-Visual Aids in Higher Scientific Education*, UGC, DES, Scottish Education Department, HMSO.

DES (1966) *A Plan for Polytechnics and Other Colleges*, Cmd 3006, HMSO.

Wolfenden Report (1967) *Parliament and Control of University Expenditure*, Committee of Public Accounts, Session 66/67, HC 290, HMSO.

National Board for Prices and Incomes (1970) Report No. 145, *Standing Conference on the Pay of University Teachers in Great Britain*, Cmd 4334, HMSO.

Rothschild Report (1971) *The Organisation and Management of Government Research and Development*, Central Policy Review Staff, Cmd 4814, HMSO.

DES (1972) *Education: A Framework for Expansion*, Cmd 5174, HMSO.

Houghton Report (1974) *Report of the Committee of Inquiry into the Pay of Non-University Teachers*, Cmd 5848, HMSO.

DES (1976) *Public Expenditure to 1979–1980*, HMSO.

UGC (1977) *Annual Survey 1975–1976*, Cmd 6758, HMSO.

Central Policy Review Staff (1977) *Population and the Social Services*, HMSO.

Oakes Report, DES (1978) *Higher Education into the 1990s: A Discussion Document*, HMSO.

DES (1978) *Report of the Working Group on the Management of Higher Education in the Maintained Sector*, Cmd 7130, HMSO.

Council for National Academic Awards (CNAA) (1979) *The Development of Partnership and Validation.*

DES (1980) *Annual Report 1979*, HMSO.

—— (1981) *Higher Education in England Outside the Universities: Policy, Funding and Management*, a consultative document, DES.

—— (1983) *Annual Report 1982*, HMSO.

UGC (1984) *Annual Survey 1982–1983*, HMSO.

DES (1984) *Demand for Higher Education in Great Britain 1984–2000*, Report on Education, Cmd 9524, HMSO.

—— (1984) *Annual Report 1983*, HMSO.

National Advisory Body for Public Sector Higher Education (NAB) (1984) *A Strategy for Higher Education into the Late 1980s and Beyond*, HMSO.

UGC (1984) *A Strategy for Higher Education into the 1990s*, HMSO.

DES (1985) *Annual Report 1984*, Cmd 9524, HMSO.

—— (1985) *The Development of Higher Education into the 1990s*, Cmd 9524, HMSO.

Jarratt Report (1985) *Report of the Steering Committee for Efficiency Studies in Universities*, Committee of Vice-Chancellors and Principals, HMSO.

Lindop Report (1985) *The Report of the Committee of Inquiry into the Academic Validation of Degree Courses in Public Sector Higher Education*, Cmd 9501, HMSO.

DES (1986) *Annual Report 1985*, HMSO.

Reynolds Report (1986) *Academic Standards in Universities, Universities' Methods and Procedures for Maintaining and Monitoring Academic Standards and the Content of their Courses and the Quality of their Teaching*, Committee of Vice-Chancellors and Principals (July).

Committee of Vice-Chancellors and Principals/University Grants Committee (1986) *Performance Indicators in Universities*, First Statement of the Joint CVCP/UGC Working Group, CVCP.

UGC (1986) *Annual Survey 1984–1985*, HMSO.

Croham Report (1987) *Review of the University Grants Committee*, Cmd 81, HMSO.

DES (1987a) *Higher Education: Meeting the Challenge*, Cmd 114, HMSO.

—— (1987b) Note by the Department of Education and Science, Changes in Structure and National Planning for Higher Education, Contracts Between the Funding Bodies and Higher Education Institutions, mimeo and undated.

CVCP/UGC (1987) *Performance Indicators in Universities*, Second Statement of the Joint CVCP/UGC Working Group.

—— (1987) *University Management Statistics and Performance Indicators in UK Universities*.

Advisory Board for Research Councils (ABRC) (1987) *A Strategy for the Science Base*, HMSO.

UGC (1987) First Annual Report on Monitoring Research Selectivity (August), mimeo.

Manpower Services Commission (MSC) (1987) *Enterprise in Higher Education*, Guidance for Applicants (December).

NAB (1987) *Management for a Purpose: The Report of the Good Management Practice Groups*, NAB.

Polytechnics and Colleges Funding Council (PCFC) (1989) *Funding Choices*, Consultative document.

DES (1989) *Shifting the Balance of Public Funding of Higher Education to Fees*, a consultative paper.

CNAA (1989) *Towards an Educational Audit*, Information Services Discussion Paper 3.

## BOOKS AND ARTICLES

Archer, M.S. (1979) *Social Origins of Educational Systems*, Sage Studies in Social and Educational Change, Vol. 9 (Sage Publications).

Argyris, C. and Schön, D.A. (1974) *Theory in Practice* (Jossey-Bass).

Ashby, E. and Anderson, M. (1974) *Portrait of Haldane at work on Education*, (Macmillan).

Bailey, F.G. (ed.) (1973) *Debate and Compromise* (Blackwell).

—— (1977) *Morality and Expediency: The Folk Lore of Academic Politics* (Blackwell).

Baker, K. (1989) 'Higher Education: The Next 25 Years', Speech at Conference, Lancaster University (January).

Baldridge, J.V. (1971) *Power and Conflict in the University* (Jossey-Bass).

Baldridge, J.V., Curtis, D.V., Ecker, G. and Riley, G.L. (1978) *Policy Making and Effective Leadership* (Jossey-Bass).

Barnett, R. (1987) 'The Maintenance of Quality in the Public Sector of UK Higher Education', *Higher Education*, 16 (3).

Becher, T. (1984) 'Higher Education Systems: Structure', *International Encyclopedia of Education* (Pergamon Press).

—— (1985) 'Higher Education Systems: Structure', in T. Husen, and T.N. Postlethwaite *International Encyclopedia of Higher Education* (Pergamon Press).

—— (ed.) (1987) *British Higher Education* (Allen & Unwin).

—— (1989) *Academic Tribes and Territories* (Open University Press).

—— (forthcoming) 'Graduate Education in Britain: The View from the Battlefront', in Burton R. Clark (ed.) *Graduate Education and Research Organisation* (provisional title).

Becher, T., Embling, J.F. and Kogan, M. (1977) *Systems of Higher Education: United Kingdom* (International Council for Educational Development).

Becher, T., and Kogan, M. (1987) *Calling British Universities to Account* (Education Reform Group).

Becher, T., and Maclure, S. (eds) (1978) *Accountability in Education* (NFER Publishing for SSRC).

Becker, H.S., Greer, B. and Hughes, E.C. (1968) *Making the Grade: The Academic Side of College Life* (John Wiley).

Bennis, W.G., Benne, K.D., and Chin, R. (1969) *The Planning of Changes* (Holt, Rinehart & Winston).

Berdahl, R.O. (1959) *British Universities and the State* (University of California Press).

Bereiter, C. and Freedman, M.B. (1962) 'Fields of Study and the People in Them', in N. Stanford (ed.) *The American College* (John Wiley).

Bernstein, B. (1975) *Class, Codes and Control*, Vol. 3, *Towards a Theory of Educational Transmission* (Routledge & Kegan Paul).

Bhaskar, R. (1978) *A Realist Theory of Science* 2nd edn, (Harvester Press).

Biglan, A. (1973a) 'The Characteristics of Subject Matter in Different Scientific Areas', *Journal of Applied Psychology*, 57 (3).

—— (1973b) 'Relationships Between Subject Matter Characteristics and the Structure and Output of University Departments', *Journal of Applied Psychology*, 57 (3).

Blau, P.M. (1964) *Exchange and Power in Social Life* (John Wiley).

—— (1974) *On the Nature of Organisations* (John Wiley).

Bleau, B.L. (1981) 'Planning Models in Higher Education: Historical Review and Survey of Currently Available Models', *Higher Education*, 10 (2).

Bliss, J. and Ogborn, J. (1977) *Students' Reactions to Undergraduate Science* (Heinemann Educational Books for Nuffield Foundation).

Bloor, D. (1976) *Knowledge and Social Imagery* (Routledge & Kegan Paul).

Blume, S. (1985) 'After the Darkest Hour ... Integrity and Engagement in the Development of University Research', in B. Wittrock and A. Elzinga (eds), *The University Research System* (Almqvist and Wiksell).

Bone, A. 'Higher Education and the Schools', unpublished.

Booth, C. (1987) 'Central Government and Higher Education Planning 1965–1986', *Higher Education Quarterly*, 41 (1).

Boys, C.J., Brennan, J., Henkel, M., Kirkland, J., Kogan, M. and Youll, P. (1988) *Higher Education and the Preparation for Work* (Jessica Kingsley Publishers).

Braybrooke, D. and Lindblom, C.E. (1963) *A Strategy of Decision* (Free Press).

Brennan, J. (1986) 'Peer Review and Partnership', *International Journal of*

*Institutional Management in Higher Education*, 10 (2) (July).

Brennan, J. and Henkel, M. (1988) 'Economics' in C. Boys, *et al.* (1988) *Higher Education and the Preparation for Work* (Jessica Kingsley Publishers).

Briggs, A. (1964) in D. Daiches (ed.), *The Idea of a New University* (Deutsch).

Bruner, J.S., Goodnow, J.J. and Austin, G.A. (1956) *A Study of Thinking* (John Wiley).

Burgess, T. (1972) *Planning for Higher Education*, Cornmarket Papers on Higher Education (Cornmarket Press).

Burgess, T., and Pratt, J. (1974) *Polytechnics: A Report* (Pitman).

Butler, R. (1982) 'The Control and Management of Higher Education in Great Britain, with Special Reference to the Role of the University Grants Committee and the Committee of Vice-Chancellors and Principals', *Oxford Journal of Education*, 8 (3).

Carswell, J. (1985) *Government and the University in Britain* (Cambridge University Press).

Carter, C.C. (1980) *Higher Education for the Future* (Blackwell).

Cave, M., Hanney, S., Kogan, M. and Trevett, G. (1988) *The Use of Performance Indicators in Higher Education* (Jessica Kingsley Publishers).

Cerych, L. and Sabatier, P. (1984) *Great Expectations and Mixed Performance: The Implementation of Higher Education Reforms in Europe* (Trentham Books).

—— (1986) *Great Expectations and Mixed Performance* (Trentham Books).

Challis, R. (1976) 'The Experience of Mature Students', *Studies in Higher Education*, 1 (2) (October).

Council for Industry and Higher Education (CIHE) (1987) *Towards a Partnership, Higher Education – Government – Industry*.

Clark, Burton R. (1978) *Academic Co-ordination*, Yale Higher Education Research Group, Working Paper No. 24.

—— (1983) *The Higher Education System* (University of California Press).

—— (1984) *Perspectives on Higher Education* (University of California Press).

—— (1987a) *The Academic Profession* (University of California Press).

—— (1987b) *The Academic Life: Small Worlds, Different Worlds* (Carnegie Foundation for the Advancement of Teaching).

Clayton, K.M. (1988a) 'Recent Developments in the Funding of University Research', *Higher Education Quarterly*, 42 (1).

—— (1988b) 'Trends in Funding Arrangements', *Higher Education Quarterly*, 42 (2).

Cohen, M.D. and March, J.G. (1974) *Leadership and Ambiguity: The American College President* (McGraw-Hill).

Committee of Vice-Chancellors and Principals (CVCP) (1990) Press Announcement, 22 March 1990: Academic Audit Unit, Director.

Crane, D. (1972) *Invisible Colleges* (University of Chicago Press).

Dahl, R.A. (1971) *Polyarchy, Participation and Opposition* (Yale University Press).

Daiches, D. (ed.) (1964) *The Idea of a New University* (Deutsch).

Dalton, I.G. (1987) 'Universities and Science Parks: A Review of the Issues', *International Management of Higher Education*, 11 (3).

Davies, J.L. (1984) 'Managing Contraction in US Universities: Lessons for Europe', *International Journal of Higher Education Management*, OECD (May).

—— (1987) 'The Entrepreneurial and Adaptive University', *International Journal of Institutional Management in Higher Education,* 11 (3).

Davis, M.C. (1979) *The Development of the CNAA: A Study of a Validating Agency,* Ph.D. thesis, Loughborough University of Technology. Also 'Final Report on SSRC Project' deposited at British National Lending Library.

Douglas, J.W.B. (1964) *The Home and the School* (MacGibbon and Kee).

Duncan, J.G. (1987) 'A Marketing Perspective', in G. Squires (ed.) *Innovation Through Recession* (Society for Research into Higher Education).

Easton, D. (1965) *A Framework for Political Analysis* (Prentice-Hall).

Elmore, R.F. (1979) 'Backward Mapping', *Political Science Quarterely,* 94 (4).

—— (1985) 'Forward and Backward Mapping', in K. Hanf and T.A.J. Tooner (eds) *Policy Implementation in Federal and Unitary Systems* (Martinus Nijhoff).

Fisher, G.C., Kapur, S. and McGarvey, J.E.C. (1978) 'Physics and Chemistry for Enviromental Scientists: The Evaluation of a Tertiary Level Science Course', *Studies in Higher Education,* 3 (2) (October).

Frackmann, E. (1987) 'Lessons to be Learnt from a Decade of Discussions on Performance Indicators', *International Journal of Institutional Management in Higher Education,* 11 (2).

Fulton, O. (1984) 'Needs, Expectations and Responses: New Pressures on Higher Education', *Higher Education,* 13 (2).

—— (1988) 'Elite Survivals? Entry "Standards" and Procedures for Higher Education Admissions', *Studies in Higher Education,* 13 (1).

Fulton, O., and Ellwood, S. (1989) *Admission to Higher Education. Policy and Practice,* A Report to the Training Agency (Training Agency).

Furumark, A. (1981) 'Institutional Self-Evaluation in Sweden', *International Journal of Institutional Management in Higher Education,* 5 (3).

Getzels, J. and Jackson, P. (1962) *Creativity and Intelligence, Explorations with Gifted Students* (John Wiley).

Giles, G.J. (1977) 'The Rise of the Polytechnics in Britain', International Conference, 'University Today', Dubrovnik 1977, unpublished.

Glaser, B. and Strauss, A. (1967) *The Discovery of a Grounded Theory* (Aldine).

Gouldner, A.W. (1957) 'Cosmopolitans and Locals', *Administrative Science Quarterly,* 2.

Gummett, P. (1980) *Scientists in Whitehall* (Manchester University Press).

Halsey, A.H. (1964) 'Quality and Authority in British Universities', *Times Higher Educational Supplement* (1 November).

Halsey, A. H. and Trow, M. (1971) *The British Academics* (Faber & Faber).

Hardy, C., Langley, A., Mintzberg, H. and Rose, J. (1984) 'Strategy Formation in the University Setting', in A. Westoby (ed.) (1988) *Culture and Power in Educational Organisations* (Open University Press).

Havelock, R.G. (1969) *Planning for Innovation through Dissemination and Utilization of Knowledge* (Centre for Research on Utilisation of Scientific Knowledge, University of Michigan).

Henkel, M. (1986) 'Exellence Versus Relevance: The Evaluation of Research', *International Journal of Institutional Management in Higher Education,* 10 (2) (July).

Hewton, E. (1979) 'A Strategy for Promoting Curriculum Development in Universities', *Studies in Higher Education,* 4 (1) (March).

Hewton, E., Becher, T., Parlett, M. and Simons, H. (1986) *Supporting Teaching for a Change* (Nuffield Group for Research and Innovation in Higher Education).

Hirst, P.H. (1974) *Knowledge and the Curriculum* (Routledge & Kegan Paul).

Jackson, R. (1988) 'Manpower Planning', *Higher Education*, Chevening Discussion Paper (mimeo).

Kells, H.R. (1986) 'The Second Irony: The System of Institutional Evaluation of Higher Education in the United States', *International Journal of Institutional Management in Higher Education*, 10 (2) (July).

Kemp, R.V. (1977) 'Controversy in Scientific Research and Tactics of Communication', *Sociological Review*, 25.

Kogan, M. (1975) *Educational Policy-Maker* (Allen & Unwin).

—— (1984) 'The Political View', in Burton R. Clark (ed.), *Perspectives on Higher Education: Eight Disciplinary and Comparative Views (University of California Press)*.

—— (1987) 'The DES and Whitehall', *Higher Education Quarterly*, 41 (3) (Summer).

—— (1988) *Educational Accountability, An Analytic Overview*, 2nd edn, (Hutchinson).

—— (1989) *Evaluating Higher Education* (Jessica Kingsley Publishers in Association with the OECD).

Kogan, M. and Henkel, M. (1983) *Government and Research* (Heinemann).

—— (forthcoming), 'Research Training and Graduate Education: The British Macro-Structure', in Burton R. Clark (ed.) *Graduate Education and Research Organisation* (provisional title).

Kogan, M. and Kogan, D. (1983) *The Attack on Higher Education* (Kogan Page).

Kolb, D.A. (1981) 'Learning Styles and Disciplinary Differences', in A. Chickering (ed.) *The Modern American College* (San Francisco: Jossey-Bass).

—— (1984) *Experiential Learning* (Prentice-Hall).

Kuhn, T.S. (1962) *The Structure of Scientific Revolutions* (University of Chicago Press).

Lewin, K. (1952) *Field Theory in Social Science*, Selected Theoretical Papers (Tavistock).

Lockwood, G. and Davies, J. (1985) *Universities: The Management Challenge* (Society for Research into Higher Education and NFER-Nelson).

Lynton, E.A. and Elman, S.E. (1987) *New Priorities for the University* (Jossey-Bass).

McVicar, M. (1989) 'The National Advisory Board Planning Exercise 1984/5: An Analysis of Educational Policy Making and Implementation', Unpublished project report, Ph.D.

Marris, P. (1964) *The Experience of Higher Education* (Routledge & Kegan Paul).

—— (1974) *Loss and Change* (Routledge & Kegan Paul).

Marton, F. and Saljö, R. (1976) 'On Qualitative Differences in Learning', *British Journal of Educational Psychology*, 46.

Metzger, W. (1987) 'The Academic Profession in the United States', in Burton R. Clark (ed.) *The Academic Profession* (University of California Press).

Middlehurst, R. (1989) 'Leadership Development in Universities, 1986–88', mimeo: University of Surrey, Department of Educational Studies.

Miles, M.B. and Huberman, A.M. (1984) *Qualitative Data Analysis: A Source Book of New Methods* (Sage Publications).

Miller, C.M.L. and Parlett, M. (1974) *Up to the Mark* (Society for Research into Higher Education).

Miller, R.I. (1986) 'A Ten Year Perspective on Faculty Evaluation', *International Journal of Institutional Management in Higher Education*, 10 (2).

Moodie, G.C. (1983) 'Buffer, Coupling and Broker: Reflections on 60 Years of the UGC', *Higher Education*, 13 (2).
—— (1986) 'The Disintegrating Chair: Professors in Britain Today', *European Journal of Education*, 21 (1).
—— (1987) 'Le Roi est Mort; Vive le Roi? Croham and the Death of the UGC', *Higher Education Quarterly*, 41 (4).
—— and Eustace, R. (1974) *Power and Authority in British Universities* (Allen & Unwin).
Moore, P.G. (1987) 'University Financing, 1979–86', *Higher Education Quarterly*, 41 (1) (January).
—— (1989) 'Marketing Higher Education', *Higher Education Quarterly*, 43 (2) (Spring).
Morris, A. and Sizer J. (eds) (1982) *Resources and Higher Education* (SRHE-NFER, No. 51).
Neave, G. (1979) 'Academic Drift: Some Views from Europe', *Studies in Higher Education*, 4 (2) (October).
—— (1986) 'On Shifting Sands', *European Journal of Education*, 20 (2–3).
—— (1988) 'The Making of the Executive Head', *International Journal of Institutional Management in Higher Education*, 12 (1).
Nixon, N. (1987) 'Central Control of the Public Sector', in T. Becher (ed.) *British Higher Education* (Allen & Unwin).
Ostergren, B. and Berg, B. (1977) *Innovation and Innovation Processes in Higher Education* (Swedish National Board of Universities and Colleges).
Parlett, M. (1977) 'The Department as a Learning Milieu', *Studies in Higher Education*, 2 (2).
Parlett, M., Simons, H., Simmonds, R. and Hewton, E. (1976) *Learning from Learners* (Nuffield Foundation).
Pask, G. (1976) 'Styles and Strategies of Learning', *British Journal of Educational Psychology*, 46.
Pearson, R., Hutt, R. and Parsons, D. (1984) *Education, Training and Employment* (Gower).
Perry, W.G., Jnr (1970) *Forms of Intellectual and Ethical Development in the College Years* (Holt, Rinehart & Winston).
Platt, J. (1976) *Realities of Social Research: An Empirical Study of British Sociologists* (Sussex University Press).
Polanyi, M. (1962) 'The Republic of Science: Its Political and Economic Theory', *Minerva*, 1 (1) (Autumn).
Popper, K. (1979) *Objective Knowledge* (Clarenden Press).
Pratt, J., and Silverman, S. (1988) *Responding to Constraint, Policy and Management in Higher Education* (Open University Press).
Premfors, R. (1980) *The Politics of Higher Education in a Comparative Perspective: France, Sweden, United Kingdom*, Studies in Politics, 15, University of Stockholm.
—— (1984) *Higher Education Organisation: Conditions for Policy Implementation* (Almqvist & Wiksell).
Premfors, R., and Ostergren, B. (1978) *Systems of Higher Education: Sweden* (OECD).
Pressman, J. and Wildavsky, A. (1973) *Implementation* (University of California Press).
Roizen, J. and Jepson, M. (1985) *Expectations of Higher Education* (Society for

Research into Higher Education).

Sabatier, P.A. (1987) 'Top-down and Bottom-up approaches to Implementation Research', *Journal of Public Policy*, 6 (1).

Standing Conference of Employers of Graduates (SCOEG) (1985) *Response to the Green Paper on the Development of Higher Education in the 1990s.*

Scott, P. (1984) *Crisis in the University* (Croom Helm).

—— (1987) 'Higher Education and the Media', *Higher Education Quarterly*, 41 (3) (Summer).

Scriven, M. (1967) 'The Methodology of Evaluation', in *Perspectives on Curriculum Evaluation*, American Educational Research Association Monograph No. 1.

Seldin, P. (1988) *Evaluating and Developing Administrative Performance. A Practical Guide for Academic Leaders* (Jossey-Bass).

Science and Engineering Research Council (SERC) (1989) Corporate Plan.

Shattock, M. (ed) (1983) *The Structure and Governance of Higher Education* (SRHE/Leverhulme).

—— (1987) 'The Last Days of the University Grants Committee', *Minerva*, 25 (4).

—— (1989) 'Higher Education and the Research Councils', *Minerva*, 27 (2–3).

Shattock, M.L. and Berdahl, R.D. (1984) 'The British University Grants Committee 1919–1983: Changing Relationships with Government and the Universities', *Higher Education*, 13 (2).

Shattock, M. and Rigby, G. (eds) (1983) *Resource Allocation in British Universities* (SRHE-NFER).

Sizer, J. (1987a) 'In Search of Excellence – Performance Assessment in the UK', *Higher Education Quarterly*, 42 (2).

—— (1987b) *Institutional Responses to Financial Reductions in the University Sector*, Final Report, DES.

Sizer, J. and Frost, R. (1985) *Criteria for Self Evaluation of Department Research Profiles. Responsible and Responsive Universities Research Project*. Working Paper, Loughborough University of Technology (mimeo).

Smith, T. (1987) 'The UGC's Research Rankings Exercise', *Higher Education Quarterly*, 41 (4) (Autumn).

Snyder, B.R. (1971) *The Hidden Curriculum* (Knopf).

Sockett, H. (1976) *Teacher Accountability*. Proceedings of the Philosophy of Education Society of Great Britain, Vol. 10.

Squires, G. (ed.) (1983) *Innovation through Recession* (Society for Research into Higher Education).

—— (1990) *First Degree: The Undergraduate Curriculum* (Open University Press).

Startup, R. (1979) 'Material Resources and the Academic Role', *Studies in Higher Education*, 4 (2) (October).

Stewart, W.A.C. (1989) *Higher Education in Postwar Britain* (Basingstoke: Macmillan).

Stufflebeam, D.L. (1969) 'Evaluating as Enlightenment for Decision Makers', *Improving Educational Assessment* (Association for Supervision and Curriculum Development).

Taylor, W. (1987) *Universities under Scrutiny (OECD)*.

Teichler, U. (1988) *Changing Patterns of the Higher Education System* (Jessica Kingsley Publishers).

Thompson, M. (1976) 'Class, Caste, the Curriculum Schedule and the Cusp Catastrophe', *Studies in Higher Education*, 1 (1) (March).

Trow, M. (1970) 'Reflections on the Transition from Mass to Universal Higher Education', *Daedalus*, 99.

—— (1974) 'Problems in the Transition from Elite to Mass Higher Education', in *Policies for Higher Education* (OECD).

—— (1975) 'The Public and Private Lives of Higher Education', *Daedalus*, 104 (Winter).

—— (1976) 'The American Academic Department as a Context for Learning', *Studies in Higher Education*, 2 (2) (March).

—— (1983) 'Defining the Issues in University–Government Relations', *Studies in Higher Education*, 8 (2).

—— (1984) 'Leadership and Organisation', in R. Premfors (ed.) *Higher Education Organisation* (Almqvist & Wiksell).

—— (1985) 'Comparative Reflections on Leadership in Higher Education', *European Journal of Education*, 20 (2–3).

—— (1989) Oral contribution, London Business School seminar.

Van de Graaff, J.H. (1976) *The Structure of Academic Governance in Great Britain* (Yale Higher Education Programme, Working Paper No. 13).

Van de Graaff, J.H., Clark, B.R., Furth, D., Goldschmidt, D. and Wheeler, D.F. (1978) *Academic Power* (Praeger).

Vught, Frans A. van (1988) 'A New Autonomy in European Higher Education? An Exploration and Analysis of the Strategy of Self-Regulation in Higher Education Governance', *International Journal of Institutional Management in Higher Education*, 12 (1).

Wagner, L. (ed.) (1982) *Agenda for Institutional Change in Higher Education* (SRHE/NFER).

Walker, D. (1989) Quoting Minutes of a Cabinet Committee, 1958, in *Times Higher Educational Supplement* (6 January).

Watson, D. (1989) *Managing the Modular Course* (Open University Press).

Weatherley, R. and Lipsky, M. (1977) 'Street-Level Bureaucrats and Institutional Innovation', *Harvard Educational Review*, 47 (2).

Weatherley, R.A. (1979) *Reforming Special Education* (MIT Press).

Weick, K. (1976) 'Educational Organisations as Loosely Coupled Systems', *Administrative Science Quarterly*, 21.

Westoby, A. (ed.) (1988) *Culture and Power in Educational Organisations* (Open University Press).

Whitburn, J., Mealing, M. and Cox, C. (1976) People in Polytechnics (SRHE).

Williams, G. (1984) 'The Economic Approach', in Burton R. Clark (ed.), *Perspectives on Higher Education. Eight Disciplinary and Comparative Views* (University of California Press).

Wirt, F. (1981) 'Professionalism and Political Conflict: A Developmental Model', *Journal of Public Policy*, 1, Part 1 (February).

Wittrock, B. and Elzinga A. (1985) *The University Research System: The Public Policies of the Home of Scientists* (Almqvist & Wiksell).

Youll, P. (1988) 'Physics', in Boys, C.J., *et al.*, *Higher Education and the Preparation for Work* (Jessica Kingsley Publishers).

Young, H. (1989) *One of Us* (Macmillan).

Zaltman, G., Florio, D.H., and Sikorski, L.A. (1977) *Dynamic Educational Change* (Free Press).

Zinberg, D.S. (1976) 'Education through Science: The Early Stages of Career Development in Chemistry', *Social Studies of Science*, 6 (2).

# Name index

# Subject index

*Note*: Page references in italics indicate tables and figures.

access 3, 48, 52, 85, 107, 187; open
31–2, 36, 44, 142, 189
access courses 83
accountability 45, 60, 67, 70, 157; and
academic planning 84–5; and
central authorities 168; and
commissioned research 117, 121;
consumerist 169, 170–1, 172; in
hard applied disciplines 91; and
individual 118, 137, 153, 172–3;
managerial mode 169–70, 172, 180;
mechanisms 171–2; modes 169–71,
175; nature 168–9; of polytechnics
143; in practice 172–3; professional
170, 172; in soft applied disciplines
92; *see also* evaluation
accountancy, status 106, 146
administration, and academic
management 72; at basic unit level
101–287; career structures 122;
evaluation 167–8; increased load
25, 85, 109; individual role 116–17,
173; lack of structures 3; power 47,
74–5, 182; *see also* management
admission, criteria 12, 24–5, 40, 93,
107, 179–80; and fall in 18-year-old
cohort 40, 85; flexible requirements
83; and manpower needs 34–5, 52,
85; reduction in numbers 42, 44–5
advanced technology colleges 30
Advisory Board for Research Councils
46–7, 54, 55, 59, 64
Advisory Council for Applied
Research and Development 59

Advisory Council on Science and
Technology 46, 55
Age Participation Rate 40
appointments 12, 69, 71, 103
assessment, student attitudes 125, 127
Association of University Teachers,
and government policy 59
audit, of universities 35
Australia, governance of higher
education 58
autonomy 3, 21 n.1, 188; basic units
100–2; individual 100–1, 111,
115–17, 119, 153–4, 156, 172, 188;
institutions 27–8, 29–31, 33, 35, 36,
38, 155, 176–8; growth 22–3;
students 126

bargaining, and change 77, 132,
143–5, 155, 174
Barlow Committee, and university
expansion 24, 27, 56
basic unit, and academic autonomy
100–2; categories 89–92; and
change 136, 137, 142, 144–6, 188;
and consumer choice 105–8; and
curriculum 94–7; evaluation 165,
167, 169; and external environment
89, 101, 105–8, 136, 148; functions
88; head 72–4, 101, 147, 171;
interdisciplinary 9, 93, 95, 96–7,
106–7, 141–2, 145, 150; as level of
organisation 8, 9, 19–20, 87–9, 176;
new 144–6; and normative mode
12, 15, 17, 87, 142, 144–6, 148–52;

education 58
Training Agency 53, 56, 62, 147

universities, federal/unitary 19, 71, 83;
freedom, *see* autonomy,
institutions; funding 34, 35–6;
imbalance of norms and operations
151; and individual 111; new
141–2, 143; technological 24, 29,
35, 42; *see also* expansion, academic
Universities Funding Council,
composition 39, 54; and evaluation
167; resource allocations 89–90,
147; and structural change 144; and
teaching function of higher
education 56
University Grants Committee, and
binary system 30, 36; as buffer
between state and institutions 35,
44–5; co-opted members 59; and
expansion 23–5, 27–9, 35–6; and
funding 26–7, 28, 34, 35–6, 41–2,
45–7; grading and evaluation 42,
45–6, 141, 167–8; monitoring role
157; and policy-making 28, 35, 39;
and research 25–6, 28, 60–1, 63;
and student numbers 42, 45; and
technological universities 29

USA, external environment 83–4, 189;
graduate schools 129; institutional
evaluation 164; interest groups 58;
private universities 6–7, 67; public
higher education system 6
utility, social 170, 186–7

values 16, 19, 21, 22–3, 48; and basic
unit 10, 12, 15, 17, 20–1, 87,
89–92, 97–8, 101, 147–52; and
central authority 13, 22, 24–6,
38–9, 54; conflicting 76, 97, 103;
and individual 20, 75, 110–11, 117,
119, 122, 152–5; and institutions
12, 20, 68, 77–80, 83, 136, 142–3,
177; of management 179–83;
market 183–6, 184; peer 11–12, 16,
21, 87, 90–2, 97, 101, 148, 177–9;
professional *see* values, peer; social
12, 23, 38, 65, 153, 177; and social
utility 186–7; of students 124–5;
*see also* mode, normative
vice-chancellor, appointment 69; and
change 135; as chief executive 47,
64, 68–71, 72, 74, 181–2

women, in higher education 37, 52